The Rise and Fall
of the
German
Democratic
Republic

Feiwel Kupferberg

The Rise and Fall
of the
German
Democratic
Republic

Transaction Publishers
New Brunswick (U.S.A.) and London (U.K.)

This book is printed on acid-free paper that meets the American National Standard for Permanence of Paper for Printed Library Materials.

Library of Congress Catalog Number: 2001052541
ISBN: 0-7658-0119-1
Printed in Canada

Library of Congress Cataloging-in-Publication Data

Kupferberg, Feiwel, 1946-
    The rise and fall of the German Democratic Republic / Feiwel Kupferberg.
        p. cm.
    Includes bibliographical references and index.
    ISBN 0-7658-0119-1 (alk. paper)
    1. Germany (East)—Politics and government. 2. Intellectuals—Germany
(East) 3. Socialism—Germany (East) 4. National socialism—Psychological
aspects. 5. Xenophobia—Germany (East) 6. Germany—History—Unification, 1990.   I. Title.

DD283 .K86 2002
943'.1—dc21   2001052541

Contents

Preface and Acknowledgements

In 1996, I wrote an article entitled, "Managing an Unmasterable Past," on the striking difference between the ways in which East and West Germany had coped with the Nazi past. The article, originally published in the journal *Society* (Volume 33, No 2: 69-79), later appeared as chapter 9 in *The Break-Up of Communism in East Germany and Eastern Europe* (Basingstoke: Macmillan; New York: St. Martin's Press, 1999), a book of comparative essays on the post-communist phenomenon.

In *The Rise and Fall of the German Democratic Republic*, I expand upon my hypothesis, arguing that West Germany approached the difficult moral, cultural, economic, and political issues of the Nazi past in a surprisingly open, honest, and self-reflective manner. By contrast, East Germany, despite its professed antifascism and its radical approach, has emerged as a hotbed of anti-liberal and xenophobic views, which serve as a breeding ground for totalitarian movements of both the Left and the Right. These historical and moral after-effects on the East German mentality are far more important than the relatively small economic differences and accompanying social problems that still exist in reunited Germany.

A few facts about my background might help the reader to understand my personal interest in the way in which East Germany coped with the Nazi past before and after reunification. I was born a year after the end of the Second World War as a stateless refugee in a camp for displaced persons in southern Bavaria, the only son of a Russian immigrant mother from a peasant family that had been deported by Stalin and a Polish-Jewish refugee father who had managed to escape the horrors of the Holocaust. Like many second-generation survivors, I evaded the issue of the Holocaust, it was just too difficult to cope with emotionally. Moreover, growing up as I did in a small town in central Sweden, where my parents were offered refuge after seven years of broken promises and thwarted hopes, made me socially vulnerable. I wanted desperately to be part of the majority in this safe and peaceful nation so I buried my doubts and anxieties for a long time.

My renewed interest in the topic developed in the early 1980s during a year spent as visiting professor at the University of Wisconsin-Green Bay on a sabbatical from Aalborg University in Denmark, where I had established myself after receiving my MA from Stockholm University a decade earlier. In Green Bay I met an American-Jewish colleague, Harvey Kay, with whom I had numerous discussions. We met almost every day, and once a month we drove in Harvey's car to Madison, where we spent the day in the huge university library. We met frequently for lunch at a Jewish restaurant where we consumed matzo balls in a steaming soup. Although I did not share Harvey's strong Marxist sympathies we saw eye to eye when it came to problems of Jewish identity in a post-Holocaust world. These discussions, sitting opposite one another in Harvey's office, in the lunch room, at the Jewish restaurant in Madison, revived in me a deep interest in that part of my family history that has been colored by the Jewish experience.

When I returned to Europe and Aalborg I resumed my main research interest at the time—Russian and East European societies, their past, present, and future. During an earlier field trip to Moscow in the late 1970s I had met my wife, who was born in East Germany a few months after the Nazi defeat and had managed to leave the GDR legally in the late 1960s. She still had family in East Germany, whom we visited frequently throughout the 1980s. Then came the extraordinary events of 1989/1990 and I decided to amplify my studies on Eastern Europe with a study of East Germany.

For this purpose I spent my sabbatical during the fall semester of 1994 in East Berlin. I had been offered generously an office and status as *Gastforscher* by Professor Rolf Reissig, Director of the Berliner Institut für sozialwissenschaftliche Studien (BISS). On several occasions Professor Reissig took time from his crowded calendar to chat and exchange views about the transformation processes taking place in East Germany, thereby contributing substantially to my understanding of the East German view of events.

At this time I became friendly with Rudolf Woderich, who was employed at the Institute. He had been one of the project leaders of a study comprising interviews with East German teachers, and later generously offered me the transcripts of some of these interviews, in addition to un-transcribed tapes that were in his possession. These original tapes and transcripts (referred to in this volume as BISS-Interview) have contributed enormously to my understanding of how a very important professional group looked upon and coped with German reunification.

During this sabbatical, my wife, who, in the late 1950s and early 1960s, had attended a *Gymnasium* (the former Grauen Kloster) situated close to the West Berlin border, began a series of taped interviews with former classmates, an idea she had conceived when she was invited to a class reunion thirty years after graduation. These interviews (referred to in this volume as Aalborg-Interview) gave me a valuable insight into what it actually meant to pursue a professional career in the GDR, how individuals coped with the dilemmas they encountered, and why reunification was seen as a major disturbance in their lives rather then as a welcome liberation from a totalitarian dictatorship.

I wrote an initial analysis of these interviews during a year-long sabbatical spent in the Department of German and Center for German and European Studies at the University of California, Berkeley, in the academic year 1997-98. The visit was made possible by a sponsorship from the former head of the German Department, Heinrich Seeba, and the acting director of the center, Beverly Crawford. The Danish Social Science Research Council paid for my sabbatical and financed most of my travel expenses. Although I intended to include the issue of the German past in the analysis, an anonymous referee at the Scandinavian sociological journal *Acta Sociologica*, to which I had submitted my paper, advised against doing so, thus that concern is strangely absent from the published article (Vol. 42, No. 3), written at a time when the question of the Nazi past was strongly on my mind.

I spent most of my year at Berkeley immersing myself in German history and, in particular, in the troubled relations between Germans and Jews. What fascinated me at the time was the fact that so many East German Jews had identified so strongly with the GDR's antifascist pretensions. I gave a public lecture on the topic, offering some preliminary explanations. These were later reworked and have been integrated into the discussion in chapter 3 in this volume of the formulation, "the victors of history." While at Berkeley, I also wrote a first draft on the issue of xenophobia and right-wing extremism in East Germany. Most of the inspiration for that chapter came from Professor Werner Bergmann, who visited Berkeley while I was there and later shared with me some of his ongoing work on the topic. My draft was tightened up and translated into an article that was published in the Danish journal *Dansk Sociologi* (Vol.11, No. 2, 2000). I have used this later version as a point of departure for chapter 8.

Even before my year at Berkeley, I had begun, and continue, a close collaboration with *Privatdozent* Dr. Erika M. Hoerning, at the Max Planck Institute for Human Development in West Berlin. I have visited the Institute a number of times since 1996 and have also occasionally invited Erika Hoerning to visit Aalborg University. She has been tremendously helpful and inordinately patient in guiding me through the tricky and dangerous terrain of German reunification, seen from a West German point of view. As a specialist in the use of the biographical method of studying the East German intelligentsia, and a generalist in terms of the social research taking place in Germany on reunification, she provided a highly stimulating and critical sounding board during numerous wide-ranging discussions, gently suggesting readings I had missed and introducing me to a host of people working in areas outside her own field of expertise. My admiration for and gratitude to her are all the greater for the fact that most of her assistance was provided while she was experiencing a period of great personal duress and illness. Our cooperation resulted in an article published in *BIOS* (Vol. 12, 1999) on the problem of the lingering loyalty of the East German intelligentsia to the socialist GDR. The main ideas in the article inspired much of chapters 4, 5, and 6 of the volume.

A first draft of chapters 7 and 9 was presented during a lecture tour of Canada and the Mid-western United States in the fall of 1999. I thank Jeffrey Peck and Laurence Macfalls, Montreal University; Scott Eddie, Michael Borneman, and Robin Ostow, Toronto University; Carl Lankowski and Brad Weaver, American Institute for Contemporary German Studies, Washington, DC; Samuel Bowles, Georgetown University, Washington, DC; Christer Garrett, University of Wisconsin, Madison; and Andreas Glaser, University of Chicago, for reading and responding to my work in progress. I also thank Hans Gullestrup, Olav Juul Sørensen, and John Kuada, Center for International Studies at Aalborg University, for their helpful comments on the first drafts of chapters 1 and 2.

Special thanks also go to Ursula Apitz and Lena Inowlocki, Frankfurt University, who, in different ways, have helped me to understand the invisible ties between the problems of German reunification and the Nazi past; to Peter Alheit, Wolfgang Fischer-Rosenthal, and Gabriele Rosenthal for valuable discussions and material on the biographical method and its use in a German context; to Irene Runge, Jüdischer Kulturverein, Berlin; Cilly Kugelmann, the Jewish Museum, Frankfurt; and Michael Brenner, Munich University, for helping me to understand the variety of Jewish views on German reunification and its relation to the Nazi past; to Director Karl Ulrich Mayer, Martin Diewald, and Heike Solga, Max Planck Institute for Human Development, for helping to change my mistaken view of how professional groups in East Germany coped with the problems of career transition; Christa Händle and Gero Lenhardt,—Max Planck Institute for Human Development; Manfred Stock and Peter Hübner, Freie Universität Berlin; and Heinz-Elmar Tenort, Humboldt University, Berlin, for sharing their expertise on educational issues in East Germany; Helmuth Wiesenthal, Humboldt University, and Wolfgang Merkler, Heidelberg University, for introducing me to the German theoretical debate on transformation; Thomas Koch and Michael Thomas, BISS, and Dirck Jäger, Wissenschaftszentrum, Berlin, for their ideas on the inextricable link between cultural and economic issues in reunited Germany.

I feel privileged and grateful for the encouragement and suggestions of Irving Louis Horowitz at Transaction Publishers during the preparation and the final stages of the book. My copy editor, Pat Tucker, has done invaluable work, for which I offer my humble admiration. She has improved the manuscript in countless ways, which has been of great service both to me and to those who will read this book.

Most of all, I thank my wife, Angela Schou, for her moral support and invaluable help in introducing me to East German professionals, for the tremendous effort she invested in conducting and transcribing interviews in German, for the numerous discussions we have had as the book progressed, and for her gentle tolerance with my numerous absences over the past years as the research drew to its close. It is to her that I dedicate this book.

1

Introduction

Cultural Studies, German History, and Moral Lessons

Beyond Postmodernism

There are currently two main approaches to the study of culture—the essentialist and the constructivist traditions (Rutherford, 1990; McCarthy, 1996). Essentialists believe culture is at the very core of one's being, one cannot escape it, cannot even think beyond it. Culture is everywhere, in time as well as in space. Once one has been born into and/or grown up within a particular national or ethnic culture one becomes a prisoner of that culture, carrying it with one or being influenced by it for the rest of one's life. Culture, consisting as it does of collective beliefs and practices, extends into all one's activities, governs all aspects of one's life and dominates one's mindset. It influences child-caring practices, gender roles, friendship patterns, family rituals, food preferences and ways of communicating. The emphasis here is on culture as an underlying structure which is more or less immune to change or only changes very slowly—the role of personal choice is minimal and the individual is fundamentally unfree and takes the imposition of the culture for granted.

By contrast, constructivists view culture less as something given and unchanging than as a conscious choice. For them, cultural beliefs and practices are not natural or primordial, they are constructs of the human mind. Since they are brought into being by creative human beings, cultures and societies can be reshaped. Individuals are not prisoners of their past, they are responsible for their personal

1

or collective destiny. The emphasis here is on a dynamic, active and creative culture. And as cultures and societies change so do individuals. The message is that people are masters of their own future, not prisoners of the past.

The constructivist revolution in the social sciences was inaugurated by Peter Berger and Thomas Luckmann who, in their pathbreaking book *The Social Construction of Reality,* offered the first powerful argument for the role of reflexive agency rather than unbending structures as the point of departure for an understanding of societies and how they work. The core of this argument was later developed by Anthony Giddens in a number of seminal works such *as New Rules of the Sociological Method, Central Problems in Social Theory, A Contemporary Critique of Historical Materialism, The Constitutions of Society, Consequences of Modernity* and *Modernity and Self-Identity*, in which he set out the contours of an anti-structuralist view of culture, society and individual socialization. Giddens's project includes and is supplemented by Ulrich Beck's important work *Risk Society*, which is strikingly similar to Giddens's view, in the tone and content of its analysis of careers and labor markets in modern capitalism (see also the accompanying volume *What is Globalization?*).

Some cultural theorists claiming to be postmodernists but confessing themselves to be constructivist rather than essentialist use the ideas of Berger and Luckmann and Giddens and Beck for purposes that are radically different from their original intentions. Neither in Peter Berger's extensive writings after *The Social Construction of Reality* nor in Anthony Giddens's project on developing a theory around the concept of reflexive agency do we find anything even resembling the inherently nihilistic idea of moral and cultural relativism to which postmodernist students of culture seem to be so strongly attracted (Sarup, 1988).

This is, I believe, one of the main reasons why Giddens has consistently refused to accept the concept of a postmodernist society. There is no such thing. We have not passed beyond modernity, and the very claim that we have is a dishonest way of preserving the antimodernist prejudices of cultural studies inherent in the structuralist or culturalist view. But whereas the antimodernist bias of structuralism originated in the fears of a discipline (cultural anthropology) of losing the object of its research, the antimodernism of the postmodernists mainly stems from a deep disillusionment with Marxism. Postmodernism is the strategy of a utopian intelligentsia that has seen its utopia vanish but is not yet prepared to ask itself why and for whom the inner connection between utopian beliefs and totalitarian regimes remains elusive. Postmodernism is a means of pretending that utopia still exists as a serious intellectual alternative, although all the evidence of the twentieth century, and in particular the German experience, points to the opposite. Postmodernism is the will not to learn from history and in particular not to learn from German history.

The attempt by postmodernism to usurp the constructivist point of view should be seen in the context of Peter Berger's clear rejection of utopia in *The Homeless Mind* (co-authored with Birgitte Berger and Hans-Joachim Kellner). The basic purpose of the book is to outline the background of political alienation and utopian antimodernism of the modern cultural intelligentsia. For Peter Berger, to be a constructionist was definitely not to be a moral relativist or intellectual nihilist. Modernity, with all its accompanying problems and dark sides, does indeed have a crucial moral advantage over traditional societies, namely the rise of free and morally responsible citizens. As an intellectual refugee from Nazi-dominated Europe, Peter Berger had experienced the crucial difference between a society in which the civil ethos was firmly ingrained in the moral fiber of a national culture and one in which this ethos was sorely lacking. This personal experience explains, I believe, why Berger never vacillated in his commitment to modernity and firmly upheld his view in spite of its increasing unpopularity with the cultural ascendancy in academia—the heartland of the intelligentsia.

The paradox is that although the postmodernist view of culture defines itself in contrast to the essentialist view, the underlying antimodernist message of cultural essentialism and postmodernist "constructivism" remains the same. As several sociologists have pointed out, the antimodernist streak among the modern cultural intelligentsia has made it strongly receptive to totalitarian utopias of various kinds (Aron, 1957; Löwy, 1979; Gouldner, 1985). On the surface postmodernist cultural theorists (Hall, 1990; 1991; Weeks, 1990; Robertson, 1992; McCarthy, 1996; Bauman, 1999) appear to have made a radical break with essentialism. They all emphasize a dynamic concept of culture, arguing that cultural identity is not stable but evolves through a series of transformations or turning points, displaying more discontinuity than continuity. Far from being essential or primordial, culture is constructed from a hybrid mixture of past, present and future. Cultural identities are constantly reconstituted or renegotiated. Instead of representing our "roots," cultural identities are shifting points of identification in time and space with nothing fixed or inherent about them. Entering the area of culture means entering the area of free choice and reflexivity.

The problem with this alternative, free-floating concept of culture is that it implies that individuals cannot transcend their own pasts because they live in the present and have no pasts to relate to. Because postmodern people are so mobile, they never stop to learn anything from collective experience. Strictly speaking, such a collective experience does not exist, as the individual constantly negotiates and renegotiates many different identities, of which national identity is only one. Since gender, ethnicity or sexual preference might be much more important for a particular individual than nation, why should he or she engage in the project of learning anything from his or her own national history or heritage?

Since identities are mere constructs, any given culture is as good or valid as any other. There is no universal truth or morality to appeal to and every culture formulates its own criteria of moral and cognitive validity. Postmodernism thus tends to take the antimodernist bias of structuralism to its extreme. Because identity (class, gender, age, sexual preference, ethnicity and so on) is constantly renegotiated by the individual in postmodern society, every attempt to reach a universal consensus on what is morally or cognitively valid must necessarily be a hidden attempt to impose a cultural understanding from the outside—a kind of cultural imperialism or chauvinism of the powerful.

Thus the postmodernist version of the constructivist view of culture does not depart fundamentally from the most problematic consequence of essentialism, its antimodernism and provincialism. On the contrary, it radicalizes the provincialism of the orthodox essentialist or culturalist view. Precisely because cultures are thought of as being mere constructs, there is no way to argue that the study of culture can help elaborate a universally valid moral narrative of humanity. Although more mobile, "postmodern man" thus ultimately remains a prisoner of the past. Postmodernism makes the very idea of universality through exchange of ideas look hopelessly anachronistic. The orthodox view of culture was based on the cosmopolitan assumption that humans as members of the same species are fundamentally alike and that cultural differences are mere variations of the same fundamental human patterns of thought (Levi-Strauss, 1977). In postmodernism this logic has been turned upside down—it is the differences that are important, everything else is subsidiary (Weeks, 1990). The very idea of postmodernism is to abandon any attempt at "Grand Narrative" in the moral realm (Lyotard, 1984).

This should be seen though in the historical context of a previous uncritical embrace of one particular "Grand Narrative," namely the Marxist or historical materialist narrative, predicting the final crisis of capitalism and the coming of socialist and communist society. Such a position would indeed look silly today. What remains, if one still harbors utopian dreams of a return to a premodern type of national community, is the postmodernist posture, which gives the antimodernist intelligentsia the satisfaction of depriving the promodernist intellectuals of the joy of intellectual victory. Postmodernism is the "sour grapes" of the antimodernist who clings to a vulgar, antiuniversalistic interpretation of Berger and Luckmann's highly original argument. There is nothing whatsoever to support this interpretation. What Berger and Luckmann emphasize is reflexive agency or the idea that individuals are creative rather than mere products of the environment. They never advance the nihilistic idea that nothing of universal validity can be learned from studying different cultures.

Cultural Interaction and Moral Lessons

For students of German history, the postmodernist concept of culture as unrelated to moral values and in particular the idea of civic ethos, the denial of scientific universality and the indifference to history as a means of moral learning has little attraction. On the contrary, the story of Germany is a perfect example of the importance of reflexive agency in history. Learning from history is what the study of German national culture is about, that is what gives it its fundamental value. The vital element missing from both the essentialist and postmodernist theories of culture is the crucial fact that national cultures are never isolated worlds, they always interact and this interaction helps them learn from the past. This cultural interaction is no mere epiphenomenon, it should be the main point of departure for our understanding of cultural dynamics and identities. Until recently, though, few cultural theorists apart from the Norwegian anthropologist Frederik Barth (1996) have taken this international or global aspect of cultural interaction seriously. Both the structuralists and the postmodernists prefer the provincial or local point of view. The main reason is, I believe, an inherent antimodernist bias in cultural studies present both in the traditional and postmodernist form although for different reasons.

The antimodernist or structuralist view originated in the professional bias of an academic discipline in fear of losing its subject matter. This explains the tone of lamentation and nostalgia in *Tristes Tropiques*, Claude Lévi-Strauss's autobiographical account of his travels among the Indian Tribes in Brazil. But the fact that a research object is disappearing in front of our eyes can never in itself be a valid claim for a particular culture to remain untouched and unchanged by forces from outside or inside. If we were to accept this plea for the cultural preservation of all our research objects, students of German history and society would find themselves in the same position as the neoNazis and supporters of the PDS in contemporary East Germany who represent pitiful attempts to cope with a GDR past (Klessmann, 1993; Walther, 1993) rooted in Nazi Germany and reproducing precisely those premodern German traditions that made a Hitler possible in the first place (see in particular chapters 3 and 8).

What is interesting is that the national cultures of Nazi Germany and the GDR changed mainly because of the impact of outside forces. In the first case it was only the defeat of Nazi Germany by the Allied forces which transformed (West) Germany from an aggressively nationalistic and racist state to a peace-seeking and cosmopolitan nation-state. In the second case, the obvious economic superiority of the West German economy (Schulz and Wielgohs, 1990; Offe, 1994) gradually eroded popular support for a regime which, until its collapse, had survived mainly because of the antifascist credentials and accompanying mythologies of its communist leaders, who claimed to represent the "Better Germany" (Meuschel, 1992; Simon, 1995).

Lévi-Strauss's mistake is that he looks upon the world from a narrowly professional point of view. Since anthropology originally legitimized itself in terms of exploring that part of the world which was seen as "primitive" and "uncivilized," the disappearance of these cultures was felt as a long term threat to the existence of the discipline itself. Lévi-Strauss's fears were unfounded—anthropology has been able to flourish because of the universality of its methodological approach which transcends its original objects. Nevertheless, the original, mainly isolationist and static view of culture has tended to haunt the profession and has become increasingly irrelevant in an age of globalization (Hannerz, 1996).

The provincial and antiglobalist bias of cultural studies manifests itself both in the extreme cultural determinism of structuralist cultural theory and in the extreme cultural and moral relativism of postmodernism. The claim for the view that individuals are totally shaped by their culture and cannot escape their past assumes that they are brought up in a culture which is left untouched by other cultures, in other words does not engage in cultural interaction. What is interesting is that the argument for cultural and moral relativism—that there are no universal cognitive or moral truths to be learned from history—is based upon the same assumption of provincial isolation. But cultures do change and moral learning does take place and one of the main reasons they do so is the interaction of traditional societies with more modern ones.

This interaction does not have to take the form of military conquest or economic impact. Sometimes the strongest impact of the more modern culture can be to function as a model of liberation or emancipation of repressed needs and wishes which the traditional society has regulated out of existence. Daniel Lerner refers to this type of cultural change in his seminal study, *The Passing of Traditional Society*. Lerner found that in all traditional societies there was a group of "moderns" who were anxious to escape from the bonds of the past and acquire the right to shape their own future. For them the encounter with modernity, although mainly theoretical and acquired through various media, nevertheless gave its members hope that their circumstances could indeed change. Similarly, access to West German television nourished hopes and dreams in East Germany of a different future from the one the communist rulers could offer its citizens (Gaus, 1986).

Coping with Cultural Prejudices

One of the main problems with both the structuralist and the postmodernist views of culture is that they make it difficult to see how cultural prejudices can be changed or modified. If cultures do not interact, individuals brought up in a particular culture are totally at the mercy of the group around them. They conform, they obey authority, their self-esteem is strongly tied to the destiny of the group, and they tend to develop strong and stereotyped images of themselves and others in order to boost their self-esteem.

This is what we should expect from a national culture, any culture. The problem is that it does not fit the German case. Although both West and East Germans tend to stereotype both themselves and the other, a comparison of the stereotypes of the two groups reveals an interesting difference (see chapter 7). Whereas East Germans believe themselves to be better than West Germans in all respects and find no reason to be self-critical, West Germans tend to present themselves in a surprisingly unflattering light. Their collective image of themselves is significantly more negative than that of the East Germans and their image of the other is significantly more positive.

This suggests a dimension, the importance of which is often ignored by both structuralist and postmodernist cultural theorists, namely that modernity brings with it a higher degree of individualization in the sense of individual empowerment and liberation from group conformity. The reason the West German stereoptypes are more self-reflexive is that the individual is less dependent upon the group for his or her self-esteem than is the East German. The question is why? How is this greater dependence upon and integration into the group among East Germans to be explained? And what are its consequences for the psychological wall that has developed between East and West Germans since unification?

How we as scholars account for the cultural differences between the two groups depends upon our point of departure or our view of the meaning of cultural studies. A cultural theorist, whether of the structuralist or the postmodernist school, would focus merely on the fact that there are indeed stereotypes among both groups. Structuralist cultural theorists would claim that this proves their main point— that individuals are prisoners of their past. The postmodernist would argue that no universally valid moral truths can be established through cultural comparison, that all cultures are valid from their own point of view and that truths are always related to the cultural context in which they arise and gain acceptance.

Both these views are unable to take account of the fact that both postwar Germanies basically rejected the cultural values of Nazi Germany, in particular its racist and militaristic dimensions, and tried to learn something from history. This raises the important question: How do we as scholars decide which of the two German states learned the right lesson or made the most accurate diagnosis of what had gone wrong in German history? To formulate the question in such a way we have first of all to abandon the deterministic idea that individuals are prisoners of the past, as this would not allow for the fact that a change of culture actually did take place, particularly in West Germany. But we have also to abandon the nihilistic postmodernist approach of moral relativism which makes it impossible for the scholar to critically analyze the reasons why East German culture preserved important aspects of the traditional German culture which produced the racism and militarism of Nazi Germany.

The fact is there is a German past from which the two states, in different ways, have tried to distance themselves. In 1945 there was only one type of German—shaped by the past. Today there are two types of Germans—shaped by different interpretations of that past. It is this element of historical and biographical reflexivity or learning that should be the subject of investigation by those who adopt a constructionist view of culture, not the obvious fact that individuals are shaped by the culture in which they grow up, nor the absurd claim that there are no universal moral values that can be used as a yardstick to measure moral progress.

It simple does not make sense to study the East Germans from either a structuralist or a postmodernist point of view. What is interesting is not that they were shaped by East German society and that the West Germans were shaped by West German society or the trivial fact that their cultures are indeed different. Difference in itself does not deserve our respect, nor is the preservation of such a difference a value in itself. What this culturally relativist posture evades is the most important fact of modern German history and culture, namely what the two postwar Germanies actually learned from the Nazi past. In order to study this, we need a firm moral foundation, a view of history that asks what kind of moral lesson a given nation learned in a particular period. What happened during those fifty years in the two post-war Germanies and why was the moral lesson that was learned so different in the two cases?

Universal Truths and the Scientific Enterprise

In order to formulate the question in this way we have to assume that there are indeed universal truths in both the cognitive and the moral fields. This is a growing insight among students of environmental problems in a global context, although they have rarely been able to convince the postmodernists (Yearly, 1996). The fear of ethnographers and anthropologists of losing their research object and thereby their careers, academic status and scientific contributions explains the antimodernist bias of the pioneers of cultural studies. In order to understand the cultural relativism and antiuniversalism of contemporary cultural studies, which have been strongly influenced by the postmodernist view of culture, we have to expand our view and look closer at the general antimodernism of modern intellectuals, which until recently (particularly among the Paris intellectuals, the creative milieu which has provided most of the leading thinkers in the humanities and social sciences in the postwar period) was strongly dedicated to the Marxist world-view. As this world-view collapsed in the nineteen-seventies and eighties, French intellectuals invented the idea of the death of the "Grand Narrative" and declared all global world-views or universal truths to be illusory. The fact that this sentiment is in itself a reflection of their deep disillusionment with the world is rarely taken into account, though, and helps legitimate the continuing strong antimodernist bias among the group.

Although French postmodernist intellectuals like Derrida and Foucault have abandoned the strong cultural determinism of the Levi-Strauss school, they have also abandoned the imminent cosmopolitanism of the latter, arguing that the search for universal truths underlying all cultures, which remained Levi-Strauss's life project, was a futile enterprise. Since there is no "Grand Narrative" in history, there are no such universal laws or truths. If everything is relative, the very idea of looking for universally valid truths outside a given cultural context is futile. But if that is indeed the case, the core of modernity—the scientific belief in human betterment through the accumulation of universally valid truths—is itself futile.

Scientific enterprise cannot be reduced to theoretical speculation or experimental work. As the two greatest theorists of science in this century, Robert Merton and Karl Popper, have emphasized, science is essentially an institution based upon certain fundamental values and norms, the most important of which is the universality of knowledge (Merton, 1968, 1973; Popper, 1972, 1966). The whole scientific enterprise stands or falls by the simple idea that it is possible to establish the validity of a particular knowledge claim, wherever it has originated, by using the same procedures, in particular the international exchange of ideas institutionalized through peer review (Coser, 1970). Science strives for the universally valid and is, by its very definition, international. Once we give up this fundamental article of faith, we are lost in a barbarian wilderness.

The idea of universalism is fundamental to modernity, it regulates not only scientific enterprise but the way in which labor markets are organized, according to the universal principle of individual merit or to the particularistic principle of ethnic or national origins. The abandonment of one often leads to the abandonment of the other. A case in point is Nazi Germany, where the decision to exclude German scientists and academics of Jewish origin from universities and research institutes was legitimated in terms of a presumed difference between "Aryan" and "Jewish" science. Since the two were radically different in kind (and the former was declared to be inherently superior) the nation would lose nothing if the best brains were sent abroad.

There was surprisingly little resistance among members of the German scientific establishment of the time to the use of modern science to legitimate a clearly antimodernist labor market policy (Jackman and Borden, 1983). Not even those academics who faked enthusiasm for the Nazi revolution seemed to be able to shake off the shameless opportunism that motivated their misguided effort (Safranski, 1998), a behavioral pattern that was repeated frequently during the Nazi regime (König et al., 1997).

We know for a fact that Einstein's decision never to set foot in Germany after the war was rooted in his dismay at the shameless behavior of his German colleagues at a time when their scientific universalistic creed was put to the test (Hermann, 1996; White and Gribbin, 1997). He never forgave their cowardice and opportunism. Nor did Sartre forgive those of his French colleagues who succumbed to a similar disease, anti-Semitism, which, as he argues vividly, expressly denies the universalistic principle of proven merit, replacing it with the particularistic argument of primordial cultural superiority (Sartre, 1965).

Mind-sets and Identity Constructs

In order to avoid the pitfalls of both the essentialist and the purely constructivist or postmodernist views of culture, we need a different way of conceptualizing it. Any given national culture has two dimensions—mind-sets and identity constructs. The advantage of this duality is that it allows for both history and biography and thereby moral teaching. Such teaching often takes place between different cultures but it does not do so in a social vacuum, it involves a degree of self-reflexivity that varies from person to person, particularly when an historical dimension is introduced. This makes it crucial to look upon culture not only as something dynamic, but also to assume that there are some universally valid truths to be gained from particular national experiences. The history of the Germans is not only of interest to Germans, it has implications for other nations and national cultures as well.

If we want to study this learning process, the duality of national culture in terms of attitudes and identity constructs has to be taken into account. Attitudes are close to what the structuralist cultural theorists meant when they talked about culture—namely collectively held beliefs and practices. At the same time it is important to emphasize the constructed nature of national cultures. This element of construction is emphasized in the concept of identities, which is closest to the postmodernist view of culture. I differ from the postmodernist view in my belief that such identity constructs contain elements of universal validity and historical lessons in which the postmodernists are not interested. Having lost their belief in one "Grand Narrative" they do not wish to see it replaced with another, particularly not one which emphasizes the values of modernity.

The basic assumption is thus that attitudes or national cultures are shaped by historical learning processes that manifest themselves in the form of national identity constructs.

National identities and attitudes do not exist in an historical vacuum. They are the outcome of intellectual attempts to make sense of history. Although interaction with other cultures is the predominant external cause of change, such change is always mediated by internal political and intellectual élites. Thus it was not only the defeat of the Nazi regime but also the way in which the political and intellectual élites in the two Germanies interpreted the meaning of this defeat that played a decisive role in the evolution of their particular national culture and attitudes (Herf, 1997).

The particular identity constructs or conscious attempts to create meaning out of what had happened and ways in which to avoid a similar catastrophe in the future had a decisive impact upon the different attitudes that developed in the two post-war Germanies. National identities are basically ways of making the past meaningful in order to give direction to the future. This in turn shapes everyday thinking and practices in schools, in the labor market, in political and cultural life, and also in the personal experiences of individuals who have "grown old together" in a particular system and have adjusted their expectations to the possibilities and risks inherent in that system (Kupferberg, 1995).

This emphasis on the role of national history and individual biographies in teaching moral lessons sets my view of national identity apart from the approach of most theorists who are mainly interested in the problem of popular identification with the identity constructs of the élites. Thus Smith (1986) emphasizes the role of historical myths which make individuals believe they have a legitimate claim to a particular territory; Anderson debates the willingness of individuals to sacrifice themselves for the nation in order to defend territory (Anderson, 1991); Ignatieff (1995) and Connor (1994) argue that beliefs in ethnic origins or "blood ties" are the most important elements in determining strong feelings of belonging to a given nation.

This emphasis on belonging is one of the issues which divides the present German nation. If a prerequisite for the cultural unity of a nation, as Deutsch (1966) suggests, is ease of communication, one of the main reasons why this type of communication has not evolved is national affinity. One of the most divisive, if not the most divisive, cultural issues after reunification is the strong presence among East Germans of feelings of belonging to the "German" nation in the historical sense and the absence of such feelings among the majority of West Germans (Scheuch, 1991; Seebacher-Brandt, 1994; Kupferberg, 1996b; Westle, 1999). How is this difference to be accounted for?

Although an understanding of the "inner wall" that divides reunited Germany is dependent on a knowledge of the identity constructs of the political and intellectual élites, these constructs are less interesting if they do not make a deep impact upon the culture or attitudes of ordinary citizens. Although current literature on national identity emphasizes its constructed nature (Eisenstadt and Giesen, 1995), there is a tendency to focus exclusively upon the role of the élites (Brass, 1991). However, if the focus is on learning processes, we are interested not only in what and how élites learn, but also in what and how ordinary citizens learn. In the case of Germany it is interesting to know something about how the thinking of the élites about the nation influenced the cultural beliefs, practices and attitudes of ordinary Germans (Schweigler, 1975).

This distinction between attitude and identity is suggested in *The Social Construction of Reality* in which Berger and Luckmann draw a distinction between a phenomenological sociology of knowledge focusing upon biographically founded constructions of everyday life (Schutz, 1973-1975) and the systematic world-views of the intelligentsia (see Mannheim, 1968; Merton, 1968; Gouldner, 1979). Later studies of the roots of particular world-views (Löwy, 1979; Gouldner, 1985) suggest that from a methodological point of view the difference is not as clear as is suggested by Berger and Luckmann. The world-views of the intellectuals can also be studied from a phenomenological point of view, which is suggested in *The Homeless Mind*. In this view intellectuals are seen in a dual cultural context— they are members of national communities but are also socialized into professional communities. This dual identity has rarely been examined as a possible source of the utopian thinking of the intelligentsia. Indeed, a focus upon the patterns of socialization within a given particular national context can help towards a better understanding of the sociological origins of the systematic world-views which Mannheim talks about.

Another reason to focus upon attitudes in the East German case is that historically they have been important in the world-view of German intellectuals. In contrast to the modern view of national identity in which the focus is mainly upon symbols and representations and more generally upon its constructed dimension, the German school, beginning with Herder, argued that nations are less intellectual constructs than they are organic products rooted in the everyday life and practices of its people. Herder, whose writing on the nation originated as a reaction to the crushing military defeats of the Germans by France in the Napoleonic Wars, "urged his fellow Germans to cease their imitation of French ways and turn instead to the contemplation of their national heritage. He called for a return to German native roots and for an emphasis on the life of the *Volk*, the common people. A sound civilization, he warned, must reflect a specific national character, what he called a *Volksgeist*, or spirit of the people. Attention to the *Volksgeist* was to become an important element of German nationalism" (Snyder, 1996: 3).

This view of the nation as something rooted in the everyday life of the people can be seen as a particular variety of the postmodernist, relativist view which rejects the universalistic intentions of modern intellectual thought as represented by the French Enlightenment. There is a clear line between this way of thinking and the direction the nationalistic cause took in Germany. As pointed out by Alan Beyerchen at a symposium on the German intellectuals or "Muses" who had to flee Hitler:

> there had long existed a deep and popular strain of anti-intellectualism in Germany. This strain was not an absolute rejection of all products of the mind but rather constituted opposition to and contempt for the Enlightenment belief that man could use rational processes to comprehend nature. It was rooted in the romantic backlash against the Age of Reason and posited an antagonism between objective, mechanistic universalism and subjective, organic nationalism. The fact that the universalism of the Enlightenment became popularly associated with the French occupation armies of Napoleon, fed the notion that internationalism was merely a way of keeping the Germans weak, divided, and at mercy of the Great Powers. (Beyerchen, 1983: 31-2)

In spite of the culturalist and reactionary implications of Herder's definition of the nation as rooted in "*das Volk*," he does have a point in the sense that nations are not exclusively the creation of intellectual and political élites. If there is to be a more complete understanding of what nations are, how they come about and why they remain nations, popular attitudes have to be taken into account. This is indirectly recognized in Renan's definition of the nation as a "daily referendum" (cit. Hutchinson and Smith, 1994: 17). Hobsbawm (1991) postulates the existence of something he calls "protonationalism" which clearly addresses the problem of how non-élites respond to the identity constructs of political and economic élites. Hobsbawm's thesis has been empirically tested by Hedetoft (1995) who tried to identify signs of such protonationalism in different European countries (Denmark, Great Britain and Germany).

German unification seemed to confirm the existence of protonationalism or feelings of "belonging" among ordinary people (Ignatieff, 1995). In spite of a separate existence in two German states for half a century, the idea of one German nation was not dead. National feelings had survived, in particular among East Germans, whereas West German national feelings were much more subdued (Merkl, 1992; Blank, 1997). The paradox was that in spite of strong feelings of belonging to the German "nation," East Germans also felt strongly culturally (Belwe, 1992; Ritter, 1996) and politically (Fuchs et al., 1997; Misselwitz, 1999) alienated from the German state of which they had recently become members. They increasingly expressed pride in the communist and socialist system they had only recently abandoned (*Der Spiegel*, 1995a; 1999) developing a distinct East German identity (Reich, 1996; Koch, 1996; 1997; 1998).

This response refutes the framework of national identity theory and forces us to regard the role of ordinary citizens in a given nation in a somewhat different light from that suggested by the school of protonationalism. The problem with the theory of protonationalism is that it tends to reduce the role of ordinary citizens to a mere endorsement of the identity constructs of the élites. Looked at from this perspective, the people basically lack the self-reflexivity and rationality of élites. They have no capacity for moral responsibility and when they act, they act not out of civic responsibility but out of pure emotion or for "patriotic" reasons. This viewpoint clearly underestimates the element of citizenship and the role of the civic ethos in the history of modern nations. If only intellectual élites are able to act rationally, the only alternative to Nazism in Germany would have been an educational dictatorship. This was the conclusion reached by the East German élites. These theories of national identity thus end up legitimizing the East German dictatorship, albeit unintentionally.

Past and Present

If we examine more closely what it is that divides East and West Germans we find that it is the question of what constitutes morally responsible actions. Although they both identify themselves as "German" in some sense (James, 1989; Craig, 1991; Watson, 1994) they have answered the question of what it means to be German after Hitler and Auschwitz in radically different ways which have had a far greater influence on attitudes than is generally assumed. My conclusion is that whereas after 1945 West Germans underwent a radical process of political resocialization, aimed at producing a strong moral or civic ethos which would function as an effective barrier against the return of a new Hitler, this resocialization never took place among East Germans, who basically remained emotionally and culturally as they were when the Nazi regime was defeated.

There are several indicators that this is indeed the case and that the main problem now faced by the East Germans is the difficulty of abandoning this construct. Thus 82 percent of them, responding to an opinion poll conducted in 1995, asserted that "life was simpler earlier" (*Der Spiegel*, 1995a: 46). This finding can be interpreted in many ways, but a reasonable interpretation is that what the East Germans liked about East Germany was not only that the individual was firmly governed by the state, but that the emphasis on the role of the government helped the individual to evade moral responsibility. The dilemma of those East Germans who wanted to have more freedom was that freedom would mean that they had to regard themselves as morally responsible citizens. As such they had to ask themselves difficult questions about what they or their parents and relatives had done under Hitler.

The hidden function of the over-regulated "tutelary state" (Jarauch, 1998) was to free the East Germans from brooding about the past, though this is rarely mentioned in the literature on German unification, which focuses instead upon economic problems and the impact of change on the labor market (Dahn, 1997; Fassbender et al., 1993; Glatzer and Noll, 1995; Hilmer, 1993; Lucas and Edgar, 1989-90; Marz, 1992; Mayer, 1994; Mutz, 1996; Schmidt and Lutz, 1995; Pollack and Pickel, 1998; Schröter, 1995; Seiring, 1995; Sontheimer, 1994; Veen and Zelle, 1996; Walz and Brunner, 1997; Zapf, 1991, 1994; Zelle, 1998). This emphasis on the present ignores the enormous importance of reflecting on the past in order to learn from it. In order to become reflexive agents we need to take the entire past of our national cultures into account. Moral evasion is a kind of refusal to learn from history and a way of avoiding the responsibilities of the free citizen and remaining a prisoner of the past.

The hidden dimension of East German history and the main lasting effect of its antifascist identity construct were the creation of loyal subjects rather than morally responsible citizens. This element however only became apparent after unification. Theodor Geiger defines attitudes as the "disposition of the thought and soul." He emphasizes that they are different from systematic world-views or constructed collective identities—"Attitudes are subjective (even if they are collective attitudes)...ideology is objective thought"—and that they are "disguised" (Geiger, 1932/87, cit. Veen, 1997: 5.) Because they are hidden they are only revealed in times of radical change. "It is precisely in times of socio-structural changes that these attitudes, behavioral dispositions and value-orientations become clear. Often they cannot follow the tempo of socio-structural change and for this reason stand out prominently in relation to the new structures. To the degree that we are talking of such long term modes of behavior, attitudes and value preferences, we often talk of attitudes" (Pollack, 1992: 489).

For this reason German reunification, looked at from a methodological point of view, can help us better to study an aspect of German history and culture which until 1989 was clearly underestimated, namely the long-term mental impact upon West and East Germans of having lived in two different systems, legitimized by two competing views of what it meant to be a German after Hitler and Auschwitz (Clausen, 1986; Knowlton and Truett, 1993).

> Questions of attitudes among social groups, regional and national communities, become virulent at turning points, incisions and breaks in social development. Disparities between everyday routines, preconscious wisdom, self-evident duties and new claims of behavior and action are experienced as increased insecurity, irritations and life crises. This is the reason that the literature about the history of attitudes uses these turning points as indicators of attitude. (Woderich, 1991a: 121)

My main methodological assumption is thus that the problems of cultural adaptation among East Germans after reunification expose the different mentalities of East and West Germans which are the result of competing national identity constructs in the post-war period. Whether there exists such a thing as an East German mentality which is distinctly different from a West German one, will emerge as one studies both their attitudes to one another and the problems of the East Germans with cultural adaptation. A postmodernist approach would most certainly have led to a different way of presenting the problem at hand. Why should the East Germans adapt to West German life, why not ask the West Germans to adapt?

Although I do not exclude the possibility that the East Germans might have brought some valuable cultural traits to reunified Germany, I cannot pretend that the moral question of what the Germans learned from history does not exist or that it is a secondary issue. On the contrary, the more I have worked with the issue of East German attitudes and identity, the more convinced I have become that it is the core issue of German unification. Having started with the assumption that the main problem was that the East Germans found it difficult to adapt themselves to the West German labor market (Kupferberg, 1998; 1999), I have become wiser.

Recent studies indicate that the East Germans, particularly members of the intelligentsia, have not fared as badly on the labor market as is often assumed (Mayer et al.1996; Diewald and Mayer, 1996). There is no compelling reason to feel sorry for them, they are not bound to be losers because of their particular cultural background. Thus a German psychologist emphasizes that "western culture...has created a human type which, with its high degree of individuality and self-orientation, also becomes an obstacle to itself. Young East Germans...are often already writing the diploma work they have been offered and see in it their hopes for the future while West German students are still brooding over whether the theme fits their 'personal profile.'" And a Swiss professor, teaching international diplomacy at the foreign ministry of Bonn believes that the East Germans will be "the better civil servants in the future" because "where systems are bureaucratic, they will have fewer difficulties learning how to adapt to politics" and because they know "how one survives in a rigid system" (*Der Spiegel*, 1995a: 53).

The main problem of German unification as I see it, is thus not the capacity of East Germans to adapt to the West German labor market. On the contrary, they might even have some competitive advantages in selected areas because they do not put the same strong emphasis on individuality, personal opinions and moral responsibility as do West Germans. What worries me is what the addition of sixteen million East Germans who have been socialized into a system emphasizing the construct of the loyal subject as the ideal of the modern citizen will have on German popular attitudes and national identity in the long run (Schneider, 1999).

2

The Unmanaged Past: Rethinking the Inner Wall in Reunited Germany

The Problem

In Leo Szilard's memoir of his time in the faculty of the Kaiser Wilhelm Institute in Berlin-Dahlem, the great physicist observes:

> I was there when the *Reichstagsbrand* occurred, and I remember how difficult it was for people to understand what was going on. A friend of mine, Michael Polanyi, who was director of a division of the Kaiser Wilhelm Institute for Physical Chemistry, like many other people took a very optimistic view of the situation. They all thought that civilized Germans would not stand for anything really rough happening. The reason I took the opposite position was based on observations of rather small and insignificant things. I noticed that Germans always took a practical point of view. They asked, "Well, suppose I were to oppose this, what good could I do? I wouldn't do very much good, I would lose my influence. Then why should I oppose it?" You see, the moral point of view was completely absent, or very weak, and every consideration was simply, what the predictable consequence of any action would be. And on that basis I reached the conclusion in 1931 that Hitler would get into power, not because the forces of the Nazi revolution were so strong, but rather because I thought there would be no resistance whatsoever. (Szilard, 1969: 95-96)

How right he was. The Weimar Republic collapsed not because the Germans had become Nazis (Brustein, 1996), but because the non-Nazis were too German. The question one can legitimately ask is how much of that traditional "German" attitude survived in the two post-war Germanies. The Israeli journalist Amos Elon, who visited Germany in the 1960s, felt that the Germans were still too German for his taste, but his feeling of being in a "haunted country" reached almost bizarre heights as he traveled through the GDR. Here the past was a painfully vivid reality, although the political leaders kept repeating that fascism has been uprooted once and for all (Elon, 1965). Schweigler, in his comparative study of national consciousness in the two Germanies in the nineteen-seventies, found, to his surprise, that cultural attitudes and practices that had long since died out in the Federal Republic, such as an unmistakably shrill "Prussian" tone of command and expectations of obedience, were still very evident in the GDR. Moreover, this seemed to be one of the reasons why ordinary East Germans felt a certain pride in their state. In contrast to West Germany, the GDR seemed to preserve a certain order and discipline (Schweigler, 1975).

The Past in the Present

In 1991, a year after German reunification, pupils between the ages of 15 and 19 from two German Länder, Rheinland-Pfalz, West Germany and Thüringen, East Germany, were asked to write a short essay on the topic "One year of German Unity—What I think about it." A thousand of these essays were collected and some were later published in a book. Although the tone and content of the essays varies some important patterns do emerge. One of these fits the hypothesis which has been well documented by extensive social research in reunited Germany, namely that East and West Germans have great difficulty in communicating with each other because they look upon the world with different mindsets - what Kelly terms "personal constructs" (Kelly, 1955; Talbot and Rickards, 1984).

The essays also suggest a lack of conceptual distinction in most sociological studies on German reunification which rarely take into account the very different reactions of ordinary Germans and the élites. West German élites have by and large been very sympathetic to reunification (in contrast to ordinary West Germans who have often resented it). There is also a tendency to undervalue the generally positive view of unification among ordinary East Germans. We should not make the mistake of identifying these views with the predominantly negative view found among East German élites. It is not insignificant that the East German élites were much more strongly committed to the idea of a socialist GDR than ordinary East Germans and that they therefore have an interest in over-dramatizing the negative aspects of unification. "Only twenty percent of the East German population vote for the post-communist party (PDS), but the motives for the behavior of this minority are something which dominates the public feeling" (Reich, 1996:133; See also Berking, 1995).

Whereas ordinary East Germans welcomed reunification but were overwhelmed by the changes in everyday life and suffered from the culture shock of adaptation to a highly modern society (Harre, 1991; Glaessner, 1992, 1993; Reissig, 1993a, 1993b; Schmitz, 1995), a substantial minority, particularly the socialist intelligentsia (the educated classes) who had been very close to the system and had gained from it (Fulbrook, 1997; Reich, 1992) would prefer to have continued the socialist experiment in one way or another and for this reason strongly resisted, on principle, the idea of reunification (Jarauch, 1994; Land & Possekel, 1994; Geulen, 1998). Interestingly this resistance has not diminished over the years, but has been kept alive by these groups, partly because of a lingering commitment to the socialist GDR (Hoerning and Kupferberg, 1999), partly because ordinary East Germans seem to have become disenchanted by West German society and have increasingly turned to a reappraisal of the "good" sides of socialist society (*Der Speigel*, 1995a; Koch, 1996, 1997, 1998).

A third aspect that emerges from the essays is the issue of the moral lessons to be learnt from the collapse of the Weimar Republic and the way in which different interpretations of what made Nazi Germany possible continue to color and influence the political climate and public communication in Germany. The lack of attention paid to this moral dimension in the sociological, socio-psychological and political science literature leaves a "lacuna" which can only be bridged by transcending the sociological/social scientific interpretation of interview material, which tends to reduce the analysis of reunification to issues related to socio-economic interests and social status (Alheit, 1995; Veen, 1995; Pollack, 1997) or to the after-effects of having been socialized in a different system with pre-modern traits (Fischer, 1992; Trommsdorf, 1995; Schluchter, 1996). What is often excluded are the moral issues of German national and personal histories (Ritter, 1996; Fischer-Rosenthal, 1995) which are at the core of a deeper understanding of the phenomenon of the internal divide between East and West Germans, the communicative or inner wall which emerged after reunification.

The Inner Wall

The East-West divide can be illustrated by the following excerpts from two essays, the first written by a West German pupil, the second by an East German pupil, both of them from working-class schools:

Since the wall was opened, things are becoming worse for all of us again. Taxes are going up and prices in the shops are rising. We therefore have to pay for the opening of the wall. I find this vile, because for many families things were going better earlier. And now it is again going down the drain. You can no longer find any apartments, because these are occupied by GDR-citizens...they imagine that we have to give them everything so they may achieve a beautiful life ... now they complain about getting so "little" money. They should be glad that they get anything at all from us. (Girl from a *Hauptschule*, 9th Grade, West Germany; cit. Böhm et al., 1993: 26)

Unity came too fast. It didn't give people in the new *Bundesländer* enough time to prepare for it or think it over. Everything happened too quickly. Suddenly all the Wessies were standing in front of the door, demanding to have their property back, those companies who earlier had produced goods that were exported suddenly were of no use etc. What in particular has disturbed me is the rise in criminal offences. Now you cannot even walk on the street after seven p.m. without being raped, robbed or brutally beaten...rents are rising incredibly, we have to pay lots of taxes and have to be careful with our money. They are robbing our money out of our handbags. (Girl from a *Regelschule*, 9th Grade, East Germany; cit. Böhm et al., 1993: 25)

What is striking about the two accounts is how differently the writers interpret German reunification. The West German girl resents it mainly because she and her family have to share part of their improving income with a new, poorer group. Her resentment has much in common with the "welfare state racism" (Wieworka, 1999) often encountered by poor immigrants from Third World countries as they try to cope with the cultural entry barriers with which rich West-European countries have surrounded themselves in order not to have to share their resources. This issue of national solidarity is tackled from a totally different angle in the narrative of the East German girl. What is construed by one group as an increasing economic burden is seen by the other as an instance of economic exploitation. It is the East Germans who are being robbed of their economic resources by West Germans demanding to have their private property back or closing factories which are said to be non-competitive (something East Germans find difficult to believe, as the same factories had earlier been exporting goods to the West; see Bislev and Hjort, 1993).

The problem of the extent to which West Germans should be taxed in the interests of redistribution of wealth (Schramm and Schlese, 1992) is not an issue for the East German girl. What is interesting is that the public discourse of the political élites as expressed in the mass media and in academic circles in reunited Germany is closer to the viewpoint of the East German girl than that of the West German girl. The East German girl's economic assessment—like that of most East Germans—is factually wrong. East German factories were able to export goods to the West because the prices of most basic goods were lower as a result of lower wages and productivity. The average living standard lagged far behind that of West Germany; owners of private property in East Germany were never owners in the legal sense - their property could be expropriated without compensation at any time, hence the restitution of legal rights to private property is in the interest of the East Germans more than that of the West Germans. Despite these errors, the views of the East German girl are more widespread than those of her West German counterpart which are largely suppressed.

What is interesting is that this suppression of views which have an unmistakably "racist" component has a clear parallel in the way in which anti-Semitism was dealt with in West Germany after the war. As Frank Stern points out in *The Whitewashing of the Yellow Badge: Antisemitism and Philosemitism in Postwar Germany*, public discourse in West Germany miraculously switched overnight after the defeat of Nazi Germany. Whereas during the Nazi regime all moral evils were projected upon the Jews (Friedländer, 1997), the removal of the Nazis from power drove anti-Semitism underground. It was prohibited by law and the German state and public sphere completely changed its attitude towards Jews.

Suddenly there was almost nothing the German authorities would not do for their Jewish co-citizens. Jewishness was no longer associated with deep shame, on the contrary it was a great honor. Jews were seen not as parasites but as useful, productive citizens who were more then welcome to contribute to German society. In short, the Germans lavished their sympathy upon the Jews and the Jews in Germany experienced the strange feeling of being elevated overnight from sub-humans to model citizens (Richarz, 1986; Burgauer, 1993; Lappin, 1994; Brenner, 1995; Kupferberg, 1997; Bubis, 1996; Bornemann, 1996).

This strong philo-Semitism so painfully documented by Frank Stern only represents public Germany though. Far from being dead, anti-Semitism has retired to the private sphere. Ralph Giordano, in his book *Die zweite Schuld* writes of the nature of the discussion in the tavern, the *Stammtisch*, where Germans are allowed to reveal their inner feelings about Jews, Nazi Germany, the Holocaust and so on. Werner Bergmann and Rainer Erb, in their book *Anti-Semitism in Germany: The Post-Nazi Epoch Since 1945*, document a substantial amount of popular anti-Semitism. About one-third of the West German population is estimated to hold views that can be classified as anti-Semitic. Not all this anti-Semitism is of the classic kind though. Bergmann and Erb identify a "secondary anti-Semitism" which can be explained as a resentment of Jews because they remind Germans of the sins of the past. Henryk Broder somewhat provocatively argues that the Germans are unable to forgive the Jews for Auschwitz (Broder, 1986) and sees the incidents of public anti-Semitism (such as the Fassbinder affair) as proof of this.

Only by taking into account this pattern of public repression of popular resentment related to racism and xenophobia in West Germany can we explain the strong sympathy for the East German view in the mass media, academic circles and politics. Although most of the privately held beliefs of East Germans about reunification, if taken at face value, are inconsistent, factually incorrect and biased, surprisingly few German intellectuals, whether in East or West Germany, have taken on the task of correcting them. This does not mean that German intellectuals agree with East German views about unification, only that it is seen as politically incorrect to undermine sympathy for the East Germans as this could be interpreted as empathizing with the type of views expressed by the West German girl. In a German context, lack of public sympathy with East Germans is potentially stigmatizing, which explains why the erroneousness of East German beliefs is largely ignored.

This is only one of the multitude of intricate ways in which the past influences the present. There is a strange paradox in the beliefs of most East Germans. Their feeling of belonging to the German "nation," manifested in such things as pride in being German, is significantly stronger than that of West Germans whose feelings of national pride have consistently been lower than those of most western nations (Scheuch, 1991; Liebert, 1991; Merkl, 1992; Blank, 1997; Westle, 1999). At the same time, East Germans often declare themselves to be "second-class" citizens who feel more "East German" than "German" (*Der Spiegel*, 1995a). Moreover they feel strongly culturally alienated from the dominant institutions of the Federal

Republic of Germany of which they have now become full citizens (Fuchs et al., 1997; Misselwitz, 1999).

Whereas a mass of data assembled by German social scientists documents the strong sense of cultural alienation among East Germans (see chapter seven), the peculiar contradiction between strong feelings of belonging to the German nation and a weak feeling of attachment to the German state is rarely examined. Normally we would expect that feelings of cultural alienation would correlate with weak feelings of belonging, but this is not the case in East Germany. In order to explain this contradiction we need to look into the history of postwar Germany and in particular how the two Germanies coped with the Nazi past.

West Germany distanced itself from Nazi Germany by creating an open, cosmopolitan society. This had the dual effect of diminishing feelings of nationalism and strengthening the values of modernity (morally responsible citizens, pluralistic institutions, a functionally differentiated social order, and so on). East German society formally distanced itself from the openly militaristic and racist aspects of Nazi Germany, but in reality reproduced the traditional provincial German culture. This strong provincialism is at the core of the East German mindset and explains why East Germans are more nationalistic (and xenophobic) than West Germans and at the same time feel culturally alienated from a distinctly modern society.

It is when we introduce the dimension of the long term cultural effects of how East German society coped with the Nazi past that the complaints of the East German girl becomes interesting. We are not merely dealing here with a predictable resistance to change or the well-known problems of a transitional society as manifested in all parts of post-communist Eastern Europe (Kupferberg, 1999). The East German case is unique in the sense that we cannot conceptualize the cultural transition taking place there without taking German history and particularly the Nazi past into account.

Henryk Broder cites as one of the most characteristic traits of the GDR the fact that its citizens were not trained to confront reality but instead superimposed a fictive reality upon the factual one and claimed it to be real.

> The point was not to approach the real world, but to make the fictional one as perfect as possible in order to leave reality behind. The creation of the GDR itself was an act of simulation of considerable originality: the first workers' and peasants' state on German

soil, which had nothing whatsoever in common with its predecessor, the Nazi state. No one felt co-responsible, neither the leadership, nor the population. The latter was also not the same as that which had so recently constituted the mass of *Volkskammeraden*. The historical roots of the GDR were placed somewhere in the time of the peasants' wars, then history made a colossal jump and suddenly the GDR fell from heaven together with NVA [the national people's army], VEB [companies owned by the people], *Volkskammer* [the parliament], the Intershops on the transit roads...and then the pretence became shameless. The government of the GDR simulated sovereignty, the parliament simulated democracy, the block parties simulated pluralism, the trade unions simulated representing the workers' interests, the factories owned by the people simulated productivity, the courts simulated independence and the party, which was always right, simulated infallibility. (Broder, 1993: 95)

The main motivational force behind this simulation was the need to escape from the moral responsibility for what had taken place during the twelve years of Nazi rule. What is rarely recognized is the impact of all this simulation upon the East German mind. The habit of pretending did not miraculously disappear after unification, on the contrary it reemerged in a new form, namely blaming the West Germans for all the problems which stemmed from it. They did so despite the fact that a huge majority of East Germans had expressed a wish to reunite with West Germany as quickly as possible.

They had hardly abandoned their people's-owned, antifascist illusion of plastic and elastic, when they started feeling cheated, misused, colonized. In spite of the fact that there had been four elections in the GDR with quite unambiguous results ... in spite of the fact that there had been demonstrations in East Berlin, Leipzig and Dresden for reunification and not in Aachen, Hildesheim and Kaubeuren, there was suddenly talk of an *"Anschluss."* (Broder, 1993: 100)

This element of pretence is evident in the statements of the East German girl. Her complaint that reunification came too fast, giving the East Germans too little chance to adapt, is common (see Belwe, 1992; Stolpe, 1992; Grell and Wolf, 1992; Moeller and Maaz, 1993; Jarauch, 1994). The problem with it is that, as Broder suggests, popular pressure for rapid unification originated in the East not in the West. In fact, according to Wolfgang Schäuble, the German Minister of the Interior at the time, popular feelings in West Germany during the spring of 1990 was increasingly anti-East German (Schäuble, 1991). Local conservative mayors too expressed the rising resentment against East German refugees. It was in order to contain these sentiments, which might have jeopardized reunification, that the political class in West Germany was won over by Kohl's argument for rapid unification. Kohl was only expressing the feelings of the large majority of East Germans who could not wait to gain access to the D-Mark, the revered symbol of West German economic strength, affluence and personal freedom (Reich, 1993; Offe, 1994). They wanted it, they got it, but they chose to pretend that Kohl, the West German political class, and more generally the "Wessies" had wanted to impose their system on reluctant East Germans who were happy with things as they were.

This brings us to a third aspect of the East-West divide, namely the issue of social control. For the East German girl the greatest culture shock was the sudden explosion of crime on the streets. Both property crimes and violent assaults suddenly became much more frequent in East Germany. What she does not mention is that most of the criminal perpetrators were probably East Germans. Where had they all been hiding, and why did they appear only after reunification? In 1992 the East German sociologist Wolfgang Engler published a book called *Die Zivilisatorische Lücke*. He takes as his point of departure Norbert Elias's (1978; 1996) theory of the process of civilization as the transition between two moral systems, one based upon external punishments or rigid social control and one based upon internal self-control, which allows for a more flexible social control. (A similar distinction was suggested by Durkheim, who differentiated between a "mechanical" and an "organic" moral order.)

This distinction emerged with the collapse of communism. It appeared that communist societies, despite the official Marxist ideology of historical progress, never transcended a rigid moral order. Morality was externally imposed rather then voluntarily internalized as suggested in Kant's theory of moral progress.

> This manifested itself at the end of 1989 when the state socialist power and the control structures in a series of East and Central European societies collapsed and the authority of the élites as well as the administrative functionaries was rapidly undermined. The statistics of traffic crimes and traffic accidents, of property crimes and personal assaults revealed that the self-reinforcing apparatuses, which had been considered to be stable and securely anchored in the personality structure, no longer functioned. And the same applies to the openly hostile attitudes towards individuals belonging to other ethnic, cultural and nation-state units. (Engler, 1992: 44)

When it comes to explaining this development, particularly in East Germany, Engler tends to avoid the heart of the matter though, namely German history and the way the East German élites coped with the Nazi past. Instead of challenging the myth of the antifascist regime as a clear indicator of a lack of an honest and thoroughgoing break with the past, he argues that the lack of an internalized morality should be seen as an effect of the unpopularity of the communist regime. "To a higher degree than...in West European societies the individual saw the state as an occupational power, towards which one at least retained the right to resistance (Engler, 1992: 45).

There is however no logical connection whatsoever between participation in a resistance movement and a lack of internal moral control. Most Western European countries had been occupied by the Nazis for years but, after a short period of lawlessness motivated by an understandable anger against collaborators, they returned to normal civilized behavior. The inability of the East Germans to restrain themselves suggests a totally different explanation, namely that East Germany, in spite of presenting itself as the "better Germany" in the moral sense (Meuschel, 1992; Land and Possekel, 1994; Simon, 1995), was a society based on rigid social control rather than flexible self control.

The problem of this underdeveloped individual morality among East Germans is one of the most sensitive issues in reunited Germany and it seems to be taboo to raise it publicly (a case in point is the public reaction to Christian Pfeiffer's hypothesis of a possible correlation between the collectivist upbringing in the GDR and the higher degree of aggression and xenophobia among East German youth). Nevertheless, Engler's suggestion that Elias's theory of civilization might help us explain something important about the state of the moral order in East Germany is worth pursuing. In fact it is indirectly supported by sociologists, who have noticed the cultural continuity between East Germany and previous cultural traditions in German history that existed long before Hitler came to power (Vester, 1995).

Ilja Srubar in his article *"War der realsozialismus modern?"* argues that the main historical impact of the GDR seems to have been to contribute to another incidence of the delayed development that is so characteristic of German history (Srubar, 1991). Gebhardt and Kamphausen go as far as to suggest that East German society actually regressed culturally after 1945. Comparing two villages, one in West Germany, the other in East Germany, they arrive at the surprising conclusion that life in the East German village despite, or maybe because of the hegemony of socialism, was kept almost unrestricted on the level of the late nineteenth century...socialism with its fundamental anti-individualist and anti-economic goal and its moralizing message of equality supported rather than disturbed the vision of a harmonious, traditional rural community. The socialist system therefore could be accepted so unproblematically in the East German rural communities because it - at least concerning its everyday effects - did not put the old order under pressure to change. (Gebhardt and Kamphausen, 1994: 9)

The retarding effects of communist rule were not only evident in the rural areas. Stefan Hradil suggests that "socialism conserved the 'specifically German cultural traditions' such as the duty-oriented Protestantism, the Prussian heritage and the state of servility (Hradil, 1995: 4). The way in which workers became tied to the factories, the place, and each other possibly gave rise to a strong collective pride among workers, which the SED saw as one of its main accomplishments (and which Wolfgang Engler uncritically lauds in his nostalgic book *Die Ostdeutschen*, published in 1999). But as Hradil remarks soberly,

although such traits might have some advantages, they do not seem to be particularly conducive to the development of individual behavior and practical subjective autonomy. From a long-term social historical perspective, which liberates the glance to see the totality of a societal culture, it becomes evident how much of the "typically German," how much of the "German *Sonderweg* has remained in the GDR: the pressure of normality, the *Innerlichkeit*, the patriarchal understanding of the state, etc. (Hradil, 1995: 10)

But not even Hradil takes the logical step of asking why the GDR preserved so much of the "cultural heritage" of the "German *Sonderweg*." Like most German sociologists, he seems to feel uneasy about introducing the issue of the Nazi past as a prime explanation for the gulf between the East German and the West German mind - a gulf so wide that the two are almost unable to communicate today. This lack of communication, the absence of an *innere einheit*, has characterized the relationship in the ten years since unification. What is astonishing is how little things have changed in those ten years. Most of what has been written is a variation on the same theme (for a recent summary, see Glaser, 1999).

So, Mikael Minkenberg's article published in 1994 expressing the view that "it has become evident that reunification has been far from completed" and that "the 'wall in our heads' seems to continue to exist in spite of the political equalization that has taken place between East and West" and that "in particular the massive demands from the East for support from the West—financial and other—in the reconstruction process" and the differences in culture between West and East Germans have led to a "growing apart" rather than a "growing together"—(Minkenberg, 1994: 169-170), might have been written in 1991 (Schlosser; Maaz), in 1995 (Thierse; Eppelmann; Brähler and Richter; Meulemann); in 1996 (Bauer-Kaase and Kaase), in 1997 (Veen) or in 1999 (Maaz).

A fundamental missing element appears to be preventing a "growing together" (Hilmer and Müller-Hilmer, 1993). My conclusion is that this element is the absence of an honest attempt in East Germany to cope with the Nazi past. Although some German scholars and intellectuals such as von Plato (1991; 1995), Henryk Broder (1993; 1994), and Peter Schneider (1999) have raised this argument, my distinct impression is that they are voices in the wilderness. Mainstream scholarship and public debate is situated elsewhere, in a sphere dominated by the social scientists and sociologists, whose main claim is that the problem of German unification is rooted in the present, not the past.

What is absent from this debate is a recognition of the strong unease felt by many West Germans who have suddenly had to share their state with a species of German long out of fashion in West Germany, a type with unmistakably similar traits to those Leo Szilard encountered in the early 1930s and which made him draw the conclusion that in such a country a Nazi movement would encounter little resistance. Interestingly, educated East Germans tend to interpret this moral unease as pure cultural arrogance. They attribute the communications difficulties between members of the educated classes in West and East Germany to a denial of East German professional competence. This difference in interpretation, one carefully moral, the other unashamedly utilitarian, emerges clearly from the following evaluations of German reunification:

> I see the implementation of reunification in an overall positive light, but have personally noticed little about it. The problems which occurred through unification should have been thought about earlier, according to my opinion. Then some of the conflicts could have been avoided...what I particularly see as negative is that the xenophobia and the brutality that comes with it becomes stronger all the time and bursts into flame. I believe this particularly to be the case in East Germany, and I believe that the cause of the hatred that many youngsters feel for foreigners is different from the one that is generally given. Through unification they have suddenly become aware of how "disadvantaged" they were earlier in relation to the West (particularly materially) and this makes them bitter and makes them aggressive. (Girl in a West German Gymnasium, 10th Grade)

I was very skeptical about the reunification of the two German states...since there are serious differences both in social relations and human mentalities. I am still skeptical. The fulfillment of unity will take a long time. There are too many prejudices (maybe also correct ones) that still dominate the encounters between East and West. Let me give an example! My mother was assigned a job in a western run tax department as bookkeeper. She has worked for a long time in her job and knows her profession. Nevertheless she was from the beginning presented as an "Osssie" whom one could fool" which led to her looking for a new, more congenial job, which she luckily also found on the difficult labor market. The East Germans are therefore seen by the West Germans as lazy, stupid...and unwilling to work, therefore the concept "Besserwessie" was invented to express this contempt towards us. (Girl in East German Gymnasium, 10th Grade)

It is interesting that these two girls, who can be considered to represent the views of the educated classes in East and West Germany, not only emphasize different aspects—on the one hand the moral issue of xenophobia and right-wing extremism which re-emerged after reunification, on the other the practical issue of having one's educational competence and professional status recognized by the new authorities—their general view of reunification is the opposite of that expressed by the girls from the working-class environments.

Here it is the West German girl who believes reunification to be the right thing from a moral point of view, although she does not necessarily agree with the way in which it was achieved. By contrast, the East German girl clearly believes that nothing good can come out of reunification—she is opposed to it in principle. Her views reflect the general lack of enthusiasm for reunification among members of the educated élites already noted, which contrasts sharply with the original enthusiasm expressed by ordinary East Germans. The East German intelligentsia did not have to wait to become disenchanted with capitalism, their disenchantment was not a result of experiences after reunification but the effect of a curious combination of utopian and utilitarian thinking.

Members of the East German intelligentsia did not particularly like the GDR—on the contrary, many of them loathed it (Land and Possekel, 1995; Dahn, 1999), nevertheless they believed it to be the "better Germany" from a moral point of view. Although the GDR did not respect elementary civil rights such as freedom of expression, organizational pluralism or independent courts, the intelligentsia nevertheless insisted that within it history had made a leap and had liberated humanity from the worst forms of repression. When one looks more closely at precisely which part of humanity felt itself to be liberated, it emerges that it is the relatively small group who profited from the system in terms of social mobility and status who became its most loyal citizens (Hoerning, 1995; Szepanski, 1995; Geulen, 1998; Hoerning and Kupferberg, 1999; Kupferberg, 2000).

The East German Mind-set

One of the main issues of contention in German sociological literature on reunification is how deep the communications divide between East and West Germans actually is and above all, how it should be explained. Most explanatory models can be divided into two camps. Whereas one gives precedence to the actual (negative) experiences of East Germans with reunification, the other argues that the most important dimension is the socialization which took place in the GDR and its long-term effect on the personality of its citizens. These positions coincide partially, but not fully, with the extent of the involvement of the respective researchers in the two preunification German states. Thus Detlef Pollack, an East German, argues that "most western observers reduce the problems encountered by the East Germans with the western system to the conclusion that they are still stuck in the GDR and its structures and that they have not yet learned to adapt to the new, social, political and legal realities" (Pollack, 1999: 2).

Pollack contests this largely western view and suggests an alternative explanation—that the factual experiences of former GDR citizens with Western society after reunification explains most of the divisions in Germany today. As proof, he cites the euphoria which characterized the attitude of the East Germans to West German society in about 1989/1990 as well as the surprisingly ease with which East Germans adapted after reunification. Both these factors, he argues, give the lie to the hypothesis that the socialization effects of the GDR were particularly strong:

> Nothing was more important for them at the time than to put the GDR behind them as far as possible and to see western institutions introduced into the eastern sector. Even though the East Germans had to learn to cope with great problems in adapting they had in the meantime become integrated into the reality of the Federal Republic. The latter had become the self-evident everyday normality which they had to master and would master. If we add to this the fact that "practically no one wants to return to the old GDR" the conclusion must be that the communications gap between East and West Germans is primarily to be explained by the actual experiences of the East Germans after reunification. The criticism levelled by the East Germans has little to do with an attachment to the

GDR, it is mainly an effect of their experiences with reunified Germany. (Pollack, 1999: 2)

It seems highly unlikely that forty-five years of Soviet occupation should have had no significant effect on the minds of the East Germans and Pollack contradicts himself by mentioning three areas in which this was indeed so, namely a strongly apolitical stance, a clear inhibition about expressing one's own personality and a tendency to blame the leadership for the failures of the system. Nowhere does he mention the role that might have been played by the Nazi past and the moral issues it raises.

The Apolitical Stance

Pollack's view of the apolitical stance of many East Germans is confirmed by comparative studies of political cultures in East and West Germany (Niedermeyer and von Beyme, 1994). His explanation of this trait, which students of German history will recognise as similar to the *innerlichkeit* which was typical of the educated classes (*Bildungsbürgertum*) from the early nineteenth century onwards (Craig, 1991), is, however, strangely ahistorical. It is explained as "the internalized skepticism against institutions" (Engler, 1996: 36; cit. Pollack, 1999: 23) so typical of GDR citizens. Pollack sees the tendency to withdraw into private life and merely pay lip service to the demands of public participation as a typical GDR product: "The lack of identification with the system in the GDR was related to a strong orientation towards private goals and values. Family, marriage, partners, but also friendships, acquaintances and social gatherings were highly valued" (Pollack, 1992: 495).

This tendency has continued since reunification. Both educated and ordinary East Germans still feel that their private goals and values are much more important then their citizenship duties, towards which they continue to do lip service despite the fact that they now live in a democracy and have the freedom to travel, freedom of expression, freedom of association, independent courts, a free press and a genuinely democratic parliamentary system. By contrast West Germans do not perceive any sharp conflict between private goals and public duties.

In an article written in 1992, Pollack noted that "the number of East Germans who feel that politicians represent their interests and show any concern for their problems is already, after a short period of democratization, very small...only one-fifth of eligible voters identify with a particular party; in West Germany the figure is two-thirds." Moreover the trust expressed in the political system by the East Germans was on average "20 to 30 percent lower than in that in the *alten Bundesländer.*" Pollack concludes that "all these data indicate that there is a huge discrepancy between the importance of these institutions to society and that which the East Germans attribute to them" (Pollack, 1992: 505).

Not only do these facts contradict Pollack's assumption that the after-effects of the socialization patterns and experiences of the GDR are insignificant, they point to a much larger issue which neither East German nor West German social scientists seem to have taken seriously, namely that the mental traits of the East Germans cannot be seen exclusively in a GDR context but have to be conceptualized in terms of German history, particularly the moral lessons they learnt from the Nazi past. Peter Gay suggests that an important reason for the collapse of the Weimar Republic was that even its adherents were not emotionally attached to republican institutions. "To the *Vernunftsrepublikaner* the Republic was, in a sense, the punishment that the Germans, aristocrats and bourgeois, deserved; it was infinitely preferable to the barbarism of the right and the irresponsibility of the left; and should enlist cooperation, even if it could not command enthusiasm." These *Vernunftsrepublikaner* were "reasonable men who had been willing to learn the first lesson of modernity, but not the second; they acknowledged that nostalgia for the Empire was ridiculous, but they could not see that the Republic might deserve passionate support" (Gay, 1969: 30-31).

The *Vernunftsrepublikaner* fundamentally shared the apolitical and often romantic utopian view of the German educated classes. Their characteristic trait was that they were sorely lacking in the civic ethos necessary to sustain a democracy in crisis. Their lack of inner conviction and leaning towards political romanticism made any defense of the Weimar Republic into a kind of lip service, while their real efforts continued to be focused upon their private, practical concerns, just as would be the case in the GDR. What is interesting is that this apolitical stance contributed strongly to the collapse of the Weimar Republic. Its survival in the GDR suggests that the moral lessons drawn from this collapse were superficial, to say the least. In fact, one of the reasons the educated classes in East Germany felt so at home in the GDR was that it fitted so comfortably into their concept of a cultivated citizen as basically apolitical and engaged in higher pursuits than those represented by a vulgar democracy.

This attitude was already in evidence in Thomas Mann's early essay, "Reflections of a Nonpolitical Man," written during the First World War. By the time Mann changed his mind it was too late, the educated classes in Weimar Germany had already spiritually capitulated *en masse* to the new savior emerging on the horizon. As Mann writes in his nineteen-thirties' essay, "Appeal to Reason," there was a strong affinity between the romantic *Weltfremdheit* and the leap into obscurity and mysticism of the Nazi warmongers. "It may seem daring to associate the nationalism of today with the ideas of romantic philosophy, but the connection is there...[and serves] to support ...the National Socialist movement from the spiritual side...we find here a certain ideology of philologists, a romanticism of professional Germanists, a superstitious faith in the Nordic—all emanating from the academic professional class." He also emphasizes that "the Germans of 1930 are harangued in an idiom of mystical philistinism and high-flown tastelessness with words like 'racist,' '*völkisch*,' '*bündisch*,' 'heroic,' which gave the movement an ingredient of cultured barbarism more dangerous and more remote from reality, flooding and clotting the brain more grievously than the *Weldfremdheit* and political romanticism that led us into the war" (cit. Craig, 1991: 209).

The apolitical stance of the educated classes in Germany, which played such a disastrous role in laying the intellectual ground for the Nazis, was never seriously dealt with in East Germany, a country which, under the cover of "antifascism" expiated the East Germans for any moral responsibility for the Third Reich and the Holocaust. To abandon it now would mean that the East Germans and in particular the East German intelligentsia would have to ask themselves what really took place in the Weimar Republic, and why it collapsed. They would be unable to lay all the blame on the ruling classes (the aristocracy, the monopoly industrialists), as the Marxist-inspired theory of "antifascism" suggests. The alienation of East Germans from the democratic constitution of the Federal Republic of Germany has very little to do with their experiences with reunification, it has far more to do with the way in which their intelligentsia claimed a moral break with the Nazi regime. The inconvenient fact is that there never was such a break. The apolitical and amoral attitude of the intelligentsia remained as it had been both before and under Hitler, legitimating their absence of civic ethos.

Inhibited Self Expression

An interesting aspect of the East German personality is a conspicuous personal modesty and a lack of interest in or talent for "impression management" (Goffman, 1959). Pollack notes that:

> many East Germans have difficulty coming out of their private niches to appear in public and present themselves. The West German style of self-presentation is seen by many as arrogant, self-righteous and lacking in sensitivity. This might be a sign of the arrogance of many West Germans but surely it is no less a sign of the underdog mentality of many East Germans. The yardstick is the modern West, the backward East is seen as the province. The East German knows that. He internalized it before the Fall of the Wall. It is not peculiar that he feels inferior in almost all areas. (Pollack, 1992: 502-3)

The explanation for this behavior, according to Pollack, is the strong social control that was exercised in the tight personal networks that played such a predominant role in East German everyday life.

> In the milieux in which one moved there was strong pressure to conform. The habits that emerged were based less on distinction, self-dramatization, self-stylization and extravagant transgressions of norms than on behavioral patterns characterized by an inconspicuous normality, adaptation to mediocrity and petty-bourgeois rigidity." (Pollack, 1992: 500; Woderich, 1991a: 25)

The consequence of this rigid social control was intolerance towards cultural deviancy of any kind, from music, clothes and hairstyles to artistic experiments, scientific curiosity and political opposition. It included not only strict regulation of travel but also state interference with the choice of careers, places of residence, living quarters, and foreign contacts.

This conformity, according to students of everyday life in East Germany (Gaus, 1986; Bender, 1992), provided both a sense of protection and an illusion of autonomy from the all-embracing totalitarian and paternalistic state. In a society where the state controls every aspect of the individual's life, it is safest to stay with people one has known for a long time. It is better to have one's friends correct one than to be called to the police station or the party headquarters. The young East German historian Stefan Wolle points out in *Die Heile Welt der Diktatur* the obvious similarities between the types of social control in Nazi Germany and in the GDR.

To cite one example, the minute control of visitors by the *Hausmeister* and the necessity to report to him in case these visitors might be enemies of the state was invented by the Nazis and taken over by the communist rulers. Pollack prefers to be totally silent on these obvious similarities although he does concede that the inbreeding in these tight, closed networks did have some negative consequences. Among other things,

> the milieu to which one had retreated was relatively strict and the different everyday worlds shielded themselves against each other and developed prejudices against each other. GDR society was not cohesive as is often claimed. The value of "helping socially weak and marginal social groups" is of less importance to East Germans than to West Germans...among East Germans the famous willingness to assist others is narrowly defined. It is related to the known circle of friends, colleagues and acquaintances and most of all has an instrumental value. (Pollack, 1992)

What he does not mention is the historical sources of this strongly practical thinking. Like most East German intellectuals, he tends to avoid the core issue of post-war German history, namely the question of what kind of moral order there was in the so-called antifascist, workers' and peasants' state.

Evading Personal Responsibility

A third trait which Pollack contends is typical of East Germans is a tendency to evade personal responsibility. In contrast with West Germans, "East Germans tend to explain both failures and successes by blaming external causes" (Pollack, 1992: 494-5). He does not try to fit this trait into his explanation of the disenchantment of the East Germans with their experiences after reunification, but argues that it is an after effect of life in the GDR. East Germans "built up a strong we-feeling which clearly demarcated itself from the leadership of the system and which acquired its identity by demarcation from 'them up there.' What united people across social differences was the feeling of being unable to do something, of being helpless and cheated." Thus most GDR citizens blamed the failures of socialism "on the incompetent leader, not the system, and certainly not on the individual himself" (Pollack, 1992: 495; see also Geulen, 1998).

Stratemann (1992), in a study done after unification, found a similar tendency to externalize the causes of both failures and successes. She too suggests that the explanation is a feeling of helplessness— individuals could do precious little in the GDR to influence their personal destinies. Interestingly, this theory conflicts with Pollack´s argument that the East Germans, after struggling for a short period, had few problems adapting to a more risk-oriented society (Beck, 1992) in which individuals were expected to take the initiative. One possible explanation for this conflict could be that there were two different groups in East Germany, those who had accumulated a great deal of cultural and social capital in the GDR and those who had not.

Predictably, the former group would have been more able to assert themselves in the new society. This distinction is not always made in the literature, which creates a great deal of confusion about the nature and sources of so-called GDR nostalgia. Dagmar Klose argues that "the two quite different models of socialization in the Federal Republic and the GDR could not be 'united,' and different value systems and mentalities evolved. Although the identity imposed by the state upon the socialist citizens of the GDR in the last instance only bore fruit among a small part of the population, a common 'East German' identity evolved out of common life experiences. One 'recognizes' oneself in familiar phrases, everyday habits, common memories. The past has dug its traces" (Klose, 1994; for an analysis of the impact of German division upon language, see Reiher and Läzer, 1996).

Klose here clearly confuses the impact of socialization, which is mainly unreflexive and manifests itself in everyday behavior, habits and mentality, with the reflexive commitment to the GDR's state ideology or its national identity constructs. Whereas all East Germans no doubt developed a particular East German mentality, only members of the educated classes explicitly identified themselves with the antifascist, socialist identity-constructs of the state. The result was that an influential minority developed a strong sense of belonging to the GDR and today have great difficulty abandoning this feeling of belonging (Geulen, 1998; Hoerning and Kupferberg, 1999). Ordinary East Germans never really belonged (Maaz, 1999), but were nevertheless strongly influenced by the GDR in their behavior and thinking.

The paradox is that the group who identified least with the GDR had the greatest problems adapting to the new system. It is mainly this group Michael Schmitz is referring to when he argues that "the former GDR citizens have a more rigid thought structure and are less flexible, demonstrate a more strongly pronounced authoritarianism, and have enormous difficulties adapting to the market economy. In spite of pressure from the labor market the East Germans rejected taking initiatives of their own and withdrew from the West German economic system" (Schmitz, 1995: 26).

Schmitz's explanation for this lack of flexibility is that it stems from the absence of personal responsibility encouraged among East Germans by the paternalistic state.

> The tutelary state raised the individual to total personal helplessness, because his or her destiny could not be influenced by personal efforts or competence. The tutelary state took care of almost everything: jobs, study, vacation, housing, leisure and consumption. The life situations of individuals were very similar. Now everything falls apart. The social structure of GDR society collapses. The competitive democracy of West Germany constantly requires individual decisions, it demands personal responsibility, which earlier few had to take upon themselves, which they now cannot implement and which they'd rather do without." (Schmitz, 1995: 25)

This picture of ingrained helplessness and dependence upon the state might be true in the case of the majority of ordinary East Germans, but it is certainly false for the minority of educated East Germans, the *gelernte Bürger* (Lay and Potting, 1995) who took great pride in their ability to shape their own destinies. Precisely because they lived in a highly regulated and protected world, with considerable personal security and few risks, they were able to use their privileges, their social and cultural capital, to beat the system and accomplish their personal goals. What is interesting in this context is the moral price individuals paid for the privilege.

In my study of the fortunes of East Berlin professionals who graduated from an *Erweiterte Obserschule* (high school) in the early sixties, I found that educated GDR citizens were perfectly able to shape their own destinies and achieve most of their personal goals and ambitions, provided they did not openly challenge the legitimacy of the system (Kupferberg, 1998). The fact that the state played a major role in the lives of individuals did not automatically make people feel helpless. On the contrary, the intimate knowledge of the way in which this interference worked helped people to create highly sophisticated strategies of adaptation with the goal of "beating the system." The subjects of my study showed amazing creativity in beating the system in one way or another. This suggests that the predominant feeling among this group of East Germans was not helplessness in the face of a rigid system, but rather personal pride in being able to beat it.

The East German psychiatrist Hans-Joachim Maaz expresses this feeling of pride, and the loss of it after unification, very well in a discussion with a West German colleague:

> Never before in my life has an historical process made me more anxious than the contemporary one. I have the impression that my understanding and control of things is much less than it was before *die Wende*. Even though I was often uncomfortable in the earlier system and often rebelled against it, even though I sometimes became desperate, angry, or filled with hate, I still knew very well: Here I live, here I have my place, here I have a certain importance— and here it is also possible to avoid the unpleasant things. In a strange way, within the repressive structures of the GDR I acquired a feeling of security and I had organized myself quite well; I lived as if the whole thing would go on forever. (Moeller and Maaz, 1993: 17)

Personal pride in beating the system was at the center of the moral reasoning of the East German intelligentsia (Dahn, 1999) and the loss of that pride after unification explains the depth of the damage to their ego. What is interesting is that they rarely reflected upon the moral choices they had made in the GDR. None of the persons in my own study felt that it was wrong that they were called on to publicly support the GDR as the price for a successful professional career. What is even more interesting is that very few German sociological studies raise this issue. Although many studies have been undertaken by sociologists from both East and West Germany on the problems of adaptation to the new labor market and there is plenty of evidence that the East Germans intelligentsia had surprisingly few difficulties in converting their educational qualifications and professional experience and in regaining their previous positions (Mayer et al., 1996; Diewald and Sørensen, 1996) there is a dearth of sociological studies focusing upon or even mentioning the moral issues involved.

The Moral Dimension

Was the moral choice made by the members of the educated classes ethically correct? Should one pride oneself on one's behavior, if that behavior is based upon acceptance of an immoral system? The curious absence of ethical reasoning among the East German intelligentsia is strikingly similar to that of German academics observed by Leo Szilard in the early nineteen-thirties and which induced him to leave Germany as quickly as possible. It also raises disturbing questions about what East German intellectuals actually learned from the Nazi period.

From an ethical point of view, the shameful behavior of educated Germans in Nazi Germany cannot be reduced to a question of collective guilt—only individuals can be convicted of criminal behavior. This absence of collective guilt does not, however, absolve the educated classes of Germany from the collective shame of having tolerated the crimes that were taking place in their midst. One could speculate that one of the reasons why these "decent" Germans were able to live with themselves and their consciences was that they separated their lives in two. On the one hand they were doing what was expected of them in terms of not openly challenging Nazi ideology and the overall legitimacy of the racist and ultimately exterminatory regime. On the other, they were priding themselves on beating a system they did not particularly like by learning how to avoid or escape from its most unpleasant features. I suggest that this was how most "decent" Germans (Baldwin, 1990) survived the war with their self-respect intact.

It is interesting that whereas in West Germany shortly after the war the political and intellectual élites began to challenge this moral strategy and to propagate a new form of ethics based upon personal moral responsibility and choice, this did not happen in the GDR because there was no feeling there of collective shame. They felt they had nothing to be ashamed of. For one thing "fascism" was a product of the capitalist system and the German people or nation had not played an active role in establishing it, and for another the GDR was led by proven antifascists, who had resisted the Nazis from start to finish. This method of absolving the East Germans from shame was reinforced by the general picture painted in the GDR of events during the Nazi years. As many observers have pointed out, there was little place for the Holocaust in the East German, antifascist narrative (Giordano, 1990; Groehler, 1994; Rosenthal, 1997; Herf, 1997). The extermination of the Jews was not allowed to trouble the conscience of the East Germans, who learned to look at the Nazi period as an example of heroic resistance led by the party of the workers against the party of the capitalists.

The result of this absence of guilt was that East Germans as a group retained their pride in being German. This pride manifested itself after reunification in widespread xenophobia and brutal attacks on foreigners on the one hand and in a longing to return to a world that was simple and innocent on the other. Most of all, they learned the habit of self-delusion, of ignoring existing empirical reality and pretending that the ideal was real and that the facts of life could be safely ignored. Thus it was easy for them to talk themselves into believing that it was the West Germans and not themselves who had pushed for reunification and that the GDR had not been the paternalistic and totalitarian regime against which they had so recently revolted.

3

Victors of History:
The Smokescreen of Antifascism

The Moral Burden

In their classic analysis of the German psyche after the Nazi defeat, *Die Unfähigkeit zu trauern*, Alexander and Margarete Mitscherlich emphasize the important role played by the cult of the Führer in Nazi Germany (Mitscherlich and Mitscherlich, 1977). This cult, and the belief in Hitler's infallibility, functioned as a protective shield against reality. By relying on the infinite wisdom of the Führer, the increasing brutality of the regime could somehow be written off as a small price to pay for the tremendous victories he had achieved and those he promised for the future. From this point of view the defeat of Nazi Germany was a major shock for the Germans as it forced them to face the terrible truth, both about their beloved Führer and about themselves.

When I read the book I immediately recognized this syndrome in the way my eighty-five-year-old East German mother-in-law speaks about the Hitler *Zeit*. Although she always asserts that she and other Germans did not know what had happened to their Jewish neighbors, who were all "highly civilized" people and whose children she had played with in school, her voice somehow takes on a youthful, excited ring when she talks about those times and especially about the way Hitler ignored the feelings of other nations with his series of dramatic moves into the foreign arena after coming to power, starting with the reoccupation of the Rhineland area where "he really showed them" that Germany was important again, a force to be reckoned with.

This frighteningly amoral view of the rights of the German nation in relation to the rest of the world did not start with Hitler but it did become more extreme when the Nazis came to power. Nor was it immediately abandoned after Hitler's suicide, the unconditional surrender to the Allies, and the Nuremberg Trials. On the contrary, Mitcherlich and Mitcherlich suggest, many "decent" Germans retained some of their enthusiasm for Hitler. Somehow they were able to divide themselves into two persons, storing their knowledge of the crimes of the Nazis and their own nationalistic euphoria in two different compartments of their minds. This made it easier for them to cope with the fact that they had been accomplices to a systematically immoral regime.

In order to understand the moral dilemma of the Germans after the war we have to assume that they must have retained some kind of conscience and that they were fully aware that they had acted immorally. If, like Goldhagen (1996), we assume that all Germans had become hardcore Nazis and that their dearest wish was to exterminate the Jews, the existence of this dilemma lacks a foundation. Only if we assume that most Germans had some kind of conscience to fall back upon does the question of how they faced the terrible truth of the Nazi regime become a social and political issue of interest and we can recognize that the memories of the Nazi years were a tremendous moral burden with which they had, in some way, to cope. What did the Germans do with that moral burden? How could educated people in particular retain their perception of themselves as a highly civilized nation in the face of their participation in the events of the dreadful Hitler years?

It appears that Mitscherlich and Mitscherlich were referring largely to West Germany where the Hitler cult, the Nazi regime and the Holocaust weighed heavily on the conscience of the defeated nation and influenced society, politics, economics, education and culture in an infinity of ways. As I have argued elsewhere, had it not been for this burden, the Federal Republic of Germany would hardly have changed so dramatically, developing in a few decades into a highly modern, international and genuinely liberal state (Kupferberg, 1996a).

East Germany did not experience this modernization—on the contrary, in most areas both the country and its citizens seem to have regressed, withdrawing and reproducing the same antimodern cultural traits and thought processes which had made Hitler possible in the first place. The prime reason for this seems to have been the absence of a strong moral pressure to remember the past. Anette Simon has suggested that in order to understand the morality of East Germans one has to take into account the fact that East Germany presented itself as a state founded and led by antifascist resistance fighters (Simon, 1995). The latter were the true "victors of history" and gave the founding of the GDR historical legitimacy.

The formula of the "victors of history" was repeated from early childhood, so that every East German child and youth became convinced that fascism was no longer a problem in the country. This was contrasted with the situation in West Germany where, it was said, there had never been a radical break with fascism.

"The transference of these criminals to the West, relieved the child." Murdered antifascists became the heroes of the GDR (the murder of millions of Jews was a side issue) and the survivors "were true to this heritage" (cit. Münkler, 1998: 25).

The basic attraction of East German communism, ugly as it was, was the repeated insistence that unlike West Germany, East Germany had coped effectively with the Nazi past (Welsch, 1991; Bergmann, 1995).

> Unlike the FRG, which underwent an agonizing period of collective soul searching after World War II, the GDR never openly and honestly discussed and confronted its fascist past. The official state line was that the socialist people of the GDR had been "liberated" by the Soviet Red Army and were victors of the war against Hitler. Instead of admitting the complicity of its own people and the danger that fascist thought could be passed on to successive generations, the Socialist United Party (SED) proclaimed that Nazism had been "eradicated" within the borders of the workers' and the peasants' state. Hitler, said the Party, was a child of capitalism, therefore fascism was a problem for the imperialist - capitalist FRG and not for the GDR. (Weaver, 1995: 152)

Or, as Peter Kirchner, chairman of the Jewish Community in the GDR said when asked about this issue in 1983: "In the GDR, we live in the knowledge that the Nazis are in the West. That is how we solve the problem" (Cit. *Traverso*, 1995: 138).

The Restoration Myth

In his ground-breaking book *The Divided Past*, Jeffrey Herf argues that whereas the political élites in West Germany came to share Adenauer's analysis of what had gone wrong in German history—

the theory which later developed into the idea of the cultural "belatedness" of the German *Sonderweg*—recognizing the strongly antiwestern, antiliberal and antienlightenment roots of German intellectual thinking and mentality (Snyder, 1952; Kohn, 1960; Stern, 1965), a similar rethinking never took place in East Germany.

Herf's reason—power politics within the East German leadership —can hardly be an adequate explanation for why they were able to relieve themselves of the moral burden of the past. He asks what would have happened if the relatively liberal and internationalist views of Marxist and leading communist Paul Merkel—whose ideas about German guilt and shame had been shaped by intensive encounters with Jewish comrades in exile in Mexico—had prevailed in East Germany? As we know they never did. Instead Merkel was imprisoned and lost all political influence for holding precisely those views (Eschwege, 1991). The question is why? In order to answer that question, we have to dig much more deeply into the problems of postwar memories than Herf seems prepared to do. Herf seems still to be a captive of the left-wing concept of a "restoration" that had purportedly taken place in West Germany but not in East Germany (Herf, 1999). He does not appear to be prepared to face the fact that this "restoration" is a myth which originated in East Germany in an effort to liberate East Germans from any moral responsibility for what had taken place during the Nazi years.

In an address to a symposium on Germany, David Gress challenged the dominant left-wing criticism of *Vergangenheitsbewältigung* in the Federal Republic as hypocritical, tackling the concept of a "restoration" head on.

> Consider: the war ended in 1945 and it was in the spring of that year that local Germans were marched through the camps of Belsen, Dachau and elsewhere by British and American soldiers to see the dead bodies, a legacy of the regime that had just been destroyed. In 1945-46, the Allies held the Nuremberg trials of "main war criminals," which were broadcast to all German homes. At least one German who later achieved some fame, the political philosopher Jürgen Habermas, has confessed that, as a sixteen year old, he performed the act of overcoming the German past with his ear to the radio listening to the trial. This, he tells us, was the critical exposure that laid the basis for what, in the context of a later episode of the drama, he names his "constitutional patriotism," his wish that Germany might join the Western community of nations. (Gress, 1995: 536)

In addition:

from 1945 to 1948, the American occupiers carried out their policy of de-Nazification which involved, among other things, asking every adult citizen in the U.S. zone of occupation what he had done in the war and classifying the respondents according to their answers, and to other evidence if available, in one of five categories ranging from "exonorated" to "heavily compromised." During those same years, both the British and the American forces began to locate and retrieve German property that had been stolen or expropriated from victims of Hitler's regime and to give this property back to the victims or their heirs. This policy continued after West German independence and evolved into the vast, incredibly costly and often traumatic exercise known as *Wiedergutmachung*, literally meaning "making good again," or compensation. In the same vein, the West German - but not the East German - government accepted responsibility for the public debts of the Reich, including its social security obligations to its citizens. Sounds like a great deal of overcoming to me. (Gress, 1995: 537)

The issue of "restoration" resurfaced after reunification, this time in the form of what to do with the property that had been nationalized during the GDR and was now being privatized again. The West German writer Peter Schneider deals with this important issue in his novel *Eduard's Heimkehr*. The way he deals with the topic can productively be contrasted with the East German writer Daniela Dahn's handling of the same subject in *Vertreibung ins Paradies*, also published in 1999 (although the book contains essays written over a ten year period). The most striking thing about the two books is that although they seem to deal with the same problem their tone and their historical and political analysis of the deeper meaning of re-privatization are strikingly different. Whereas Daniela Dahn's book basically repeats the myth of a historical "restoration" in West Germany, later extended to East Germany, Peter Schneider offers a deeper, more honest presentation of the moral issues involved.

Schneider notes a curious alliance among the "defenders" of national property, namely the local East German police force who refuse to be told by a "Wessie" what their job is, and a group of spoiled anarchists from West Germany who have occupied the house in central East Berlin that has been inherited by the returned Eduard. What unites the two groups is their lack of concern about legal procedures. Nothing could be further from their minds than the idea of a liberal constitution or a *Rechtstaat*. To Dahn, whose fame and moral authority rest upon her previous book, *Wie bleiben hier oder Wem gehört der Osten*, the idea of a *Rechtstaat* is a joke. What she does not say is that she did not have to wait for re-privatization in East Germany to arrive at that conclusion. Like the East German policemen and the West German anarchists, she was deeply convinced that private property was theft, something that had been demonstrated years before by the philosophical father of anarchism, Proudhon. And although the official Marxist state doctrine of East Germany condemned anarchy as a petty bourgeois deviation, it nevertheless shared the same contempt for legal procedures in solving issues of private property.

For both the East German communist policemen and the West German anarchists, all property of any significance belonged in principle to the whole nation and not to any single individual. Although the GDR went to extremes in this respect, expropriating almost anything of value - factories, estates, houses—contempt for law did not emerge in 1945 with the arrival of Soviet troops insisting upon the immediate expropriation of the property of "war criminals" (the major industrialists and estate owners who, according to Marxist theory, were the true culprits behind the Nazi phenomenon)—it started in 1933 when the Nazis came to power. This inconvenient truth is the core of the intellectual insight contained in Peter Schneider's novel. The idea of abandoning legal procedures in dealing with the rights of private citizens was not an invention by the "victors of history," the German communists who had the victorious Red Army on their side, it had defined the Nazi regime from the very start.

The Nazis limited themselves to abandoning legal procedures against two groups they defined as the mortal enemies of the regime, namely the communists and the Jews. The former were put in concentration camps, the latter were gradually deprived of any protection by the law. They could not practise their professions, intermarry, receive public education and health services, use public facilities, and finally and logically they were deprived of the right to live. Somewhere in the long gradual process of abandoning the principles of the *Rechtstaat* this particular minority who were being systematically denied the "right to have rights," as Hannah Arendt expresses it (Bernstein, 1996; Young-Bruehl, 1982) the Jews also lost their right to own businesses such as shops, factories, publishing houses, newspapers, export-import firms, and so on (Mosse, 1987).

The fate of these prosperous Jews was never of particular interest to the anarchists and Marxists, hence they became invisible. Adherents of the GDR (in both East and West Germany) thought that private property was theft. In other words they neither saw nor cared that they were continuing on the path laid down by the Nazis.

If some people for some reason did not share the same fundamental rights as everyone else there had been a fundamental break with the *Rechtstaat*. Since the wealthy were a favorite target of the GDR authorities in their attempts to weed out undesirable elements, most of the accumulated illegalities of the regime affected them. As it became increasingly clear in the spring of 1990 that the system was about to collapse, the Modrow regime desperately wanted to save as much as it could. The result was the enactment of two laws. One retrospectively gave inhabitants of houses that had been expropriated from their rightful owners the right to live in these houses indefinitely, the other, *Treuhandanstalt*, was aimed at preventing nationalized productive property, particularly in industry and agriculture, from being re-privatized.

This attempt to legalize theft was not a very good way to return to the *Rechtstaat* and was unacceptable both to the first freely elected East German government and to the Federal government that took over responsibility in East Germany in October 1990. Whereas Peter Schneider in his novel firmly places himself in the *Rechtstaat* tradition, Daniela Dahn refuses to recognize the legitimacy of the *Rechtsstaat* which to her is as much of a joke as it is to the East German policemen and West German anarchists in Peter Schneider's novel. Interestingly her Marxist approach also leads her to reduce the highly complex issue of unification, which after all is as much about morality and legality as it is about economics, to a question of the wealthy robbing the poor of their hard-earned savings. Somehow this reasoning seems to have a strong affinity with the amoral utilitarian thinking which was typical of the German mind before the Nazis came to power. Which makes one suspect that the popularity in East Germany of Daniela Dahn's philosophy might indicate a similar absence of a strong moral foundation.

The Victors of History

The crucial point about the way in which the past was managed in the two postwar Germanies is not whether the West Germans behaved perfectly – they most certainly did not – but rather that the aspects mentioned by Gress (above) indicate the presence of a very strong moral pressure, initially exercised by the Western forces of occupation but later taken over by the West German government itself.

Although one might disagree with certain policy decisions of the

Adenauer administration—such as allowing individuals with a problematic past to achieve high positions in government —one can hardly accuse either the government or its followers of trying to evade moral responsibility for the events of the past. Paradoxically, the strong criticism raised by the Left in the sixties of attempts to evade the burden of the past signifies to the continuing role played by this moral burden in post-war Germany. Although the *Historikerstreit* seemed to indicate a lessening of the burden, the swift reaction by Habermas and others indicated that the intellectual élites would not allow the issue to fade away (Maier, 1988; Baldwin, 1990).

The GDR, on the advice of the Soviet leaders, never recognized the unconditional capitulation of Nazi Germany as a defeat for the German nation. Although the German army had struggled bitterly to the end against the Soviet forces, particularly on the Eastern Front and around Berlin (Kuby, 1965), the concept of the antifascist state was based upon the myth that East Germany belonged to the "victors of history"—a formulation East German rulers never tired of repeating.

Thus Walter Ulbricht in 1960 emphasized "the great and strong community which has radically uprooted fascism" (cit. Schubarth et al., 1991: 5). In a speech in Moscow in 1964 he stated as a matter of fact that "those who ally themselves with the Soviet Union and the other socialist countries find themselves on the proven ground of the victors of history" (cit. Schubarth et al., 1991: 6). His successor, Erich Honnecker, in a speech on 5 May 5 1975 reminded his listeners of the historical meaning of the end of the Nazi regime: "This thirtieth anniversary after liberation sees us all...as the victors of history" (Schubarth et al., 1991: 6).

The widespread acceptance in East Germany of this myth was partly a matter of national pride. For a German who wanted to be proud of his or her nation, it was a bitter pill to swallow that there had been no armed resistance in Germany to the Nazi regime as there had been in other Nazi-occupied countries. Although tens of thousands of political prisoners had been temporarily or permanently placed in concentration camps and millions had been dragged from their homes to be killed in extermination camps, these proofs of inhumanity had not been enough to convince the Germans that their future lay in opposing rather than supporting the regime.

This fundamental but remarkable fact explains, I believe, why even those who defined themselves in opposition to Hitler lacked the moral authority necessary to build up a viable alternative to his rule. Thus those aristocratic forces within military intelligence who had tried to turn against Hitler at the end of the war were mainly motivated by the same utilitarian reasoning as the rest of the nation. They had hoped to convince the Allies to let Germany keep as much as possible of the territory it had conquered and were surprised at being rebuffed. Without external support and logistics, this internal opposition of course stood little chance of getting rid of Hitler and was forced into a desperate and foolish effort to change things by an attempt upon Hitler's life (Powers, 1997).

The discussion among exiled intellectuals who defined themselves as "antifascist" also somehow managed to evade the moral issues involved. As the war progressed, the main issue became how the German nation could avoid being "punished" for the deeds of the Nazis. Bertold Brecht during his Hollywood exile had heated arguments with Thomas Mann about the plans of the Americans for postwar Germany (Lyon, 1980; Frey, 1976). In his diary Brecht wrote: "one has to make a distinction between Hitler and Germany" (Lehnert, 1976: 69). Brecht's patriotism made it difficult for him to recognize the bitter truth - that there had been no popular resistance to the Nazis and that the Allies could, for that reason, do as they pleased since there was no moral authority to negotiate with. One of the few exiles to recognize this fact was Mann who, in explaining why he did not want to participate in the "Free Germany" movement argued:

> And finally my view is that one has to leave it to liberal America to warn against a destruction of Germany; according to my point of view, it does not become us immigrants to advise America about the treatment of our country after the difficult and still distant victory. Among German leftwing socialists there is a kind of patriotic fashion, to insist that 'nothing should be done' to Germany. That is not my feeling at all. After all that happened, I do not want to protest against what the allies do with Germany when the country is finally forced to its knees. Of course one would wish that they will not do anything that cannot be repaired, stupidities that might influence the future. But from a purely moral and pedagogical point of view, its [Germany's] fall and its punishment cannot be deep enough after the shameful arrogance, the desert like wrath of superiority and fantasies of violence this people has produced in its intoxication. (Lehnert, 1976: 71)

Although the expression "victors of history" tried to appeal to national pride, its origins can be traced to Soviet and German communism. It was a useful myth used shamelessly to rewrite the story of the German communist movement. This use of history for self-

serving purposes is wonderfully illustrated by the following quota-
tion from an interview with Klaus Gysi, a leading communist in the
new government:

> We predicted that whoever voted for Hindenburg would choose Hitler. That was cor-
> rect. We predicted that whoever voted for Hitler would vote for the War. That was also
> correct. Now we return to the collapse of fascism at the end of the War. And we are on
> the side of the victors. Or in other words, we belong to the victors of history, point one.
> Point two: We must of course reeducate the people. (cit. Land and Possekel, 1994: 21)

This method of reasoning appealed particularly to a dedicated
cadre that until 1945 had been consistently wrong about almost everything and was a victim of its own undisguised lust for power. The
German communists had not been particularly eager to fight the Nazis
in the late 1920s and early 1930s, as the Nazi movement grew ex-
plosively, mainly because the communists were busy fighting the
Social Democrats for leadership of the labor movement. When they
changed their policy and abandoned the disastrous theory that the
"social fascists" were the main enemy it was too late to organize
effective resistance. They now took comfort in the prediction that
Hitler's rule would be short lived, that the future belonged to the
proletariat which would establish its dictatorship as the capitalist
economic system went into its death throes.

The fact that Hitler meant war did not play any significant role in
communist propaganda until Nazi Germany broke the Molotov-
Ribbentrop pact and attacked Stalin's Russia. Barely having survived
the onslaught and having turned the initial immense losses into a
triumphant victory, Stalin ruled all of Eastern Europe and was eager
to put communists in charge everywhere to serve as a buffer zone
against another surprise attack. Communist rule in East Germany
fitted into this equation, but in order to avoid too much popular resistance from a suspicious and unwilling population, it had to be
won over so Stalin found it useful to forget the shameful past and
concentrate on the glorious future. This line had already been ham-
mered out in Moscow before the return of the hardcore communist
exiles who were put in power on behalf of the Soviets. Surprised by
their good fortune, these consistent losers grabbed eagerly at the
straw of victory.

A third group to whom the idea of being declared "victors of
history" had a strong appeal was the Jewish returnees who decided
to make East rather than West Germany their home. For them the

attraction of the formula derived from a different moral burden—
they suffered from a deep shame about their ethnic and religious
background. It is well known that despised minorities sometimes
assimilate the prejudices of the majority against their own group.
Given the strong tradition of anti-Semitism in Germany, and especially after what had happened during the Hitler years, Jews who
wanted to escape their Jewishness were attracted by the GDR, which
allowed them to cope with their shame.

A case in point is that of Salomea Genin, who was born in Germany to an immigrant mother: "I wanted to have roots, but not Jewish roots," she said. These feelings originated from her early experiences in Nazi Germany where "to be Jewish was something abomi-
nable, this deep truth is something I learned from the Nazis in Berlin
before my sixteenth birthday. I also had a disturbed relationship with
my Polish-Jewish mother. By distancing myself from her, I also distanced myself from one of her traits—being Jewish." After she escaped to Australia, her search for identity led her to communism and
she later returned to what she had come to define as her true home:

> I didn't need the Jewish stuff and I didn't want it and I was not an Australian....when I
> was 21 I knew what I wanted: to become a Jewish communist. So I planned my journey
> and after many years of effort I came to the GDR as a 30 year-old, but only with the
> help of a very important friend. I was happy to feel at home at last in this antifascist
> state...here human dignity was respected, fascism had been banned forever, and with it
> anti-Semitism. It was worth living here, to work, to engage oneself - for the state, for the
> individual. Here it didn't matter that I was a Jewess, just as little as it mattered to me.
> (Genin, 1994: 383)

Genin's is a clear case of the Jew wanting above all to escape the
burden of being a Jew in a world that allowed the Holocaust to happen (Wyman, 1998). A somewhat different case is that of Frau Eisler
who returned to East Germany in 1949 from the U.S.A., probably
because she feared the rising anticommunism, which threatened her
professional prospects and impinged upon her civil rights. "I feel
like an equal member of society here. I feel safe and I am taken care
of...my journalistic work is a big source of satisfaction. I also sit on
the committee for antifascist resistance fighters, and I am grateful
for the care and for the manner in which they are treated here" (cit.
Bornemann, 1996: 151).

Unlike Genin's story, Frau Eisler's contains no elements of self-
hate. They have been replaced by the discrimination she experienced in America as a communist, rather than as a Jew, which made

the choice of East Germany seem both rational and emotionally fulfilling. What she does not reflect upon is the vulnerability of people
like herself in East Germany, where joining the "victors of history"
was no guarantee against racial and ethnic persecution. Eschwege, a
German communist who returned to Dresden from Palestine, was
told about the "violent anti-Semitism" in the Soviet Union after the
war. "When I first came to Dresden, whole groups within the Soviet
army consisted entirely of Jews; for example, all the cultural and
political officers were Jews. At first I didn't understand it, but then I
found out that because of the anti-Semitism in the Soviet Union,
many Jews were not demobilized after the war, but remained in the
army because they felt more secure there" (Ostow, 1989: 138).

This vulnerability was experienced particularly by those Jewish
returnees who rose rapidly in the state apparatus of the new communist regime (Ostow, 1996a). About 3,500 mainly politically motivated Jewish returnees settled down in the East Zone and the GDR
after the war (Burgauer, 1993: 155) and a large part of this group
"rapidly took over functions in the state administration and later state
government, SED's *Staatspresidium* and later the *Vereinigung der
Ferfolgte des Naziregimes* [VVN - those who could prove that they
had been discriminated against under the Nazi regime and who were
entitled to certain privileges] as well as in the *Länder* and city administration, economy, culture and media" (Goldenbogen, 1996: 12).
One of them, Clara Berliner, proudly expressed the feeling of triumph she felt as she returned. "You have to understand that here we
are the victors and we are in power" (Ostow, 1989: 87).

As the anti-Semitic show trials in Eastern Europe, which began
with the Slansky trials in November 1952, reached East Germany,
Jews in visible positions began to experience what it meant to be a
"victor of history." In his autobiography Helmut Eschwege admits
that the self-proclaimed antifascist state suddenly turned against the
Jews in its midst. Many of them were arrested and interrogated and
some were kept under lock and key for long periods. When they
were finally released they were broken people and society had turned
its back on them.

Bruno Goldhammer, editor in chief of an illustrated journal had to
"sit for years in a lonely cell. He was constantly interrogated in order to force him to make false accusations against friends. His wife
divorced the 'party enemy,' he lay helpless in his cell, crippled by

heart attacks" (Eschwege, 1991: 69). Another prominent Jew, Leo Löwenkopf, who had been a top functionary in the GDR and President of the National Bank in Sachsen, was released after a few months in prison. "He left prison as a broken man. To cheer him up, the board of the community arranged a birthday party for him a few weeks later in a hotel in Dresden. As always we invited the leading people from the party leadership and the ministries, but the majority did not show up. The solidarity under oath only lasted seven years, now it was suddenly forgotten" (Eschwege, 1991: 71). The communist leadership in East Germany welcomed the Jews as long as they had a use for them. When the "victors of history" changed their minds and turned against their Jewish comrades the East German leadership followed swiftly, proving that it too had remained fundamentally German in outlook and behavior.

A fourth group for whom the concept of the "victors of history" had a certain appeal seems to have been the physically handicapped. Although they were "Aryans" in the ethnic sense they must have felt themselves to be useless outsiders in a Nazi Germany single-mindedly dedicated to the aim of winning the war. A society like the GDR in which everybody could be made to feel useful - provided they did not question the legitimacy of the state—must have seemed a vast improvement to them. An example of this is found in the story of Ilse who, despite her handicap, was offered a position as manager of a large bookstore in the center of East Berlin:

> I agreed with a great deal in this country. And our country, as I saw it, overall made an effort to build up an antifascist order. That was at least the founding idea. And that made everything that was difficult for an individual like me easier. Because when you were depressed about anything which you were dissatisfied with you could always say to yourself, this is not as bad as under Nazism ... and on top of that came of course that because you had lost everything, this liberated a lot of activity. To start all over again is a wonderful thing. (Hoffmann-Pawslowsky and Voigt, 1995: 34-5)

What Ilse does not mention is the very need to be useful in order to feel accepted by society. The GDR expanded the sphere of the useful and was in this sense a more generous and liberal society than Nazi Germany. Seen from that point of view, Ilse's experience is similar to that of Frau Singewald, a Jewish survivor of a concentration camp outside Auschwitz. After she was liberated by Russian troops and could return to her home country, she joined the ruling party. "It was a good feeling to take part in the political work because I could do something to build up a state where there were no longer any barriers for us as human beings and no questions" (cit. Goldenbogen, 1996: 126). Being on the side of the "victors of history" helped Frau Singewald to obliterate a past in which some individuals had been excluded even from the right to be useful.

In doing so, however, she, like many others, stopped asking awkward questions about the possible similarities between the Nazi regime and the GDR, whose self-proclaimed humanism was always narrowly defined within a strong practical and productive context (Lenhardt and Stock, 1997).

Convincing an Unwilling Population

The main reason the formulation the "victors of history" played such an important role in the foundation myth of the GDR was less to do with the feelings of these small minorities than with the fact that it gave the SED a tool with which to legitimize its unpopular rule over an unwilling population which longed for the freedom and prosperity that was so obviously missing from the Eastern Zone. In her article "*Antifascismus und antifascistische Widerstand als politischer Gründungmythos*" Herfried Münkler argues that the main function of the promotion of East Germany as an antifascist state was to induce a minimum of loyalty in its unwilling citizens by relieving them of the moral burden of the Nazi past. This was done by reducing uncertainty and simplifying political choice in an attempt to make the founding of the GDR appear to be irreversible. Although from the start its status and survival were shaky because the division of Germany was so clearly dependent upon the decisions of the former Allies over which the SED had little or no control, it was important for the SED to pretend that nothing would change and the GDR would exist forever.

The "victors of history" formulation fitted into the Marxist theory of the objective laws of history, according to which socialism was bound to win over capitalism. No matter how bleak things looked, the party was armed with a scientific world-view and would, as Klaus Gysi stated, triumph in the end. The foundation of the GDR confirmed this basic truth and helped renew faith in the party. It expressed the determination of the SED never to give up power or to show any sign of weakness. This determination lay behind Honecker's refusal publicly to admit that the refugees who had left the GDR in droves in the late summer of 1989 would be missed—a denial that would later be turned against him later in the internal power struggle that ended with his dismissal from all his positions (Schabowski, 1991).

But for the most part, the GDR used the "victors of history" concept as a symbol of the fact that if the Republic were to end, it would be with a bang. It solved the problem of reducing uncertainty by associating any threat to its existence with the threat of a nuclear war between the super powers. By and large, it seems that the SED was highly successful in this respect. An East German dissident intellectual, Christoph Dieckman, who was involved in the alternative movement, the *Basisgruppen*, that grew up in the 1970s around concepts like "Peace," "Justice," and the "Preservation of Creation," wrote:

> Yes, it did nauseate us, the vulgar ideological trash, the opportunism of the fellow travelers, the nonsense of the ideological indoctrination [*Parteilehrjahre*], the presentation of the colors, the parades, the over-regulated everyday life, the arrogant treatment by the state of the people it was supposed to serve. But we did not run away, and not only because Hungary was still closed. GDR seemed to be a state that would exist; it also made historical sense in a bipolar world, and we could not have forecast that history would give up this East-West [antagonism]. (Land and Possekel, 1994: 60-1)

Diekman, like most of his dissident friends, could not imagine that the East-West conflict would end some day. For the GDR this conflict, and the underlying threat of a nuclear Armageddon increasingly became the only significance of the "victors of history" formulation.

According to Alexander and Margrete Mitscherlisch, for most Germans the Nazi defeat was inexplicable and resulted in a loss of purpose. The reiteration of the "victors of history" concept was aimed at helping the East Germans cope with this loss of purpose without dwelling too much on difficult moral issues. Von Plato (1991) states that most Germans after the defeat of Hitler talked about their role in purely functional terms, as though it had not involved any moral considerations at all.

Individuals defended themselves by saying that they had only "done their duty" and that most of their activities were "nonpolitical." After 1989, East Germans used almost exactly the same arguments to evade moral responsibility for their role in the GDR dictatorship.

> Today one hears similar expressions to those expressed after 1945. "Not everything was bad." "I only did my duty." "We didn't know anything." "It was necessary to join the party to gain influence," "to help my family," "to advance my career," "my idealism was misused," "with us everything was nonpolitical," "I have nothing to accuse myself of, I couldn't change anything anyhow." (von Plato, 1995: 14-15)

Most East Germans feel no shame at all about the compromises they made, in fact it is seen as a grave injustice and a sign of arrogance for West Germans to raise the issue at all.

That one was held responsible simply because one had lived in the system at the same time as a political leadership one did not particularly like and now should be punished once more for their faults, is a frequently repeated rationalization that helped the person to reorient himself both after 1945 and after 1949. (von Plato, 1991:12)

Karl Popper, in his brilliant criticism of "historicism" in *The Open Society and its Enemies* and *The Poverty of Historicism*, states that the main problem with any view of history which reduces progress to a question of which class happens to be in power is that such a view is basically amoral, equating as it does might with right. To do the right thing according to such a view is to do the rational thing, that is to obey the powers-that-be, no matter who they are or what they do. Thus individuals can never do wrong as long as they do what they are told.

As Christa Wolf points out, the only thing the East Germans had to do was to obey the new rulers, and their consciences were automatically clear.

This formula has contributed to making the understanding between generations more difficult. At a certain time which cannot be determined a small group of antifascists, who governed this country extended its consciousness of victory to the whole population. These "victors of history" for this reason stopped confronting its real past, the past of the fellow traveler, the seduced, the believer in the time of National Socialism. Their children they mostly told little or nothing about their own childhood and youth. Their bad consciences made them unable to resist the Stalinist structures and ways of thinking which for a long time were regarded as proof of "party commitment" and "political loyalty." The children of these parents, who are now wholly "children of the GDR" ... could not give their children enough courage ... and apart from the eagerness to get high marks, could not endow them with values, towards which they could orient themselves. (Wolf, 1990a: 11)

A third function of the antifascist foundation myth, according to Münkler, was to help the East Germans in their choice of fundamental political loyalty. After the war there were two competing foundation myths in Germany. On the one hand there was the West German myth which based itself upon the idea of the moral responsibility of the German nation and the need to break with the "*Sonderweg,*" and on the other, the East German myth which denied this responsibility, blaming the immorality of the capitalist system rather than admitting that the behavior of Germans during the Nazi regime did not conform to normal moral standards. Whereas the East German regime deserved the loyalty of the East Germans because it made them the "victors of history," the Federal Republic did not, because there the people in power "had not really broken with the past and therefore did not deserve the loyalty of the democrats" (Münkler, 1998: s20).

This suggests that the myth of the "victors of history" also served as a point of departure from which to stigmatize the competing liberal democracy. Although the Federal Republic was a German democracy, indeed the only German democracy and, as it turned out, a highly stable one and a world apart from the Weimar Republic, its existence threatened the shaky legitimacy of the GDR which had to be strengthened by the myth of "restoration" in order to produce the necessary minimum of loyalty. As Münkler suggests, the importance of this counter-myth helps to explain another strange aspect of East German society, namely the weak or absent political opposition. This is what Christa Wolf hints at when she suggests that the "victors of history" formulation had the effect of making the individual helpless to resist the state.

Wolf suggests that the expiation of guilt did not work perfectly in East Germany. An element of decency remained among at least the educated East Germans who did not find it so easy to live with their consciences. This vague feeling of having done wrong rarely led to open criticism though or to active opposition. Dissidents who challenged the dictatorship of the party had to struggle with the knowledge that they would immediately be stigmatized as supporters of the restoration of capitalism that had taken place in West Germany. A former school friend of my wife, an East German computer expert who had been deported to West Germany in early 1988 and now lives in West Berlin, told me over dinner in the fall of 1994 when I was living in East Berlin, that before he was evicted he and his wife had spent a whole night of interrogation at the Stasi headquarters. The question they were constantly confronted with was whether they advocated a similar restoration to that which had taken place in the Federal Republic. Only after they had repeated their denial over and over again were they released, and a few days later they were ordered to leave the GDR.

The Question of Impact

Many East Germans today vehemently deny that these policies, directed from above by an unpopular and socially isolated party, had any impact upon the East German mind. Daniela Dahn, assures her readers that whatever one can accuse the East Germans of, it was not moral complicity. On the topic of "GDR identity" she writes: "I have difficulties with the word identity. It insinuates that the persons identified with something. The best thing about the GDR was that the population was against it" (Dahn, 1999: 104). This is alas the right answer to the wrong question. The problem was not lack of popularity—many Germans did not particularly like the Nazi regime either, nevertheless they accepted it and made no attempts to resist it. That is the nature of moral complicity. In fact, only people who are moral enough to see that a particular system is wrong can be accused of moral complicity—the rest are simply criminals.

The moral effects of the GDR upon the East German mind should not be measured by studying those who were personally guilty of crimes against humanity but rather by looking at the distortion of morality among individuals whom one would have expected to be decent and moral. One such group is East German teachers, who managed the transition to the new system most successfully (Diewald and Mayer, 1996; Pritchard, 1999). In fact the predominance of teachers with a GDR background in East German schools is so marked that scholars and politicians are worried about its possible effects upon future generations brought up in East Germany (Gruner, 1990; von Ollberg et al., 1993; Döbert and Rudolf, 1995; Benner et al., 1996).

Although a great deal of research has been done on East German schools and teachers, most of what I have read has shied away from the problem of the moral after effects of living in a state whose legitimacy was founded upon a myth. East German scholars, although no doubt highly competent to study the issue in some depth, have often been under great pressure to establish a foothold in the West German system in which they as "outsiders" have a natural handicap against the "establishment" (see Neckel, 1997). The result is that they have concentrated on what they consider more pressing issues, such as the insecurity many East Germans felt in trying to get a foothold in the new system (see Koch et al., 1994). Established West German researchers seem to have been worried about the possibility of losing the goodwill of their research object, and have tended to suppress their feeling of unease (see in particular Hoyer, 1996). Some West German scholars have even "gone native" and become so captivated by the nostalgic stories East German teachers have to tell that they have completely identified with their longing (Händle, 1998).

There are, of course critical studies, but these focus mainly upon the authoritarian and conservative pedagogical outlook of East German teachers (see Stock, 1996; 1997; Gehrmann and Hübner, 1997; Neumann, 1997) and rarely venture into the highly contentious issue of the way in which the "victors of history" concept has influenced the moral thinking of East German teachers.

In the absence of such studies I have had to rely upon two group experiments, one planned and carefully organized, the other unplanned but no less interesting.

Case One: Playing Concentration Camp Prisoners

A role-playing experiment conducted some time after reunification and involving students from teacher colleges in both East and West Germany, revealed interesting differences between the ways in which the two groups perceived the Nazi past. Each group was asked to improvise a role-play situation involving a concentration camp. The West German students produced a play showing demoralized and abandoned prisoners waiting to be taken away to a certain death. They had no doubt that the play must be about Jewish prisoners. As a group selected for extermination merely because they happened to be Jews, their death had no meaning. They could of course try to escape, but given the mixture of hostility and frustrating indifference among the German population the idea of resistance or escape was a gamble against impossible odds.

By contrast, when the East German students did their role-play, they presented an entirely different scenario. The prisoners they portrayed were neither demoralized nor abandoned. They were too busy organizing collective resistance. Although this carried considerable risks, the situation was not hopeless. The world outside had not abandoned them, they still had some degree of social capital left, which they were determined to use.

Certainly escaped German communists would have stood a far better chance than Jewish escapees. There was a possibility that the population outside the camp would take them in or pretend that they did not know that they were enemies of the state. They would have time to contact the communist underground network, create new identities for themselves or, if necessary find a route out of the country. Anna Segher's novel *The Seventh Cross*, which was widely read in the GDR describes just such a situation.

The West German professor who conducted the experiment was amazed at its outcome which made it clear that East German propaganda had been taken seriously by the GDR's citizens. What he does not mention is that the experiment also revealed that people who had grown up in the GDR had never been exposed to the realities of Nazism and saw the situation in concentration camps as a struggle between heroic German communists and German Nazi bullies for control of the future of the country. Reality had been presented to them in a way that evaded the terrible truth of what the Nazi regime had really meant.

Such a message was, of course, pleasing, because it relieved them of a moral burden. As Herf writes (1997), even the rituals of memory in the two Germanies reflected different narratives. In the Federal Republic ritualized gatherings commemorating the concentration camps were times of deep and shared mourning, with leading representatives of the West German state sharing feelings of irreparable loss with the leaders of the Jewish community. In the GDR similar occasions were triumphal, a celebration of the heroes who had sacrificed themselves for a higher cause—the new, supposedly democratic German Republic. Their sacrifices had not been in vain, the antifascist heroes had become the "victors of history."

Case Two: Making a Moral Choice

A few years after reunification a group of about 100 East German teachers in Berlin-Brandenburg took part in a week long internship course, dedicated to the issue of coping with the past. The basic material to be discussed during the week was the film *Mefisto*, in which Brandauer plays a left-wing actor called Höfgens who, after the Nazis have come to power, is offered the job of stage manager at the most important theater in Berlin. The film is based upon a novel by Klaus Mann, but it is not mere fiction. Both the novel and the film are closely patterned upon the life and career of the famous German actor Gründgen. The film was shown on the first day of the course and the idea was to analyze its meaning from a variety of angles—psychological, social, and so on. The core question to be answered was whether such a person should have been given a similar job in the Deutsche Theater in East Berlin after the war?

Presenting the question, Jan Hoffmann, the leader of the institute which had organized the course, emphasized that the participants should not rush to reach an answer. He had assumed that the answer would be 'no'; that a man who had compromised himself so completely and in public, would probably not even try to apply for such a job, particularly in East Germany which prided itself on rooting out fascism. Hoffmann's intention was that the participants should try to understand why Höfgens, alias Gründgen, had acted the way he had; to explore the temptations and sources of moral complicity in a totalitarian dictatorship which made people act against their consciences.

To his surprise, the teachers thought it a waste of time to spend a week going into Gründgen's motives for working for the Nazis. The answers, they felt, were too banal and self-evident to bother about. By the end of the first day the teachers had reached a unanimous conclusion: they had no problems at all about the man being employed in the Deutsche Theater. They gave four reasons for their decision:

> Reason number one: The man was competent. Reason number two: During the dark years of Nazism, he had dedicated himself to art and culture, which was a rarity at the time. Reason number three: During this time he had done what he could, within his ability, to mention and sometimes help other colleagues within the profession. Reason number four (the best): ...he didn't hurt anyone. (BISS- Interview)

The interesting thing about this experiment is (a) the clear self-deception and rationalization about Gründgen and his motives; (b) the ease with which the teachers could identify and reproduce their rationalizations; (c) their complete identification with these rationalizations. Clearly the person whose moral behavior was to be evaluated had not thought about other people, he had wanted to save his own skin and favor his own career. What he did or did not do to art, professional colleagues and Jews was irrelevant. He acted amorally in accepting the job in the first place, although he no doubt tried to rationalize his decision through arguments similar to those put forward by the assembled teachers.

The teachers did not have to spend a whole week thinking about the situation, assisted by experts from the social sciences, in order to reproduce his rationalizations for serving the Nazi regime—in the story of Gründgen they recognized their own situation. Intellectuals were faced with the same moral dilemmas in both Nazi Germany and the GDR and reacted to those dilemmas in the same, shamelessly opportunistic way.

When we consider these two experiments together, an underlying pattern emerges. The amoral, strongly pragmatic thinking of people like Gründgen did not disappear in East Germany after the war for the simple reason that the antifascist regime did not present Nazi Germany to the East Germans as a moral problem. There was no radical break with the Nazi regime, the educated classes remained as pragmatic as they had been under that regime. They had not particularly liked Hitler and some of them, like Gründgen, were ideologically opposed to the Nazi world-view, but cared more about their careers then about the moral stature of their country. As for their Jewish colleagues, they chose to leave them out of the equation altogether.

Similarly, the educated classes in the GDR did not particularly like Ulbricht or Honnecker. In fact, they loathed both of them and thought they were incompetent (after all, Honnecker was a mere *Dachdecher*, as my East German mother-in-law likes to say) but they valued their careers too much to do anything foolish. Despite their compromises, they saw themselves as decent people. They did not want to admit that they had found an accommodation with a totalitarian dictatorship, and they stopped expecting the democratic republic that the GDR promised.

How could they preserve this feeling of moral decency? The answer again lies in the myth of the "victors of history." East Germany might be a loathsome state but West Germany was even worse. At least in East Germany one had got rid of all the fascists. While the West Germans brooded about the fate of the helpless Jews, reduced to pieces of flesh that could be manipulated at will, the East Germans took pride in the image of an heroic and courageous antifascist resistance movement, presumably saving the honor of Germany. There the memory of history caused feelings of shame, here it evoked feelings of pride, allowing the East Germans to rid themselves of the moral burden and the memory of the millions of humans slaughtered by the German state simply because they happened to be Jews.

4

The Workers' and Peasants' State: The Myth of the Marxist Utopia

Totalitarianism and Self-Deception

In her book *Anatomy of a Dictatorship: Inside the GDR 1948-1989* the English historian Mary Fulbrook writes that a crucial difference between the Nazi and GDR dictatorships was the levels of popular support attracted by each.

"Imposed under conditions of defeat and military occupation, the rule of the SED never achieved the degree of genuine popular support enjoyed by Hitler...yet the communists wanted at least the appearance...of comparable mass support." Although they made "comparable 'total claims' on individuals" and employed "comparable organizational means to try to incorporate people into some sense of 'national community,'" they only succeeded "in obtaining...the outward compliance" of the population. The major political pattern was accommodation rather than enthusiastic support. " By the 1970s many East Germans had come to some sort of modus vivendi" with the East German regime which at the time seemed to have reached a degree of stability "never achieved by the volatile, expansionist and destructive Third Reich" (Fulbrook, 1997: 285-6).

How are these similarities and differences between the two German dictatorships to be conceptualized? Fulbrook rejects the concept of "totalitarianism" as too simplistic and prefers the more neutral term "dictatorship" which allows for a more "differentiated analysis of a complex reality" (Fulbrook, 1997: 283). Such a broad concept does not, however seem very useful, it is too imprecise and it leaves out the problem of managing the past in post-war Germany. Why was the GDR so consistently unpopular and rejected by the majority? West Germany was imposed from the outside under similar conditions (Fulbrook, 1992) but its popular legitimacy was never seriously threatened (the only social group that rebelled there was the short lived student movement in the 1960s, a phenomenon that was not strictly German but was common to all Western countries).

According to Hans-Joachim Maaz, "until *die Wende* in the fall of 1989 the West was 'the projected better'" (Maaz, 1999: 117). For ordinary East Germans the Federal Republic was the country of their dreams, unreachable but nevertheless preferable, "a country beyond the seven mountains that the GDR citizen could dream about, the end station of his longings and desires." Although this was an illusion it was a necessary illusion "which made it possible for him to endure the realities" (Belwe, 1992: 15). The so-called stability of the GDR also turned out to be an illusion. The problem of the concept of totalitarianism in a GDR context (Jesse, 1998) is not that the authorities did not try to create a totally compliant population, but that they tried very hard and never succeeded. The totalitarian ideal of the totally committed and captive citizen remained a utopian dream, the simulation of a reality that looked very different (Bessel and Jessen, 1996; Wolle. 1998).

Unlike ordinary East Germans who resisted the GDR, members of the educated classes, the "intelligentsia," were, as Fulbrook observes, largely co-opted by the communist state. Within this group it was the cultural intelligentsia, the "intellectuals" in the Western sense who were most involved (Grunenberg, 1990).

> The pinnacles of the cultural intelligentsia were of great significance in the history of the GDR. Returning exiles such as Bertold Brecht or Stefan Heym, though restrained and doled out to the public in selective, limited doses, were very important in establishing a degree of legitimacy for the anti-fascist state; critical writers of a slightly younger generation, who were themselves to a great degree products of the GDR itself, such as Christa Wolf, for all their veiled and partially self-censored critical comments nevertheless lent the GDR a degree of international acclaim and credibility. (Fulbrook, 1997: 78)

A somewhat different pattern emerged among the less visible elements of the intelligentsia—individuals with *Gymnasium* level education or above who had entered professions like law, medicine, religion, the natural and social sciences, the humanities, engineering and, to some extent, teaching. This group was originally indifferent or hostile to the communist state, in fact "in the fifties, it was particularly from the ranks of the professional classes that the *Republikflüchtlinge*, those fleeing to the West were drawn" (Fulbrook,

1997: 79). The situation changed, though after the Wall was built in 1961, forcing those who remained to adapt themselves to the new realities as emigration to West Germany was no longer an easy option (Mietzner, 1998). This, combined with intensified "cadre training and political control, eventually came to mean that the intelligentsia in effect constituted conformist pillars of the system rather than a potential opposition...in contrast with the more critical and independent role of the technical and cultural intelligentsia in Czechoslovakia and Poland" (Fulbrook, 1997: 81).

Jan Faktor (1994) points out that this crucial difference between the intelligentsia in East Germany, even those who saw themselves as dissidents, and those in most other East European countries existed right up to the collapse of the GDR. They simply ignored the intellectual rethinking and development that had taken place in Czechoslovakia after 1968, when the mood among intellectuals definitely shifted from Marxism to liberalism. Although people like Havel and other leading dissidents in Czechoslovakia were cherished as heroes by East German dissidents, the latter did not seem to be aware of the intellectual break with Marxism that had taken place among the educated classes in Eastern Europe during the 1970s and1980s (Kupferberg, 1993).

Paradoxically the intellectual odyssey of these East European intellectuals had led them to share the dreams of ordinary East Germans—dreams of a decent and free life based upon the elementary respect for civil rights that had been denied to them in their own countries. Like those ordinary East Germans the East European intellectuals had reached the conclusion that the prosperity of western countries had its source in the existence of these rights. The East German intelligentsia, on the other hand, appear to have had what Veblen called a "trained incapacity" to understand this. "My East German friends were still unmistakably impregnated by the 'faith'" (Faktor, 1994: 30).

The Role of the Teachers

Thinking back on her role in the GDR, Gisela, an East German teacher, admits that "as teachers we idealized many things, because we did not notice many things. Today when I try to get a grip on it, I think we always tried to find excuses in front of our pupils...I also largely identified with many things that in our state...on the other hand I always said to myself: things were going...we were doing well in those years. We had social security, we had our apartment, we received our incomes, we did not suffer, we had a car. Taken as a whole we had everything" (Geulen, 1998: 265).

What is interesting about this personal narrative is that members of the East German intelligentsia did not merely pretend that they lived in a workers' and peasants' state (as they pretended that the Nazi past was a West German problem), they actually deceived themselves into believing it. They also believed that the GDR was a state in which ordinary East Germans had no real reasons to be dissatisfied. Despite the fact that working-class East Germans obviously dreamed of something very different from communist rule and a socialist economy, East German teachers continued to insist that socialism represented a meaningful existence for them—the very epitome of their dreams and longings.

The intellectual origin of this self-deception was their belief in the liberating effects of Marxism which they rarely mention today, partly because it reminds them of their complicity with a totalitarian regime, and partly because it was an integral part of their identity (Giddens, 1991; Cerulo, 1997). They were strongly committed to it (Kanter, 1968; Hoerning and Kupferberg, 1999) and for this reason have great difficulty abandoning it (Ebaugh, 1988).

Where did this belief emanate from and how was it maintained despite the mass of contradictory evidence? In Gisela's case, two aspects emerge. One is the professional role of teachers in the GDR. Gisela was expected to deceive herself. The measurement of reality from an ideological standpoint rather than from empirical facts, was a predominant trait among East German professionals and suggests a parallel evasion of moral responsibility. In her memoir, Gisela defends her lack of interest in ascertaining the true situation, claiming: "We did not notice many things." This argument is strikingly similar to the way in which Germans rationalized the policy of exterminating Jews during the Nazi regime. They did not notice many things either, particularly the sudden disappearance of their erstwhile neighbors and friends.

The other argument relates to living standards and social security. Here the suggestion is that ordinary citizens in the GDR had no reason to be dissatisfied with what the GDR offered its citizens. This argument seems to be a nostalgic distortion of reality. Citizens of the

GDR complained constantly about the many irritations of daily life caused by a malfunctioning economy, and they became increasingly envious of West Germans who did not seem to have these problems. This despite the fact that according to the "objective laws" of history, capitalism was dying and was being replaced by socialism, the "victor of history."

The Church and Socialism

One of the most intriguing aspects of the GDR was the role played by the Protestant clergy. Initially hostile to the communist regime, it accommodated itself and seemed to take pride in sharing a belief in the utopia represented by the regime (Eppelmann, 1993; Kælble et al., 1994; Land and Possekel, 1994; Maier, 1997; Fulbrook, 1997). Although the church's conversion to a belief in the Marxist utopia only occurred late—in the mid-1960s—it is amazing that it took place at all. Retrospectively this conversion has been legitimized as being a purely pragmatic arrangement. The formulation adopted at the time—"church in socialism"—was, according to Manfred Stolpe, the leading representative of the Protestant Church communities in the GDR, intended to defend civil rights rather than to legitimize a society in which these rights had been abolished. "'Church in socialism,'" says Stolpe, was seen as a commitment to action that drew the church into society: to help to improve and reshape it in a way to make it more human and to give the individual more opportunities to participate and more freedoms" (cit. Land and Possckel, 1994: 57).

What Stolpe does not mention is the effect of this self-deceptive accommodation. It brought about a dramatic change among leading East German theological scholars who began to reinterpret Christian theology in order to make it fit into a Marxist framework. Although Marxism is disdainful of the rights of the individual, proposing to abolish them in order to liberate the proletariat and all of humanity—a point of view that is diametrically opposed to Christianity which as an historical movement has always insisted upon the inviolability of the rights of the individual—the recently converted Marxist theologians suddenly espoused this view. The Marxist utopia, as many East German intellectuals had come to understand it, legitimized the abolition of civil rights, seeing them as integral parts of an anachronistic bourgeois civilization. Nevertheless these theological thinkers suddenly found Marxism to be a perfect vehicle for the struggle for exactly these rights.

Thus Gottfried Forck admits: "I recognized myself very well at the time in the formulation...that socialism should be improved within our area." Forck believed he had "discovered that Marxism was a humanistic doctrine. A doctrine that really concerns individuals and therefore has a certain right to be taken seriously." He claimed that a regime that had become unpopular precisely because of its lack of humanity nevertheless represented a higher form of civilization than one that was uncompromising on the issue of civil rights. "I really thought...I did not like dictatorial communism—I thought it was possible that in this dictatorially deformed political system there was hiding a socialist system, or whatever one calls the alternative, that it was one's duty to revive, and that one could posit in contrast to the somewhat anachronistic middle classes in West Germany" (Land and Possekel, 1994: 57-8).

Although there were different reasons for the extremely strong element of self-deception among the East German intelligentsia, there was an overall consensus among them that the GDR, with its presumed potential for human freedom and creativity, genuinely represented a radical new beginning that made it morally superior to West Germany. Although they were aware that many of the rights and liberties denied to citizens of the GDR had long been the norm in western societies, these rights were still seen as anachronistic. The GDR - a society that intentionally denied individuals elementary civil rights such as freedom of expression and assembly, freedom of movement and choice of home and occupation as well as entrepreneurial and political freedoms—was nevertheless mysteriously seen as offering something more valuable and for this reason was to be supported.

A Neglected Group

Jarauch suggests that the intellectual self-deception of the East German intelligentsia should be seen in the context of the Nazi past, and in particular the way East Germany had coped with the heritage that had led to Hitler and the Holocaust.

The attempt to renew the GDR led to a widespread search for a "Third Way" between communism and capitalism. Motivated by the failures of "actual socialism," this quest for an alternative path was conditioned by German division. In neigboring countries,

Czechoslovak repression and Polish martial law had shocked intellectuals into abandoning the idea of "socialism with a human face." Yet in East Berlin, dissenters from Robert Havemann to Rudolf Bahro continued to dream of democratizing Marxism. (Jarauch, 1994: 77)

Although members of the East German intelligentsia I have interviewed are often embarrassed to admit that they believed in the Marxist utopia, the fact remains that right up to the sudden and unexpected collapse of the Wall they were committed to the ideals of the GDR and to the conviction that they truly lived in a workers' and peasants' state in which the system, if not perfect, at least demonstrated its deeply liberating and progressive potential. As one intellectual interviewed by Geulen put it: "In principle we had the ideals, if you can put it like that, the ideal that socialism would lead to the liberation of man...from exploitation...That was the point of departure of politics" (Geulen, 1998: 205).

Geulen offers several reasons for the total commitment of intellectuals. Among them are the important socializing effect of the educational system, the ethical attraction of the Marxist utopia, the need to emphasize the ethical values of a socialist society to make the GDR look better than the Federal Republic, and the belief in the existence of "objective laws" according to which socialism was an historically superior mode of organizing production that would inevitably surpass and replace the morally inferior and crisis-ridden capitalist system. Another explanation is the hypothesis that the intellectuals felt secondary to the "ruling class" and needed to establish their own identity and importance as the group most strongly dedicated to the deeply liberating ideals of Marxism (which for some frustrating reason seemed to remain more theoretical than real).

In fact the intelligentsia were by no means second to the "ruling class" and one of the reasons they became so dedicated to socialism in the first place and clung to it to the very end, seems to be have been the extraordinary career opportunities the GDR offered talented children from their ranks (Solga, 1993; 1994; 1995; Hoerning, 1995) and the strong group pressures to conform imposed by these opportunities. The peculiarities of German history have to be taken into account in order to make sense of this phenomenon (Niethammer, 1991; von Plato, 1991). Another aspect was the welcome opportunity to police ordinary East Germans, thereby acquiring a level of moral authority. By playing along the East German intelligentsia increased their level of self-deception, and completely obliterated the fact that it was legitimizing a regime that had abolished elementary civil rights. A third aspect, which is of a more general sociological nature, is rooted in the role of professionals themselves and the crucial importance of knowledge as a means to power and social status.

Career Considerations and Group Pressure

The conviction that the Marxist utopia was potentially liberating was widespread in Eastern European countries (Kupferberg, 1999). In East Germany it seems to have been particularly strong though in all professional milieux. Thus Renate Schönfeld, who eventually became a priest and a convinced Marxist, reveals in her autobiography how the combination of career considerations and accompanying group pressure—the fact that there were so many Marxists in the environment of a young person striving to enter a professional career—led to her conversion. Like most professionals she had to gain work experiences outside her chosen field as a gesture towards the "ruling class" before being allowed to apply for entry to an institution of professional education. The only exception was teaching, where there was a constant dearth of applicants, particularly men. She first encountered this group pressure, which was typical of all professional institutions in the GDR, early in her career when she worked as assistant nurse at the highly prestigious research hospital Charitee.

> Practically all nurses and doctors were members of the SED. I wasn't really raised as an anticommunist, but I had a certain fear of contact, which I was fully relieved of through the common work. They were good and reliable colleagues. (Szepanski, 1995: 89)

It did not take long for these excellent relations in the work sphere to spill over into her social life and she began to socialize intensively with "antifascists who were communists"(Szepanski, 1995: 192).

This group pressure intensified when she moved to Greifswald where she studied for the priesthood. She joined the youth organization, FDJ, and, after two years took the logical step of joining the party. The ideal of the liberating role of the Marxist utopia played an important part in her decision.

> During this time I met students from the "Third World." Their descriptions made concrete what I had understood theoretically. Also my view of the GDR and the social-

ist countries changed. Until then I had enjoyed the advantages of this society such as free study and a scholarship that I did not have to pay back. In spite of my good will, I stood apart from social and political developments. This changed when I recognized that this more just society that at the end of the 60s gave many developing countries hope, also deserved to be supported by Christians. For this reason I took the decision to become politically active in the GDR. This decision decisively changed my life. I no longer looked upon things from the outside. I had made up my mind, against capitalism and for socialism. (Szepanski 1995: 1991)

Another type of group pressure allied to career considerations is illustrated by the case of Hansi. He had graduated from a *Gymnasium* in 1963, but had interrupted his studies as *Gymnasium* teacher. Having gained experience as a building worker, he eventually became a social studies teacher at a vocational school for building workers. Like Renate Schönfeld, Hansi had originally been skeptical about the GDR, mainly because he had pacifist inclinations. For this reason he refused to enter military service, which did not exactly improve his opportunities (it was not uncommon for young men who wanted to increase their professional career chances to volunteer to serve three years as reserve officers as a proof of their patriotic commitment to the socialist state). Hansi had refused this option and instead spent his obligatory time as a *Bausoldat* (a military engineer, trained not to shoot but to build) and behaved rather badly. Having resigned himself to being kept out of a regular professional career for many years, when he reached his thirties he decided that it was time to settle down and finished his academic studies. For this purpose he entered a part-time graduate program which might lead to promotion and more stimulating and better-paid work. During this time he finally decided to become more committed to the Marxist belief system:

Interviewer: "Did you join the Party?"

Hansi: "Yes, in 1975, because I thought that socialism in and of itself was not such a bad idea. But look what they have done with it.....I must say, they deserve to be punished. A useful social model, but no one knew how it should work and to sell something like that to us, what a bad thing."

Interviewer: "Do you think that you could have changed something? Or didn't you see things in these terms?"

Hansi: "No, not that I could have improved anything. They were for it, hence you are also for it." (Interview in Berlin by Angela Schou, 1994)

Again career considerations and strong group pressure stand out as the most potent motive for conversion to the Marxist belief-system. Hansi's conversion came later than that of Renate Schönfeld and it seems to have been more reluctant. He is quick to distance himself from a doctrine he only hesitantly espoused, mainly for career reasons. During his school years he probably pretended to believe in the Marxist utopia because such a belief was necessary in order to gain entrance to a *Gymnasium/EOS* and to be allowed to pursue a professional career. The (East) German educational sociologist Manfred Stock states that

> the attribution of career opportunities by the state was tied to political criteria. *Aufstiegsorientierte* [pupils who wanted to pursue a professional career and therefore needed a higher education] had to declare themselves in agreement with the interpretation of political legitimacy as seen by the state, even more because the channels for social mobility from the seventies onward became even narrower...for pupils who had no career plans, this need to subscribe to the idea of legitimacy ceased to be an issue. A decision not to conform did not affect the careers of pupils who had decided to enter vocational education. (Stock, 1996: 628-9)

Family Background

There were other forms of group pressure. In those families where a parent had experienced a leap in social mobility because of joining the party before or after 1945 children were under strong pressure to conform in order not to jeopardize their parents' careers (Engler, 1992). A case in point is that of Jenny, my wife´s best friend in *Gymnasium/EOS*, who, after my wife had received permission to leave the GDR in 1968 (she had married a Danish communist and the son of a member of the Danish resistance movement) was told not to contact her friend ever again, as this would hurt not only her own career chances, but those of her father.

He had been a laborer before the war but, as a loyal party comrade, was given the chance to study law and ended up as a judge, a position he thought was more important than the friendship of two girls. His daughter evidently agreed, or at least that was what she convinced herself to believe.

A similar case is that of Lisbeth Mühle (born 1928). Her career in the GDR went from "farm worker over several qualification stages to *meister* [foreman] in a large factory. This function gave her responsibility for production but maybe an even greater responsibility for people" (Szepanski, 1995: 139). The result in her case was a strong feeling of gratitude:

> I have always said that I have become what I have become through the Party ... it wasn't only through the Party, my will was also present. It is better to say with the help of the Party. With five children, alone in the capitalist state, I would have given up. I would still be gliding around on the field as a farm worker. (Szepanski, 1995: 135)

Although not an intellectual, she is a member of the large group of unskilled workers for whom the GDR represented a degree of social mobility unheard of in the very rigid German society that had existed up to the Nazi takeover.

The GDR's radical attack on the social structure seemed by many at the time to be more systematic and honest, which made it easier for the state to enroll a small portion of the mobile working class in its ranks (Niethammer, 1991). Nevertheless, as the regime stabilized and the children of the new intelligentsia it had created grew up, the social pressure from parents in this previously highly mobile group made it impossible to uphold the radical policy of broad recruitment. On the contrary, as the economy stagnated the social structure became less and less open (Huinink and Mayer, 1993; Mayer and Solga, 1994) with the paradoxical result that by the time the GDR came to an end the socialist intelligentsia, largely though not exclusively recruited from outside this group, had practically closed itself off from newcomers (Geissler, 1993; 1996).

Inadequate statistical material makes it difficult to calculate the exact figures, but according to Rainer Geissler, the proportion of children from workers' families in higher education in the GDR dropped from 53 percent in 1958 to a maximum of 7 to 10 percent in 1989. The corresponding figures for West Germany show an increase from 5 to 15 percent in the same period. In 1989 the rate of reproduction among the intelligentsia in the GDR amounted to 78 percent. Geissler concludes that "at the end of the GDR the social selection on the way to the universities was even sharper than that in West Germany; the proportion of children from workers´ families was smaller than that in West Germany, the proportion of children from academically educated/professional families was about twice as large" (Geissler, 1996: 265).

Stock comes to a similar conclusion. In the nineteen-sixties the proportion of children of the intelligentsia entering universities and *fachhochshulen* (the equivalent of American Colleges) "increased tremendously: from 27.9 percent in 1960 to 52.7 percent in 1965," whereas the proportion of children from workers' families dropped dramatically, "from 58 percent in 1958 to 30 percent in 1967" (Stock, 1997: 315). The visible trend towards social reproduction, mainly based upon self-selection, intensified in the 1970s and 1980s. "In 1982 the proportion of workers' children declined to between 10 and 15 percent and 69 percent of students in higher education had parents with a university or *fachhochschule* degree. In 1989 approximately seven to ten percent of the students were children of workers and 78 percent had parents with university or *fachhochschule* qualifications" (Stock, 1997: 319).

These figures suggest that members of the intelligentsia had a dual reason for being particularly grateful to the GDR, namely the enormous broadening of career opportunities for the generation that had been young in 1945 and a policy that made it possible for those parents who moved into the intelligentsia effectively to exclude children from the "ruling class" from gaining access to higher education in this so called workers' and peasants' state.

For this it had to pay a high price though. It had to transform itself into a pillar of conformity in a state with obvious totalitarian ambitions. The group pressure to conform was enormous, which explains the hundreds of thousands of "conversions" to Marxism within this particular group. People who had no ambition to become professionals or who thought it was not worth the trouble were not placed under any pressure so the number of conversions within the "ruling class" was much smaller.

The Outsider

One group with no particular reason to be grateful comprised families with members who had belonged to the Nazi party. Although some former Nazis were later integrated into the communist state, many Nazi functionaries, particularly professionals, lost their jobs or had to face the fact that their career chances were not particularly good during the first years of the communist regime. One such person is Ali's father who had held a high-ranking job as tax inspector and had joined the Nazi party. In the spring of 1945, one of many older men called in to do military service in a last desperate attempt to stave off defeat, he had been captured by the Red Army. When he returned from the prison camp, he had to make do with a job as a laborer.

What is interesting is the reaction of his son. Instead of feeling angry and hostile towards the communists, Ali sided with them. In an interview, he reveals that there was a "class struggle" in the family. Ali was generally called "the Red" in his class at the *Gymnasium/EOS* because he had become a candidate member of the party at a very young age (the norm was twenty-five, he was seventeen). Ali was an outsider at school—his classmates did not trust him, because of the intensity of his beliefs. Whereas most students in his class only pretended to believe in the liberating role of Marxism—as a rule people only "converted" when they entered a professional milieu in which the pressure to conform was almost impossible to escape—Ali's political conversion had come earlier and was genuine. While the others more or less mechanically repeated how grateful they were to be living in a socialist state where education was free and you did not have to repay your scholarship, Ali really meant it.

His gratitude derived from the vulnerability of his position and was driven by fear rather than by group pressure. Children of Nazis lived in terror of being disadvantaged or discriminated against because of their family background and felt particularly grateful towards the state when this did not happen. They were under stronger pressure than anyone else to conform to the fundamental concepts of Marxism. For members of this group, acceptance to higher education and a professional career was no doubt felt as a kind of liberation. Unlike most of the new socialist intelligentsia, they did not experience it as liberation from a humble class background but as liberation from the burden of having been born to Nazi parents.

Historical Mission and Social Importance

The impact of German history upon the belief in the liberating effects of Marxism is also revealed in other ways. Klaus Gysi, in his explanation of the significance of the "victors of history" myth, emphasizes two other aspects. There was an acceptance that the communists had the right to rule against the express wishes of the population because their world-view had allowed them correctly to predict historical events (the presumed insight in the "objective laws" of history). The people who had refused to listen to their warnings had to be "educated" because the events that had led to Hitler had clearly proved their ignorance and lack of a fundamental understanding about what was best for them (Henrich, 1998). Who would educate them? Those who were in possession of the scientific understanding of the laws of history, the proven "victors of history"—the party of the working class.

It was inevitable that East German professionals would quickly grasp the message and flock to the "workers' and peasants' party" to become part of the wiser, morally superior élite, who knew what was best for the ordinary people. The paternalism inherent in this philosophy appealed particularly to the writers, actors, directors, professors, teachers, journalists, and so on who could identify with the Marxist language of the GDR because it seemed to endow them with an historical mission and at the same time portrayed their role in society as socially and politically important.

This feeling of historical mission and social importance is reiterated frequently in the personal stories of East German intellectuals. What is interesting is that this attitude is not found only among those intellectuals who were integrated into the party apparatus and thus tended to identify completely with socialism. Those who felt that they had no power at all and were merely fulfilling their function as critical intellectuals justified their attitude in terms of the same moral-pedagogical mission and the importance of their role. Thus Christoph Diekmann (born 1955) who participated in different *Basis-gruppen* states:

> many of my generation who, as artists, teachers, journalists or in another manner wanted to make evaluations, took their status seriously. ... even when we were most bitterly critical of the state we had to assess it in terms of what it could become rather than what it was. In spite of all the perversions there were still openings for socialism, it was not completely closed. (Land and Possekel, 1994: 68-9)

Frank Adler and Rolf Reissig, who were highly critical of the way Marxism was interpreted by the East German leadership, emphasize that although the idea of the historical superiority of socialism "in the light of present events...appears to be an illusion" this illusion played an important role among Marxist social scientists, who believed that "socialism with all its conspicuous faults, defects, irrationalities" nevertheless, "partly because of its reality and effect on world history" but "primarily because of its 'uncultivated' potential for an opportunity for free and equal development for all" was the system that harbored "more hope and greater visions of the future" (Adler and Reissig, 1991: 6). The emphasis on a grand historical mission in itself strengthened the sense of enhanced social importance among social scientists. What could be more challenging than to work towards such a vision?

It is interesting how the Marxist interpretation of history, society and consciousness underpinned the paternalistic task of the "tutelary state" (Jarauch, 1994; 1998) and allowed the cultural and pedagogical intelligentsia to take upon itself this historic task. This element of enhanced social importance that derives from taking upon oneself such a mission is, however, rarely stressed in contemporary sociological literature about this group and its role in the GDR. Thus Muszinski, in his analysis of the role of the teachers, uncritically accepts their representation of themselves as powerless tools of an impersonal system:

> The teachers in the GDR were exponents of the system, if they wanted to remain in their profession. Formal discipline had a high value, yes a value in itself, that corresponded to the authoritarian character of the system; the pedagogical forms of teaching had as their goal processes of control...in relation to parents teachers were persons of authority ...from above GDR-teachers and pedagogues were subjected to the tutelage of strict control from the school and the party. (Muszinski, 1995: 11)

What this one-sided analysis of the role of the teachers in the GDR leaves out is the sense of importance derived from the feeling of having a mission. The fact that this dimension was missing in West Germany made many West German academics and professional groups look to East Germany with great envy. The fact that in the GDR leaders achieved their status at the expense of the civil rights on which the greater freedom and prosperity of western societies is founded appears to have been ignored. The role of the enhanced status of the intelligentsia in the GDR in turn helps to explain why this group has, since reunification, been so reluctant to abandon its belief in the liberating effects of Marxism.

The most frequently reiterated complaint of East German teachers since reunification has been that they feel dissatisfied in their jobs and have a problem finding meaning in what they do (Hoyer, 1996; Hübner and Gerhmann, 1997; Neumann, 1997). This level of dissatisfaction can obviously not be explained by the labor market situation which is exceptionally good for this group, nor by income levels which, as some teachers admit, are much higher than they were, allowing them to live a life of unexpected luxury. Nor can it be explained by mere career concerns. Teachers who have advanced in their careers and been appointed to positions of leadership express the same dissatisfaction with the current situation as those who have experienced difficulties having their qualifications and experience recognized (Koch et al., 1994). Even more confusing is the fact that reduced control from above and access to more modern and exciting pedagogical materials do not appear to have brought increased job satisfaction.

Part of the dissatisfaction can no doubt be explained by the authoritarian, technocratic attitude of East German teachers (Hübner and Gehrmann, 1997). "Discipline and order, set curricula, the fixed contents of textbooks...still have an unbroken charm for many former GDR teachers" (Neumann, 1997: 400). But these attitudes only make sense in terms of an "educational dictatorship" (Grunenberg, 1990) which views teachers as moral guides in a tutelary state in which they must observe and correct people who do not know what is best for them.

Even those who, like Christoph Diekmann (above), might disagree with the political leadership, still find their mission in a society of morally irresponsible citizens very intriguing. This explains why even the cultural intelligentsia felt that the GDR was a better place to live than the Federal Republic. After all, who needs the cultural intelligentsia in a society firmly based upon civil rights where individuals can enjoy their freedom without the need for someone else to symbolize their longings by provoking the powers-that-be and transgressing certain taboos?

In the GDR such freedom was a professional privilege. In the rest of the western world it was a civil right shared by everybody.

Gina Pitsch, a performing artist who recited and sang her own poems and songs, describes the feeling this way: "Because nothing was printed in the newspapers any more and even the truth was something you did not believe in because it was so covered with lies, we artists, particularly those making political art, were somehow expected to ignore all possible taboos and say on the stage what could not be published." Her highly critical production, *Pas de deux allemande*, was performed no fewer than ninety-five times in one year. She performed mainly in the cultural houses that were controlled by the Pioneer Organization and even gave a performance during a youth week arranged by the *Zentralrat* of the FDJ. Although in principle there was strict political censorship, this was not always implemented and the public enjoyed it tremendously: "We had a unique opportunity to attract attention from an educated, politically conscious and critical public. I can only dream about that today. We will never have that again" (Szepanski, 1995:297-298; for similar sentiments see Christa Wolf's autobiographical novel *Was bleibt?*).

Under socialism undivided attention and appreciation was given to performing artists and to established writers such as Stefan Heym and Christa Wolff who were known for their critical views. People like them were believed to have moral authority. To some in western liberal democratic societies where the highest recognition to which a writer or artist can aspire is the status of celebrity or star this appears to be an enviable situation. While some stars are idealized and endowed with mystical qualities others are seen as fundamentally ordinary people (Morin, 1971; 1977). They have no moral authority whatsoever.

For this reason, Western intellectuals are often attracted to socialism and support Marxist states. Once individuals are given the freedom to travel, to vote, to choose their field of study and their career, and more generally to express themselves freely and associate with whom they choose both in private and public life, writers and artists inevitably lose their exalted role - they are no longer looked to for moral guidance.

This pattern can be observed in all post-communist countries. Former moral authorities like Václav Havel in Czechoslovakia, Aleksandr Solzhenitsyn in Russia, Gyorgy Konrad in Hungary, Adam Michnik in Poland, and so on, no longer command the attention and interest they once did. As the societies have matured they have been replaced by stars and celebrities.

The Totalitarian Temptation

Until the collapse of the GDR and the accompanying reunification the belief of East German intellectuals in the liberating effects of the Marxist utopia was shared by large numbers of intellectuals in both Eastern and Western Europe. What made the East German intelligentsia unique is the stubbornness with which it has stuck to its Marxist beliefs in the face of the collapse of communism and the fall of the Wall. This suggests that historical factors have tended to strengthen some of the sociological factors at play. What are these factors? Why has Marxism become the "opium of the intellectuals" (Aron, 1957; Colquhoun, 1986)? Some writers (Löwy, 1979;

Gouldner, 1985) argue that there is a romantic, anti-capitalist streak in modern intellectuals that attracts them to totalitarian utopias. Kolakowski believes that it is the combination of romanticism and rationalism that makes Marxism so attractive (Kolakowski, 1977; 1980; Kolakowski and Hampshire, 1977).

The problem with these and similar explanations is that they focus on the "ideological" aspects of Marxism. Peter Berger however argues that knowledge is always situated in the everyday life contexts of societies and social groups (Berger and Luckmann, 1966; Berger et al., 1973). This suggests that a more phenomenological study of what intellectuals actually do when they engage in intellectual activity might be more profitable. Such a study would look beneath the orthodox Mannheim approach to the sociology of knowledge (Mannheim, 1968; Merton, 1968) that attempts to deduce ideologies from class interests (an approach that in itself does not transcend the Marxist paradigm and is thus inherently vulnerable to its utopian self-deceptions).

Such a phenomenological analysis would look more generally at the East German mind and might shed more light upon the intriguing and largely unanswered question of the fascination with Marxist totalitarian utopianism that characterized the intelligentsia throughout the twentieth century, until the fall of the Wall made that kind of thinking too obviously anachronistic. I am suggesting that it might be profitable to look more closely at the professional activities of these intellectuals.

In *The Captive Mind*, his classic "inside" analysis of the intellectual fascination of Marxism, Czeslaw Milosz introduces the intriguing argument that what makes Marxism so attractive to intellectuals is the combination of a lust for power and relief from social isolation. Because Marxist philosophy functions as a state language (Marxism-Leninism) it unites the worker and the intellectual—they become parts of the same communicative code. The striking characteristic of this code is its emphasis on abstraction and theoretical arguments. In other words, we are dealing with a highly intellectualized system of communication, in which professionals tend to feel naturally at home, whereas workers will feel at a disadvantage. The particular experiences, competencies and preferences of workers are only represented in this language in a distorted and artificial way.

A similar point was made by Bakunin in his criticism of "scientific socialism" as a socialism that prioritized theory and intellect (Bakunin, 1979). He predicts that an attempt to implement a classless society will lead in reality to the opposite—the absolute authority of intellectuals (which he believes to be the worst kind of control because of the abstract nature of intellectual thinking). Foucault in his writings from the nineteen-fifties and onwards, restates Bakunin's thesis of the particularly dangerous marriage of knowledge and power, but without acknowledging the originator and without mentioning the particular context in which it was phrased (Foucault, 1969; 1977; 1979).

For Foucault, the idea of knowledge as power or power as knowledge is mainly used in the context of a critique of the medical and law professions in western societies. He appears to be indifferent to the fact that power discourses have played a much more important and far more disastrous role in communist societies and seems to be content to assume the traditional role of the western intellectual - strongly critical of his own society, with the result that other much more imperfect societies are looked upon with far less critical, even naïve eyes (for a discussion of this paradox, see Paul Hollander's seminal work, *Political Pilgrims*).

What is interesting is that when one analyzes the role of professional groups in communist societies, one finds the opposite—they are highly critical of western societies and almost naïve in their acceptance of their own. How is this paradox to be explained? How can the same sociological group behave so differently in two different kinds of society? Might it have something to do with the nature of the group itself? Obviously medicine and law are not the only professions where knowledge serves the group's drive for power. All professionals use their specialized knowledge to achieve authority and control (Hughes, 1964; 1984). Sociologists of the professions have observed that their special status in society ultimately depends on the trust society invests in their presumed expertise which is elusive, "esoteric" and impossible for outsiders to penetrate (Elzinga, 1990; MacDonald, 1995).

In Marxist societies this level of control seems to be much stronger than it is in pluralistic societies in which professional groups have less power than business people and are also subordinate to a democratically chosen political élite, representing the moral, legal and political views of ordinary citizens (Huszar, 1960).

This lack of power is a constant source of complaint among most professional groups. Marxism represents a totalitarian temptation precisely because it promises to eliminate these rival groups—business people trying to guess what customers would like to buy and political parties trying to guess what voters would like to have on the agenda. Instead of having to guess what the "masses" think and aspire to, professional groups in Marxist societies can monopolize knowledge production and use it to steer society in whatever direction they believe is best.

The role of the expert in a free and democratic society is, as Max Weber pointed out a long time ago, to analyze the consequences of actions, and on the basis of that analysis advise the role players but leave it to them to make the decisions (Freund, 1968; Aron, 1976). In post-war Germany, many intellectuals believed this to be a risky endeavor, after all the Germans had recently proved their inability to make rational choices. The result was that the temptation of paternalism was particularly strong and seems only to have died out with the collapse of the GDR (Hacker, 1994). Suddenly the West German intelligentsia began to realize that the GDR had been an "education dictatorship" and that belief in Marxism simply served to legitimate the moral complicity of the East German intelligentsia with an amoral regime with obvious similarities to Nazi Germany.

For East German intellectuals the fact that the lure of totalitarianism seems to have endured is indicated by their evident preference for the Marxist PDS, the successor party to the ruling SED. Most observers believe that the preference for the PDS among professional groups is either related to their need to protect their own interests (Falkner and Huber, 1994), or is a combination of ingrained habits and bad experiences.

> Having identified strongly with the East German state in the past, they feel bound to its principles. They often experienced material losses during the reunification process, because they lost status and privileges. Because of their high educational level, the majority of them manage relatively well. The size of this segment is about 10-15 percent of the East German population and all signs indicate that they are identical with the core voters of the PDS. (Veen and Zelle, 1996: 13; see also Falkner and Hübner, 1994)

If it was mainly a question of loss of status and bleak prospects one would expect that the younger professionals would abandon the PDS and start voting for the Green Party as is the common pattern in West Germany but there is no sign of such a change. On the contrary, a recent analysis of voting patterns in the reunited city of Berlin (Wüllenwerber and Bauer, 1999) shows that despite the fact that the future for young East German professionals does not look particularly bleak professional groups continue to be the core supporters of the PDS.

In 1999, the average unemployment rate in Berlin was 15.9 percent. Interestingly, the highest unemployment figures were to be found not in East Berlin, but in West Berlin. In traditional working class districts like Kreuzberg, Neukölln and Wedding unemployment rates were respectively 25.2 percent, 22.2 percent and 22.1 percent. In contrast, the highest unemployment rates in East Berlin were in Prenzlauer Berg, Köpenick and Weissensee (17.9 percent, 16.0 percent and 15.8 percent), areas that have traditionally had a high concentration of East German professionals such as artists, civil servants and employees of the Stasi. Whereas the traditional working class districts in the west, with a much higher degree of unemployment, tended to vote for the conservative party, the professional districts in the East with a significantly lower unemployment because of higher educational levels, supported the PDS.

It is not only older East German professionals who demonstrate this preference. In Hellersdorf, the newest district in Berlin and home to the youngest Berliners with the highest level of education, 42.5 percent voted for the PDS. "According to the mayor of the district, Uwe Klett (PDS), 'the future of the city lies here. The policies of the next decades will take place right here.'...most of Klett's supporters are successful here. In East Germany PDS is also the party of those who are better off" (Wüllenwerber and Bauer, 1999: 66).

This preference among younger East German professional groups with the potential for a brilliant future suggests that paternalistic thinking is ingrained in East Germans and that for this group a free market economy and a democratic polity is suspect and to be avoided.

5

Die Wende:
Exit, Voice, and Collapse

Exit and Loyalty

During the 1980s belief in the liberating role of Marxism waned in the GDR. Secret studies done by the Youth Institute in Leipzig indicated a dramatic decline in loyalty to socialism among young workers and pupils in vocational schools, although young people embarking on professional careers proved to be more tenacious (Friedrich, 1990; Gensicke, 1992). Their loyalty only dissipated in the summer and autumn of 1989, mainly in reaction to the collapse of authority. The rapidly declining power of the socialist state which was reflected in the exploding Exit Movement (Hirschman, 1993) caused deep distress among the older, more established members of the East German intelligentsia, who were still strongly committed to the continuing existence of the socialist state and insisted on the importance of staying and supporting it (Joppke, 1993).

Jutta's response is typical of this reaffirmation of loyalty among the East German intelligentsia to the socialist ideal and the antifascist state (Hoerning and Kupferberg, 1999) and their corresponding hostility to the Exit Movement:

I must say, *die Wende** - if you can call it that - I only accepted it hesitantly. That is in the beginning I watched these masses with sadness and dismay, when they left the country ... because I still thought: "There are so many possibilities, that haven't been tried yet, which actually gives us the chance to make something better out of this." (Geulen, 1998: 252)

Tlim, who was studying to become a teacher in Dresden in 1989, confesses that she was

*Turning point

not as brave and defiant as one could have wished ... at the time I could not understand how so many could go to the Czech embassy or over the green border with children and so on. Then I always said to myself, well things are not going that badly for us ... if this massive flight had not occurred and also this brutality with the kids, then perhaps it would not have gone so far. (BISS-Interview)

Another young teacher in Dresden talks of the reaction in her school after the summer vacation when it emerged that some teachers were missing. At a meeting called by the director a unanimous resolution was passed condemning those who had deserted the socialist fatherland in its time of need. At the time the pupils were very restless which affected the atmosphere in the school. Standards of discipline declined sharply and the teacher confesses that she decided to take part in the demonstrations herself, to show her solidarity with the pupils (BISS-Interview). Her behavior seems to have been atypical though. Most teachers instinctively sided with the state.

We had always believed in the ideal and thought, well it isn't beautiful this socialism in the GDR but it still offers better opportunities to achieve our goals and that, according to the logic of history, it should in time become something we believe in. (Geulen, 1998: 215-216)

Ali, who had been in Moscow in the summer of 1989 visiting a friend, had not been informed of what had started as a series of occupations of the West German embassy in Czechoslovakia and had escalated to a free flow of GDR citizens through the recently opened borders into Hungary and Austria. When he returned, his world had changed dramatically:

Ali: "A [Russian] friend had visited me and I traveled back with him in his car. That was in July. And at that time there was no sign in the GDR of what would happen. I came back in the middle of August, turned on the television, and there were already all these stories about Czechoslovakia, Hungary."

Interviewer: With the Exit wave?"

Ali: And it was a shock.

(Aalborg Interview)

Until this Exit Movement in the late summer of 1989, German intellectuals had relinquished none of their belief in the liberating role of Marxism. A teacher, born in the 1950s, talks of his "total identification with the state of the GDR...that reached its peak in 1976 after I had been in school service for a year." According to the same teacher "this identification with the state of the GDR, with the ideology of the GDR, had an unambiguous impact upon me during my studies" (Geulen, 1998: s212). There were moments of doubt among Marxist adherents but they had little effect upon the basic affirmation of the socialist ideal.

> There was a fundamental identification...there were always doubts where one asked oneself: What are the reasons for this or that. There was hardly anyone who didn't have these doubts. But the fundamental identification was there, that is for certain. (Geulen, 1998: 215)

This loyalty to the ideal explains the lack of empathy of this group with those of their co-citizens who demanded access to the elementary civil rights regarded by citizens of the supposedly reactionary and protofascist Federal Republic as natural and inviolable. The intelligentsia lived in a closed sub-world of their own and most of them regarded the Exit Movement with considerable skepticism, sadness or shock believing that if one wanted to improve socialism it was irrational and self-defeating to abandon the GDR, as this only strengthened the reactionary forces that aimed to unmake the objective laws of history.

Voice and Collapse

The Exit Movement represented an imminent threat to the very existence of the GDR because it gradually eroded its authority. For this reason some members of the intelligentsia were not only saddened and dismayed by what had happened, they felt increasingly frustrated because the socialist state was powerless to stop the Movement from getting out of control. Martin, who was "sitting in front of the television when these waves of exit took place," thought "this cannot be possible, when they climbed over the wall in Prague...I thought, hey, they have to do something, I thought that all the time. This cannot be true...no. This was humiliating for the state." Sabine "felt mad at our people, at our government, for not doing anything, yes that nothing happened. We were totally dismayed that nothing happened, that nobody did anything." Like Martin, Sabine felt that the dignity of the state was at stake. "For me this movement was without dignity...yes for me...this was the ultimate lack of dignity" (Geulen, 1998: 252).

Geulen maintains that the intelligentsia was mentally unprepared for the Exit Movement. Their world "literally broke apart" (Geulen,

1995: 249). These feelings of frustration increased as the Movement entered the "Voice" phase, with people taking to the streets demanding far-reaching reforms. Herr Gross, a physical training teacher from Sachsen-Anhalt, talks of his expectations of an imminent crackdown and his surprise when it did not come.

> I thought constantly of what would happen if a military conflict broke out...My wife always said "Well, maybe you will be lucky and you will not be called up to the *Mot-Schützen* [Motorized divisions]." But I was always certain that they would call us up. (BISS-interview)

Much to Hr. Gross's surprise the order never came. When the Exit Movement transformed itself into "Voice" (at the time of the first Monday demonstrations in Leipzig and the founding of the *Neues Forum* which demanded a dialogue with the authorities and a broad extension of civil rights in East Germany) the response of the communist authorities was to reject the demands for public dialogue and civil rights. At the same time they were apparently too internally divided and paralyzed to dare give orders for a military crackdown (Barhmann and Links, 1994; Maier, 1997) on the lines of the feared "Tiananmen solution." This "solution" had been praised during a recent visit to Beijing by Egon Krentz during his recent visit to Bejing in a statement for which the East Germans never forgave him and that undermined any trust in the new leadership that had replaced the old Honecker hardliners.

The change in leadership, which appears to have come about through an internal conspiracy among the top leadership (Schabowski, 1991), did little to restore trust and only had the effect of undermining the authority of the state even further. Egon Krenz spent most of his time visiting factories in the GDR to elicit public assurances about the continuing commitment of the workers to socialism (Bahrmann and Links, 1994) but these turned out to be a mere pretence. The ultimate test came when the new communist leadership deceived themselves into believing that socialism had proved itself to be so superior that they had nothing to fear by allowing the East Germans freedom to visit the capitalist Federal Republic and see for themselves what it was like (Gysi, 1995).

This fatal mistake led to the ultimate collapse of the GDR, a result that was certainly not the aim (Hertle, 1996) of a communist leadership whose mistake was an inability to distinguish between genuine belief in the socialist ideal and the simulated adherence (Lane, 1981) of ordinary East Germans. For Hr. Gross, this outcome signified that the world had gone mad. The military crackdown never came, and suddenly it was all over. The Wall had been breached, East and West Germans were embracing each other out of pure joy and Hr. Gross, sitting in front of his television in Saxen-Anhalt, far away from the decisive events, did not understand a thing.

Instead of reimposing its impressive discipline and authority, the GDR as a state was totally humiliated, leaving Hr. Gross feeling numb and shocked.

> My wife always said "They will call you in. Be prepared, it won't be long before they will call you in." There was nothing about it in the newspapers, though. I wondered about that. Particularly when the situation got more tense. When it started in Berlin with the Wall, where everyone was sitting on the Wall, in Bornholmer Street, where it was opened—I saw my own brother on television, he lives in Berlin—I thought: "Now it has gone too far. Now it will only take hours, then you will be called up and then it will break loose." (BISS-interview)

Hr. Gross believed the humiliation of the socialist state could not go on forever, someone in the state apparatus had to react and restore authority. Though the prospect scared him since he would be one of those who would have to shoot demonstrators in the streets, he did not question whether it would be right to shoot his co-citizens for demanding elementary civil rights (Colletti, 1974; Kundera, 1987). His anger and frustrations had grown so strong that it seems he would have been prepared to kill his own brother if he had been called upon to do so. His dismay at the growing popular movement that threatened his very existence and everything he believed in was so strong that he became increasingly incapable of assessing realistically what was politically possible in the new, radically changed situation. Little did he sense that at the time of the opening of the Wall the communist authorities were acting out of desperation and intellectual confusion, searching in vain for a way to regain the initiative and restore the authority and historical legitimacy that was all but gone (Gysi, 1995; Sabath and General, 1994).

Die Wende

A few days before the final collapse of the GDR, several hundred thousand East Germans gathered at Alexanderplatz to express their belief that *Die Wende* truly represented a turning point in the history of the GDR, in the sense that socialist ideals had been offered a new chance to prove themselves (Jarauch, 1994). Stefan Heym spoke of a "window that had been opened, letting the foul smell of the GDR out," and several leading intellectuals, including Christa Wolf, circulated an appeal *Für unser Land*, arguing against an imminent "sell-out of socialist values." The overwhelming response of the intelligentsia to the idea of a renewal of socialism in the GDR raised hopes that later turned out to be yet another incidence of self-deception (Findes et al., 1994; Wolle, 1998).

Jutta reveals that she felt "euphoric" on 4 November 1989:

> I thought, these people are not stupid. They have a sound instinct, they are intelligent, and with them one can hope for a better socialism. I really meant that up to February - when even Modrow himself said it - that one could democratize socialism, that one could improve it, if one got rid of all the old men and we at last came to power. (Geulen, 1998: 253)

Marina Weyrach, who was working on her doctoral dissertation on the topic of international law and civil rights, also describes this time as period of euphoria followed by deep disappointment. "We thought: Now the new time is coming." She had been appointed to the parliamentary committee investigating possible charges against the deposed leaders (Klemm, 1991) whose old-fashioned patriarchal rule had reached ridiculous levels (Eberle and Wesenberg, 1999). There was a widespread feeling at the time that the failure of socialism was basically a generational problem. If the new generations was allowed to occupy positions of power everything would change (Geulen, 1998). This is why "the time of the investigating committee was the best time for her. 'It was the revolution.' She thought it was being implemented. She visited all the prisons, she went to the psychiatric institutions, she talked with people, investigated, drew up charges. 'Then came the election. ...We were all disappointed at the time'" (Pohl, 1994: 100).

The first free elections, held on 18 March 1990, liberated the East Germans from the need to simulate loyalty to the socialist system. For the first time they were allowed to express their preferences freely and openly (Scheuch, 1991; Glaessner, 1992). It should be emphasized though that the break with pretence had in fact taken place when the Wall was opened. Although this was an emotional rather than a rational event, it did have a rational impact upon East German citizens, who could now compare their private dreams about the capitalist systems with reality. The comparison, says Manfred Stolpe, had a dramatic effect, convincing a large majority of ordinary East Germans that they had been right in rejecting the socialist utopia as unrealistic. By contrast with socialism, capitalism worked, it fulfilled its promises:

> The GDR-Germans profited massively and directly from observing the West. And that had a decisive impact. What one saw and experienced personally—the efficient western system, the widespread prosperity, the supply of consumer goods, as well as the external aspects such as order and cleanliness, the fact things were looked after - with one stroke all this convinced the East Germans: This is what we want to have. We want to take part in this, no more experiments...one saw and experienced a Germany that one would like to have, and the millions who had never had an opportunity to look around found that this country behind the now open border was not strange country to them. It was an existential experience, something different from the abstract one mediated by western media...more then half the population did not have western relatives ...they only knew their GDR world, and that world, having been touched by the other world, now really seemed like a gray prison. (Stolpe, 1992: 184-5)

Recognizing Defeat

Not all members of the intelligentsia saw *die Wende* as a new opportunity for socialism. On the contrary, some appear to have realized early on that the rebellion of the majority in the GDR signified that the effort to impose a socialist system upon an unwilling population had ended and that most people would prefer to have a well-functioning capitalist system rather than to start on a new experiment. The sociologist Hildegaard Nickel, in her account of how she experienced *die Wende*, emphasizes that "I was aware that this state could not be saved under any circumstances...this recognition hit me like a blow in the stomach." Nickel had not signed the appeal by Christa Wolf and other prominent intellectuals to save the GDR and she was convinced that "everything will be different ... it is of a fundamental nature." Nor was she surprised by the result of the elections. "I couldn't argue for it," but she was convinced that a "Third Road" (a combination of Marxism with civil rights) was out of the question. "It was no coincidence that it was the intellectuals who wanted it" (Szepanski, 1995: 101).

Her unusual evaluation of the situation can partly be explained by the fact that she lived very close to the border, and thus could not help observing the behavior of ordinary East Germans in the first days after the Wall was opened.

I saw a stream of people—you cannot imagine what took place here at the border crossing. The children came by bus as far as the corner, and though the school is actually further away, they all climbed out at the bus station before the school and ran across the border passage. Throughout the day, I will never forget it, there was always a parade of demonstrators on this street, and the nearer they came to the border crossing, the more the tempo was speeded up, as if the people feared that when they arrived it would be closed again. (Szepanski, 1995: 101)

The massive popular move to cross the border before the GDR authorities changed their minds should have been obvious to all the intelligentsia, but the hordes of demonstrators did not fit into their Marxist and antifascist belief system so most of them pretended that things had not changed radically and that the masses could be convinced to give the GDR another chance to prove itself. As indicated above, this belief was tied to the conviction that the incompetence of the older generations was to blame for the distortion of the ideals and that there was nothing fundamentally wrong with the ideals themselves.

Many intellectuals were incapable of acknowledging defeat, hoping that some miracle would take place. The elections failed to provide that miracle and the result was a strong feeling of disenchantment, particularly among those who had been most active in working towards a "Third Road" (Jarauch, 1994; Findes et al., 1994; Maier, 1997).

The reason Hildegard Nickel was able to recognize the defeat of the socialist state was clearly related to her understanding of the deeper motives behind the obvious disenchantment of ordinary East Germans with Marxism. This disenchantment was far from new, it dated back to the workers' rebellion in 1953 that would have put an end to the Marxist experiment had it not been for the presence of Russian troops. People like Nickel had been able to deceive themselves about the extent of support among ordinary people because of the closed world in which they moved. In her case, she had even been alienated from her working mother who, like most East Germans dreamt of West Germany. Eventually she was to move there, leaving her daughter behind, to pursue her professional career.

Hildegaard Nickel's career had not been devoid of problems. She had been one of a team of sociologists, led by Arthur Meier who, in the 1980s, had conducted a very revealing study into the way in which young East Germans experienced the school system in the GDR (Meier et al.,1983). The results were not well received by Margot

Honecker who was Minister of Education at the time. She ordered that the study should not be published or the results disseminated. The disappointment with this centrally imposed censorship of research made Nickel change her field of study to gender - a less contentious area in a society that took great pride in its promotion of the role of women, but she soon discovered that the supposed emancipation of women in the GDR was more simulated than real (Nickel, 1990).

Her personal experience drove Hildegaard Nickel to take a more realistic view of events. As she admits, the loss of belief in socialism was a major shock: "The opening of the Wall upset me immensely. ... I literally collapsed. I have heard that the same thing happened to others. I literally could not move." The shock affected her back and temporarily immobilized her. "Someone phoned me and asked: 'Hey, what's the matter with you?' I said I couldn't move ... but blamed the back" (Szepanski, 1995: 100). Only later did she realize that her physical response had been a reaction to the loss of an ideal.

She began to look at her experiences in the GDR in a different way. "Earlier I wasn't aware of what I was missing in the GDR, I repressed ... many things. For instance that I was not allowed to publish, to say anything. I now feel the fact that I can publish my research results as a fantastic liberation" (Szepanski, 1995: 110). She talks now not only about the repression of civil rights as the price for trying to impose an ideal upon a recalcitrant reality, but also about the fact that she had deceived herself. "I had the feeling that I had rationalized and repressed a great deal during the GDR, for instance the fact that I wasn't allowed to visit my mother or that I had to keep the results of my investigations into the sociology of education secret" (Szepanski, 1995: 100).

A somewhat different feeling of liberation is expressed by Ali (see above), whose initial response was shock and who then wanted only for it all to be over as soon as possible. Unlike Herr Gross, who was still deeply committed to the socialist ideal and was prepared to pay the price to keep it alive, Ali's fervent hope was that the "victors of history" would recognize that they had been defeated and give up peacefully.

> Ali: "There was a time when I thought it might develop into a civil war."
> Interviewer: "When was that?"

Ali: "It was about October, November 1989. Maybe even in December. At the beginning of December, I think it was, I felt bad. Most of all one didn't know what would happen next. Therefore I felt very happy when the Party dissolved itself...you know that SED had a conference. Then the Party comrades took their banner, went around the house and returned as PDS...I didn't take part in this change and actually felt relieved."

Interviewer: "Did you leave the SED then?"

Ali: "No, it ceased to exist."

Interviewer: "And have you tried to become a member of the PDS since then?"

Ali: "No, no, I do not have any illusions about the PDS." (Aalborg-Interview)

Instead of being concerned about the humiliation of the Marxist state, expecting and wanting the state to avenge itself upon a rebellious people and reinstate communist authority, Ali was concerned that reactionary forces would attempt to strike back. As the danger of such an event receded, he felt immensely relieved and happy, indicating that for him personally the Marxist project had come to an end. He was not so sure about his former comrades though. Although they had acknowledged defeat they continued to deceive themselves, harboring illusions about having another chance at some time in the future. It would be without him though—his path and theirs had now definitely separated. No more experiments. He no longer believed in the liberating role of the Marxist utopia or at least he could no longer mobilize any enthusiasm for it. He had become estranged from Marxist beliefs, an ex-Marxist or ex-communist, like so many other members of the twentieth-century intelligentsia in Eastern and Western Europe before him (Lessing, 1994; 1997).

6

The Dismantling of the GDR: Saving Careers and Legitimizing Biographies

The Trauma of Reunification

In his self-critical book about the role of the East German intelligentsia in the GDR, *Abschied mit den Lebenslügen: Die Intelligenz und die Macht*, Jens Reich, one of the founders of *Neues Forum*, argues that for a majority of the East German intelligentsia, German reunification was experienced as a trauma:

> A restructuring of the collaborating society is taking place, in which the intelligentsia is no longer able to play its traditional role as a creative, moral, pedagogical and scientific élite. Unexpectedly a whole cocktail of different defects is being attributed to us in a variety of individual mixtures: professional incompetence, social rootlessness, loss of moral credibility, political betrayal, and most of all there are suddenly too many of us. A mass army of frustrated intellectuals has arisen because of unemployment, pressure to retire early, restructuring, closures, delays in appointments and Abwicklung [dismantling] ... that this situation might be the reward for the long complicity with the command system is never taken into account but is denied by the enraged [intelligentsia] with a high degree of emotion. (Reich, 1992: 13-14)

The trauma of *Abwicklung* has been noted by several observers, both foreign academics and West Germans (Meyer, 1993; Markovits, 1993; Schluchter, 1994; 1996; Bürklin, 1996; Wolf, 1996; Maier, 1997; Solga, 1998). Strangely, none of them seems to have noticed the hidden connection between the purely practical goal of saving careers and the highly emotional denial of complicity with a totalitarian system suggested by Reich. It seems clear though, that any objective analysis of what took place after unification has to take as its point of departure the way the East German intelligentsia had constructed its self image in the GDR and the deep crisis of identity that followed upon the unexpected and unwanted collapse of the state (Kupferberg, 1995; Hoerning and Kupferberg, 1999).

They had built their personal careers in the GDR on the assumption that, since they were "victors of history," the state would provide a stable framework that they could always rely upon. Never in their wildest nightmares could they have imagined that the socialist GDR would one day have to capitulate to the capitalist Federal Republic. Hans-Joachim Maaz suggests that, most members of the intelligentsia believed, as he did that "I had organized myself well and lived as if all of it would exist forever" (Moeller and Maaz, 1993: 17). What is interesting about this thinking is that they do not see the problem as the fact that they had accommodated themselves to the demands of the regime but that this accommodation had been disturbed by a development that was neither anticipated nor desired.

It is this that explains their trauma. The fact that they would have to rethink their career plans is not enough to explain the depth of their resistance to reunification. On the contrary, as one starts looking at the way in which different groups within the intelligentsia coped with their career problems after reunification it appears that overall they did remarkably well. A group of researchers at the Max Planck Institute, on the basis of a large, statistically representative study of personal destinies on the labor market, arrived at the somewhat surprising conclusion that the educated group suffered much less from the transitional problems of adaptation to a new system than ordinary East Germans who did not have educational credentials or certificates:

> The greatest stability is manifested by those with occupations within the public sector, and in particular in areas that were "taken over" to a large degree—for instance the school system and kindergartens—or by those that were expanded or rebuilt, for example local administrations. The greatest instability was found among unskilled and skilled labor and persons in leading positions, by which we do not mean "certified" occupations. It is surprising how well economists and engineer-economists could hold [their positions]... although one would have expected a higher loss of qualification in this occupational group." (Mayer et al., 1996: 26)

Another surprising result of these investigations is that women in the professions emerged as the "winners." "If one compares women and men it turns out that the interpretation of women as the 'losers' of reunification is wrong. Women who were professionals, para-professionals and skilled workers held onto their positions better than men, significantly better in para-professional occupations—essentially kindergarten teachers, teachers in elementary and junior high school, and workers in the health field."

Two reasons are given for this: "women because of their strong presence in the public sector [the rules of take-over in the Unity Contract largely protected public employees of the GDR against dismissal when the two public sectors merged] could protect and even improve their positions in comparison with men, who confronted greater risks in industry," and "more men than women were employed in sensitive security or political positions" (Mayer et al., 1996: 26, 29).

If the "trauma" of the East German intelligentsia had only been a question of practical and rational career considerations, schoolteachers would have been quite satisfied with reunification since the overwhelming majority of them were indeed "taken over" by the public sector. Most studies indicate though that dissatisfaction is extremely high in this group. It is in this particular milieu that GDR-nostalgia and pride in the socialist system seem to have their strongest adherents, so the problem of adjustment is primarily a question of coping emotionally. Schneider suggests that this emotional element is at the root of the attempt to retain a belief in Marxist utopianism. "The prospect of a new series of experiments in building socialism apparently does not scare them [the East German intelligentsia] off" (Schneider, 1999: 222).

Scapegoats of the Nation

Although publicly East German intellectuals seem to abide by a tacit agreement to deny emphatically that there might be a connection between career concerns and moral complicity with the totalitarian regime, their private views tell a very different story. According to Jan Hoffmann, one of the main reasons why they were not happy about the prospects of German unification was their concern about possible reprisals for having legitimated a highly unpopular system that survived only through a combination of pretence on the part of the unwilling majority and self-deception on the part of the all too willing intelligentsia.

> Independently of the ... individual degree of distance from the political system of the GDR, the autumn of 1989 was seen as scary, irritating or actually unwanted by the large majority of the pedagogical intelligentsia, and here I mean both scholars and teachers. They had adapted to the framework of the system and had performed the clearly defined

social functions that they could live with and that they thought they could cope with …
and if this … is correct, then when later they became very insecure, they feared losing
their jobs and they feared that they would become the scapegoat of the nation. (BISS-
Interview)

Hoffmann's hypothesis about this widespread fear of reprisals is
confirmed by Jenny, who, at the time of *die Wende* was an employee
of the East Berlin administration, working with financial issues:

Interviewer: "Now a totally different question. How did you experience the day or the days, when the borders were opened.
Did anything in particular happen?"

Jenny: "Yes, insecurity … at that moment you could not predict
at all how things would develop. Because after all you had
worked in the state apparatus. And I mean that an administration is necessary in the future as well, that is evident. But
whether they were going to take over one's colleagues or
not, how it would be in the future, that was something I worried about a lot...one simply said, what will the future bring,
what happens to the profession, to the children? Will they
keep their jobs or will the jobs go down the drain? Those
things were all in the stars. There was a lot of insecurity."
(Aalborg-Interview)

Jenny's feelings were reflected in her emotional detachment from
the behavior of the general population. "When you saw how they all
ran over, to get the *Begrüssingsgeld* [welcome money] and stood
there for hours, I hated that. And when you saw at the underground
stations, as they went through how overcrowded they were, then I
said to myself, you can wait." (Aalborg-Interview). Which she did,
for over a month. She and her husband did not visit West Berlin until
shortly before Christmas that year. The year 1989 did not end on a
happy note for her and her family. They had never asked for or
dreamed of being able to visit the West. On the contrary they had
deceived themselves that they had all they could possibly need in
the GDR. The idea that if one had an important job in the state apparatus one had no need for civil rights is linked to the formulation of
the "victors of history."

As it turned out things were not so bad. Like so many women
employed in public administration, Jenny was "taken over" by the
city administration of Berlin just as the Unification Contract had
promised. Moreover she could use her contacts to arrange jobs for

both her daughters. Only her husband who, although he had no educational qualifications had risen to the position of manager because of his party membership, had to return to the electrician's job for which he was qualified. This particular family fitted perfectly into the general pattern noted by the Max Planck Institute. Other professionals from the class of 1963 interviewed for this study showed mixed patterns of adaptation:

- Christel, a physician and general practitioner, was able to continue with her career. Reunification made it possible for her to open a private clinic enabling her to become self-employed and avoid the possibility of being forced out of her profession by the restructuring of the medical system.
- Ali, who had been a *Gymansium/EOS* teacher, remained a teacher at *Gymnasium* level after unification. But since one of his teaching areas was Russian, he had to reeducate himself as an English teacher in order to be fully employed because of the sudden drop in demand for Russian teachers in East Germany.
- Gisela, who was married to a self-employed signboard manufacturer, had to put in more hours in her husband's business, because competition suddenly became much tougher and the future of the firm was less secure.
- Hansi, who had almost reached the top of his profession as a vocational training teacher, had to start all over again because the western system of vocational training was different from that in East Germany. After a series of short-term assignments he finally found a stable job as teacher in a prison for delinquents.
- Dieter, who had been educated as construction engineer and worked for a firm producing industrial paint, became involved in different projects, mainly related to the environmental clean-up of heavily polluted industrial areas.
- Dietmar was educated as a research librarian and had worked within a very narrow field - copying and translating articles from Eastern Europe on the construction of factory buildings within the Comecon (a trade organization for communist countries) system. At the time of the interview he was still looking for a job in which he could use his skills.
- Gudrun had been working in the local administration as a *Fachberater* (professional consultant) for about thirty *Kinderkrippen* (crèches) in Köpenich outside Berlin, and was "taken over" by the new city council and placed in the municipal department for youth and family.
- Rüdiger had worked as an accountant at a racetrack outside Berlin, a job he lost after reunification. After a period of unemployment and trade union activity, he accepted a job as chauffeur for a drug company, with hopes of advancement in the future.

- Gerhard, who had been evicted from the GDR in early 1988 together with his wife and children, had lived in West Berlin ever since and had had no difficulty finding a job as a computer engineer.
- Wolfgang, who had escaped from the GDR in the late nineteensixties and settled down in West Germany, had become a highly successful financial manager, changing jobs at will to enhance his career.

On the whole, adaptation to the Western system did not seem to present an overwhelming problem for most of these professionals. Emigration to the West before the collapse of the GDR seemed to be a great advantage and increased the chances of career advancement in the new system. Some professionals suffered severe setbacks in their careers, others adapted very quickly. Those who were "taken over" by the West German system, public administrators and teachers, experienced the least disruption. The results of the Max Planck research suggest that educational certificates functioned as a safety net for most of them.

What is most interesting though is that career difficulties and new opportunities were strongly related to a combination of public regulation and market forces. There was no question of punishing East German intellectuals merely because they had been conformist pillars of a totalitarian system (with the possible exception of Jenny's husband, the manager who had achieved his position mainly because of his party connections). Fears of "moral cleansing" of the hundreds of thousands of professionals who had been party members or had otherwise identified themselves publicly with the totalitarian regime turned out to be unfounded. Far from becoming "scapegoats," the East German intelligentsia emerged as the clear "winners" of reunification, in comparison with less fortunate compatriots who had no educational credentials to fall back upon.

The Return to Scientific Universalism and Open Recruitment

There was certainly a moral element involved in the restructuring of the academic and scientific landscape. This restructuring is often presented as mere "modernization" of East German higher education and research and an attempt to raise it to the level of that in West German universities and research institutions. However, it also involved a decision to return to the universal principle of employment on merit rather than to retain the practice which appears to have been the guiding principle in the GDR of giving the children of the intelligentsia the best opportunities. The decision to open the reduced number of positions to free competition came as a major shock to East German scholars:

> Although there were numbers of admission to higher education and a rigorous planning regime in the GDR, the authorities were powerless to stop the continuous growth of the "intelligentsia." The social pressure to go into occupations with high prestige and relatively easy working conditions was strong. The authorities never succeeded in diminishing bureaucracy and over employment—the apparatus was always more tenacious. Then came the new bill. There were too many institutions and within them too many employees, too few of them qualified. (Reich, 1992: 18)

Although academic positions were not particularly highly paid—skilled workers could often earn more, particularly by supplementing their incomes by offering services on the black market—parents were anxious to secure entrance to higher education for their children and for them to achieve academic positions which had a high status in German society. The East German educational sociologist, Manfred Stock, explains this preference for academic positions as a particular lifestyle preference among intellectuals which was related to the emphasis they placed on good books, classical musical, art museums, serious drama, political cabarets, and so on, rather than on status symbols such as expensive furniture, fashionable clothes and smart cars. He describes this choice as a "social distinction strategy."

The careers of professionals were tied to

> corresponding cultural standards in the homes of their parents. Access to such objects as books and musical instruments differed according to the educational qualifications of the parents. There were similar distinctions in the way in which families communicated and in their styles of upbringing and the corresponding linguistic competencies of the children. The composition of peer groups ... was very homogenous in relation to social background. (Stock, 1997: 329)

The main problem for the East German intelligentsia was that their status was not discernible. Members of the West German intelligentsia, as they advanced in their careers, were able to combine culture and an enhanced material lifestyle which reflected their exalted status. By contrast, East German intellectuals who wanted to become members of the intelligentsia had to live the lives of eternal students, living in cramped apartments and working hard, without any visible incentives, to improve themselves.

The result was that they were not particularly admired by their neighbors who could not understand what they got out of life:

> When an employee with an academic diploma drove his daughter to the music school in a Trabi [the cheapest and most common car in East Germany] the neighbors in the newly built apartment block could hardly regard this as an elevated lifestyle, especially if the factory worker could afford a better car as well as access to spare parts that the former could only dream of. The Trabi could not be represented as a sign of understatement, because it was always assumed that buying one was not the expression of free choice. In this way the norm of limited individualism was reflected in the construction of the "lifestyle" of the intelligentsia. (Stock, 1997: 330)

This understated lifestyle probably explains the dramatic change that took place in the recruitment to the intelligentsia. Increasingly, as the incomes of skilled workers surpassed those of intellectuals, professional careers lost their attraction for working class families and their children. Stock believes that this explains why there was an "increasing correlation" between "social background, school achievements and accompanying educational careers" (Stock, 1997: 329).

Given the dominance of children with this background in the institutions of higher education in the GDR, the pressure upon the authorities to allow children a) enter higher education; b) to pass the exams and c) to get a job appropriate to the educational investment of the child (and his or her parents) must have been enormous. Parents who were members of the intelligentsia afforded their children a strong sense of security and a guarantee that the child would be able to continue the family tradition (Hoerning, 1994).

The loss of this feeling of protection and security explains why German reunification was traumatic for those intellectuals whose careers had relied mainly upon such family connections. Having always been able to circumvent merit as a selection mechanism, they were suddenly and brutally reminded of it and it came as a shock which

> can be explained by the fact that many believed that the transition would be a new start with time to adapt. There would be a respite during which they would be spared, particularly as there were no immediate competitors...open competition for positions on the federal and international market meant that chances even for well qualified and politically neutral scientists and engineers from the former GDR were reduced to zero. Individually those who were affected argue that it was not their fault, they did not deserve it and they feel discriminated against, cheated, colonized. Many persist in stiff-necked pride, others react with deep depression, others still with opportunistic adaptation. (Reich, 1992: 14)

Loss of Protection

The importance of the protection of a powerful family member and its function in replacing criteria of merit is illustrated by the careers of Gerhard and Rüdiger (for a third interesting case involving a former dissident who rose rapidly up the career ladder as a party functionary because of the protection of his father, see von Wensierski, 1994: 124-138). Both of them attended the very prestigious *Grauen Kloster Gymnasium* in East Berlin, to which the East German artistic and political élites preferred to send their sons and daughters. Gerhard's father was a professor of theology at Humboldt University, Rüdiger's mother was a well known linguist. Though Gerhard was a dissident—he sang forbidden songs in school and was a believing Christian—this did not prevent him from enjoying a successful career in the GDR. He became a computer engineer and would have remained in the GDR had he not been arrested as one of a group of dissidents who disturbed the official Rosa Luxemburg demonstration (held on the anniversary of her murder by Freikorps troops) by quoting one of her most provocative remarks - that freedom is always the freedom to think differently.

Rüdiger was no dissident. On the contrary he was a committed Marxist, but not of the right sort, as it turned out. Like Gerhard, his most important asset was a parent with good connections (in his case a mother who was a writer) who kept a close eye upon her erratic son. After Rüdiger had graduated in 1963, he worked for two years as an assistant nurse at the famous research hospital, Charitee, in Berlin. Since entrance to medical school was highly competitive, he could not use his connections for that purpose. Instead he became an agro-technician, specializing in animal production. His first job after graduation was at the central trade union of potato workers, because, as the cadre leader said, "he knew something about agriculture." Everything went well, until Rüdiger criticized the efficiency of Soviet agriculture which, according to the functionary in charge of personnel issues, caused so much anger that Rüdiger had to leave. As compensation he was offered a job as manager of an agricultural cooperative outside Rostock on the Baltic Sea. Feeling sure that he could find something better he declined the offer.

After he had spent a year in intermittent employment in small jobs, his mother intervened and got him a job as an accountant at the central racetrack at Hoppegarten outside Berlin. Here he remained until reunification, when he lost the job. After another year of drifting he finally accepted an offer to work as a chauffeur for a drug company in the hope of getting promoted to an office job in the future. Given the feeling of professional security he had experienced in the GDR and the trauma of suddenly finding himself after reunification without a safety net—this time his mother was helpless—it is understandable that he idealized the GDR:

> What advantage did I get out of *die Wende*? Many of my friends of my age or a little older have become unemployed...no young person in the GDR had any kind of problem with his education, more advanced study, work, academic study, and so on. There were no problems. Of course some could say that because of their political opinion they couldn't do this or that. Well, of course it was somewhat regimented. But in principle anyone could get a vocational education. And it was also possible by different means to get access to advanced studies. And all of this was free. (Aalborg-Interview)

A Carefree Existence

Although only in exceptional cases did the East German intelligentsia pay for their complicity with a totalitarian regime with their careers, they nevertheless had to face the morality of this complicity and to cope with it in one way or another. They had somehow to legitimize their personal histories. This "biographical work" (Fischer-Rosenthal, 1995) has rarely been put into perspective by German social researchers, who have focused almost exclusively upon the career concerns of the group. Nevertheless it is strongly present in the stories of East German intellectuals who feel they have to defend what they once stood for. One of the most popular rationalizations has been to represent the GDR as a state that protected its citizens, making life as secure and carefree as possible, something that the West German state is constitutionally unable to do.

The fact that this carefree existence was not the result of mere generosity but had its price, namely participation in public rituals of simulation or self-deception, is frequently conveniently omitted. A case in point is that of the artist Barbara Thälmann:

> I am an unmarried woman with two children, who has a profession, who lived in a system that never forced me to make a choice... I never in my life faced a decision...I could always, even when I hadn't earned money for three months—sometimes I didn't receive any income for six months, for instance when one of my programs was banned—pay for the kindergarten, always pay my rent, and I could always give my children clothes and food, and when they were seen as specially talented by the school they were supported by the state. (Szepanski, 1995: 72)

Barbara Thälmann is happy to remember how the family policy
of the GDR helped support her artistic career, but forgets to mention
that as an artist she had to be careful not to annoy her government,
or she would soon be deprived of her right to work as an artist or, as
in the well-known case of Bärbel Bohley, would be forced to take
her artistic interests with her to another country. For other East German intellectuals, defending their way of life means to repeat the
mantra that the GDR was one of the most progressive societies in
history. This is the way Gisela Oechselhauser, who after reunification was appointed director of Distel, the famous political cabaret in
East Berlin, remembers the GDR:

> This system...that out of the best of intentions took too much care of the people and held
> it captive also had the advantage that there were some things you didn't have to decide.
> One certainly had the same status as a patient at a hospital, that was not so good, but one
> didn't have to make decisions about certain things. I mean that both in a positive and
> negative sense. For instance one never had to make decisions about the right to an
> apartment, work, pension. I see that as immense human progress. (Gaus, 1999: 106)

Oechselhauser's view of this "immense human progress" presup-
poses a rather narrow definition of humanity, excluding as it does
the large majority of the East Germans who felt less liberated than
imprisoned by that existence. It excludes the overwhelming majority who did not identify with its Marxist ideals and who dreamed of
a different, freer, more prosperous life. Ordinary workers of course
also complain about the loss of a carefree existence, but the crucial
difference is unlike the intellectuals they pretended to believe in the
Marxist utopia but they were not deceived by it.

It appears that intellectuals did not value personal freedom and
consumer choice as much as non-intellectuals, that they rationalized
the absence of freedom and prosperity as the price that had to be
paid for becoming a part of the intellectual class. Their Marxist radicalism was rooted in their position as eternal students who never
harvested the full intellectual and material rewards of investing in a
professional career, but had to be satisfied with restricted freedom
and cultural consumption.

This is also the reason why free provision of culture and education plays such an important role in their personal stories when they
compare the GDR with the Federal Republic. The freedom and prosperity of the latter is constructed as vulgar or beneath them, because
it is associated with a lack of appreciation for the choices they made

when they drove their children to music school in their Trabies. Thus Frau Posselt, a teacher, in talking about herself emphasizes the continuity of her previous lifestyle and values:

> We already had the apartment before die Wende. The only thing that is new now is...a washing machine and that I can buy [musical] instruments that were unavailable before. That has changed for me, and books, and professional journals. Well, but lastly also on the personal level, it has become somewhat materially oriented. I don't like that at all, and therefore many things have fallen apart here. Yes, it is only a question of material things. My opinion is that as a teacher I earn more than enough. No one in this world should earn more money, because it is enough for a life and for a beautiful life. And also, because the world has suddenly become too materialistically oriented, and that only creates frustration and does not create relations that are positive at all. (BISS-Interview)

Frau Posselt still looks at the world through the narrow vision of a student who was never allowed to grow up and get used to the idea that professionals do not have to make a choice between education and wealth; that this choice was imposed upon them by an restrictive and badly functioning Marxist society. Her remarks also suggest that the East German intelligentsia need time to adjust to the new reality and, as this adjustment takes place, some of them will no doubt change their ideas about social distinction, bringing them closer to intellectuals in West Germany, a development that is probably already taking place. This does not, however, make any difference to the emotional shock that has less to do with considerations of career and social distinction than with how individuals legitimate their ways of life.

Abandoning Utopia

In order to understand the emotional depths of the identity crises of the East German intelligentsia, it is not enough only to look at their concerns about their careers. Once must also look more closely at the type of ideology that made it possible for them to deceive themselves into believing that they were doing the morally decent thing rather than actively supporting an unpopular regime. This rationalization was made possible by the belief in the liberating effect of Marxism. Most of what we know today about the GDR and how it functioned confirms that it was a highly repressive society, a dictatorship with strong paternalistic and totalitarian traits (Bender, 1992; Kaelbe and Kocka, 1994; Bessel and Jessen, 1996; Fulbrook, 1997; Jarauch, 1998). In reality the effect of Marxism was the opposite of what the Marxist ideology proclaimed—it crushed the dreams and hopes of ordinary people.

This is another reason why those who lived privileged lives in the GDR (and still live privileged lives after reunification) feel such a strong need to justify themselves. Members of the intelligentsia are indeed privileged in the sense that their talents may be noticed and their work talked about. These rewards are hinted at by George Orwell, who admitted that his main motive for becoming a writer was a "desire to seem clever, to be talked about, to be remembered after death, to get your own back on grownups who snubbed you in childhood...it is a humbug to pretend that this is not a motive, and a strong one. Writers share this characteristic with scientists, artists, politicians, lawyers, soldiers, successful businessmen—in short the whole top crust of humanity." As he frankly acknowledges, this deeply selfish motive distinguishes intellectuals and other privileged groups from the rest of humanity. "The great mass of human beings is not acutely selfish. After the age of thirty they abandon individual ambition...and live chiefly for others, or are simply smothered under drudgery. But there is always the minority of gifted, willful people who are determined to live their own lives to the end, and writers belong in this class" (Orwell, 1968: 3).

Such selfishness can be earned through talent and hard work. The privilege of living a life that matters, that makes a visible impact, if only upon one's students, patients or clients, does not necessarily present a moral problem. It only becomes a problem if the person knows that it is not simply a question of talent and hard work but of prostituting him or herself in one way or another. For this reason the collapse of the GDR represented not only a career problem but also a moral problem for many intellectuals and privileged persons. One of them was Katarina Witt, the world-renowned ice skater. Her career as an international skater, which began in 1988, a year before the collapse of the GDR, was hardly touched at all by the change and she suffered no setback in her career.

> I was a child of the GDR, and experienced it as a very happy childhood. I was lucky enough to be able to perform in a sport and be supported. The sports system which existed there supported my talent. I also had the state to thank for the level that I had achieved at the time. For this reason I cannot say that it is all old cheese, let us get something new quickly, something different and better. I went through the school system of the GDR, I learned a lot and thought: This is simply the better system. And I hoped: Maybe it can work, that two different states can exist side by side. (Gaus, 1999: 18)

What Katarina Witt is expressing is a strong feeling of guilt for supporting a system that was rejected by an overwhelming majority of the people. It was precisely because of this gap between reality and the utopian ideals of the state that the system could not survive in the end. The most fervent wish of ordinary East Germans was to replace the Soviet system with something resembling the system in the West. The conviction that the GDR indeed represented something better and something that would outlast the capitalist system was so outrageously wrong that it could only take root and survive within the relatively privileged and tightly sealed worlds of the professionals. Although the "ruling class" participated publicly in the charade of the GDR as a "workers' and peasants' state," in private their minds and dreams were elsewhere. The concept of socialism as historically superior and morally better never really took hold among ordinary citizens who had too much commonsense to believe in such a myth.

The GDR was a totalitarian state trying to impose an ideology upon a people, an attempt that led to the systematic elimination of elementary civil rights and the crushing of the civil society that had reemerged after the defeat of Nazi Germany (Staritz, 1995; Herf, 1997). Whatever the members of the intelligentsia might have thought about the desirability of living in a state devoid of elementary civil rights, they managed to persuade themselves that it was morally right to support the system because it defined itself as a "workers' and peasants' state." Since it represented a much higher justice, moral decency, honesty, and respect for individual opinions and choices could be sacrificed.

The Failed Experiment

While some East German intellectuals described the collapse of the GDR as a "failed experiment" (Reissig and Glaessner, 1991), a leading Marxist, sociologist Arthur Meier, argued that they should stop deceiving themselves.

What is falling apart in front of our eyes is not just a particular form of socialist statehood, which has recently been made light of by interpreting events as the end of Stalinism or bureaucratic-administrative rule, it is the collapse of real socialism itself, determined by inner causes...those who believed that until now there has been no socialism, only a perversion of it created by its leaders, are mistaken once again...it would be a naïve self-deception...to pretend that real socialism had never existed...real socialism does not experience a transitional crisis from which a "third road" can emerge, but a revolution that follows upon many years of continuous stagnation that seals its ruin. (Meier, 1990: 3)

In spite of these attempts at radical rethinking and intellectual renewal it seems as though the practice of blaming the system not the ideal for what happened to the GDR is still rife. Gisela Oechselhauser represents a widely held view when she argues that:

This state, the GDR, and the ideal of socialism do not have much to do with each other. I soon found that out. The ideals are attractive to me though ... the ideal that one can do something good for people, let them live for instance, so that if I have food, others may not starve to death. (Gaus, 1999: 100)

Nevertheless this was exactly what happened both in Stalin's Russia and Mao's China where people were deliberately allowed to starve to death because they were seen as an obstacle to the implementation of the ideal. And as to merely letting people live, one wonders how Oechselhauser brings this conviction in line with the deliberate shooting of refugees caught trying to cross the border to West Germany illegally.

There is no contradiction between ideals and reality in Marxist states, the problem is the self-deceptive belief in the liberating effects of the system, which forces people like Oechselhauser to pretend that bad things never happened and could not happen. Other members of the East German intelligentsia are less sure and more open to these difficult existential questions. Ellen Brombacher, who was born and brought up in West Germany until her father, a committed communist, brought her with him to live in the GDR, seems to have brought with her an element of self-criticism which is missing from Oechselhauser's story.

Naturally it is an enormous problem for me that what we tried and what I was part of, has collapsed. The whole socialist attempt ... has collapsed. When I try to make up the account, I think ... we have to find answers to questions like: Why did it happen? What did we do wrong? What were the problems within the system? Could it work at all? How have I acted, what were your faults? (Gaus, 1999:127)

Although Ellen Brombacher does not, like many others, try to blame previous generations, there are some inherent limits in her way of approaching the problem. What she wants to know is whether and in which way the experiment might have been successful. She deplores the "failed experiment" but would rather it had succeeded, which means she would be prepared to try again if given another chance. She does not seem to acknowledge that the basic lesson of the communist experience is that it will always end badly. The problem is not that the system has collapsed but that the attempt to implement it was inhumane. The solution is not how to make the system succeed but to abandon it all together. But, as Peter Schneider points out, East German intellectuals are more concerned with justifying their own actions than about saving humanity:

> A lot of intellectual people wagered their sanity and their lives on a utopia, of which the most important characteristic compared to other utopias was an economic thesis. Only through the subjection of private property to the means of production can one reach a just society, they believed. Now they do not want to understand why their utopia failed. They understand nothing about economy, have never interested themselves in these things, and are proud of it. They have made a finding about the cause of death although they have only investigated the corpse from a distance. The experiment itself did not fail, it was sabotaged by hostile forces and driven to failure. Let us not have any illusions. These self-righteous individuals are not concerned about the good of humanity, but with justifying their lives. They would rather lead humanity into a new experiment with catastrophic results than admit that they made a mistake. (Schneider, 1999:222-23)

The emotional logic behind this continuing utopianism is that in postponing the implementation of the socialist state to the distant future one does not have to account for its consequences in the present and the past. This has the intended effect of protecting the East German intelligentsia against charges of moral complicity with an experiment that has probably cost more human lives and suffering in the twentieth century than its rival, racist utopia of the right (Lessing, 1997).

Schneider contends that the problem of moral responsibility is a shared one. "There will be no dearth of voluntary participants from the West. They have only seen the blessings of socialism through a train window, like images of a passing landscape" (Schneider, 1999: 222). What he is suggesting is that Western Marxists have sometimes been even more radical in their utopianism than Eastern Europeans.

It was the former who, in the nineteen-sixties and seventies regarded China and Cambodia as the *avant garde* of Marxism, far surpassing Eastern Europe in its attempts to liberate the people from their allegiance to the last vestiges of a bourgeois civilization. The Chinese "cultural revolutionary" and the Pol Pot's Khmers Rouges were the more authentic Marxists and for this reason they evoked the unbridled enthusiasm of the Western European left-leaning intelligentsia for a short time, until the horrific consequences of their unbridled fanaticism were revealed and accepted, shocking many leading Western intellectuals into a deep, self-critical rethinking. These insights, which were at the heart of some serious rethinking among the Marxist intelligentsia in France (see in particular the works of the "new philosophers" such as Glucksmann, 1977, 1979 and Levy, 1975), have only rarely emerged in the German debate from which some of the most serious questions have been omitted, a further indication of the strong influence of the country's history upon current thinking about the past.

7

The "Elbow Society":
East German Group Mentality and Cultural Alienation

The Problem of Group Membership

Both sociologists and social psychologists agree about the importance of the social influence of groups upon individuals. But whereas the latter tend to emphasize the potentially repressive and irrational impact of group membership, the former believe that it can in fact be empowering and enlightening. Individuals cannot avoid being members of a group—human life has a strong social component—the question is how the quality of that membership impacts upon personality and identity. Both disciplines indeed have a point.

A series of classic experiments on the effects of group membership upon individual thinking and actions (Wetherell, 1996; Bauman, 1993) has shown that individuals who are placed in situations where there is a great deal of group pressure to conform tend to abandon their intellectual and moral independence in order not to draw attention to themselves. These results are confirmed by daily experience. When group pressure is heavy (for instance in a boarding school, a military training camp, or a political or religious sect) the main preoccupation of the individual is to escape being ridiculed, deprived of the company of his or her fellows, or attracting the wrath of the group by insisting that he or she is right and the group wrong.

Other experiments, which have been verified in the literature on ethnic prejudice and nationalism (Baird and Rosenbaum, 1992; Ignatieff, 1995), indicate that stable group membership or a feeling of "belonging" are an important source of self respect independent of the individual's personal contribution to the group. Such collective pride and shame varies with the fortunes of the group, and in order to increase collective pride and decrease collective shame individuals tend to develop stereotypes both about the group's adversaries and about its members (Tajfel, 1978; 1982; Tajfel and Turner, 1979).

Given the strong influence of group membership upon individual thinking one may legitimately ask how individualism in the sense of non-conformist, anti-authoritarian, self-critical and tolerant thinking is possible at all. Where does it come from? The way sociology approaches this problem is by reformulating it as a question of social change or the transition to modernity. According to Simmel, modern culture in the sense of city life (Simmel, 1968) and the spread of the market economy (Simmel, 1978) has the important but often neglected effect of strengthening personal identity and weakening the role of the group. It also brings with it a host of negative cultural aspects, but this does not diminish its major advantage—the release of the individual from the pressure to conform.

In an article *"Bemerkungen zu sozialetischen Problemen,"* written in 1888, Simmel suggests that individuality as we know it is directly affected by the range of our associations (Levine, 1991). The broader and more diverse our social contacts, the more we become individuals in our own right (Simmel, 1890). This idea is further developed in Simmel's book *Soziologie* (1908) in which he analyzes the process of individualization as an effect of (a) a changes or regulations through which individuals become legally responsible for their own acts; (b) a change in the nature of intellectual activity, allowing individuals to have their own opinions; and (c) a change in patterns of socializing towards voluntary associations based upon common interests.

Simmel attributes the sociological roots of the individualization process mainly to the third factor. In his study on the effects of the market economy he argues that the expansion of trade has an important cultural effect as individuals enter commercial relationships with strangers, outside their own group. From that point individuals are no longer merely members of the group in which they have been socialized and whose culture they have acquired, they have become members of several more or less distinct groups or intersecting "circles" with different, competing cultures (Coser, 1969). This expansion of the number of groups and cultures with which individuals are in touch has the important psychological effect of making them less dependent, practically and emotionally, upon one particular group or culture (Levine, 1991). The quantitative expansion of group membership influences its quality. The less power the group or culture has over the individual the more freely he or she thinks and acts. This, according to Simmel, is the secret of the individuality so characteristic of modernity. The first step towards individual liberation is to break the monopoly of any given group or culture over the individual mind. Only when the individual is invited to participate in competing groups or cultures can he or she truly be free.

Simmel's insight has an important, but rarely noted consequence for the modern concept of citizenship, based upon equal rights before the law. As Hannah Arendt suggests in *The Origins of Totalitarianism*, the Nazi phenomenon, and totalitarianism in general, can be understood as an onslaught on the French Enlightenment belief in the rationality of modern man. This anti-paternalistic thinking paved the way for a social order in which every citizen was in principle seen as equal before the law, being endowed with the same civic rights as his or her neighbor. A person's position on the social scale, whether he or she was a peasant or a monarch, did not allow the one a liberty denied to the other. Liberty was the privilege of individuals, not social groups. For this reason the Nazi phenomenon could easily be recognized as a massive onslaught on the principle of equal rights before the law.

What is interesting in the German case is that this attack on equal rights, although instigated by the Nazis, was implemented by a state bureaucracy with a strong legal base. In his essay "Prussian Conservatism," Talcott Parsons describes the dominant culture of German society as permeating its bureaucracy as well as "combining a belief in patriarchal authoritarianism with an emphasis on legalistic formalism. The need for order and strong rule is important, and there are considerable Lutheran undercurrents" (Tudor, 1974: 164-5). Or, in Parsons's words:

> This world is dominated by sin, mitigated only by the restraining influence of ordained authority. Society is not and can never be a Kingdom of God on Earth, but it is fundamentally a vale of tears. In its application to the role of authority, this pattern favors a certain realism, for instance with respect to the advisability of adequate military protection of one's territory but its benevolent patriarchism readily slips over into a kind of harsh authoritarianism and even into cynical pursuit of power in defiance of the masses of the people. Government is to it a grim business. (Parsons, 1964: s109-110)

It is not difficult to understand that the Nazis, with their imperial-ist goals and open anti-Semitism (the two were frequently seen as interdependent—in order to become an effectively imperialist na-tion the Germans had to get rid of the Jews in their midst) found a fertile ground for their propaganda. They came to power on the prom-ise of restoring the lost order longed for in particular by the middle classes (Lipset, 1983; Rutkoff and Scott, 1986). Kracauer, in his study of German films during the Weimar period, concludes that these films predate Hitler in the sense that they symbolically cope with all the major themes that legitimated him—the danger of unbridled lib-erty, the knowledge that one cannot escape fate, and most of all, the need to succumb to a harsh authority, as the only alternative to chaos (Kracauer, 1971; Huaco, 1965). "German films explored the...theme of the individual faced with the alternative of tyranny or chaos" (Hall, 1999: 256).

Having accepted the need to succumb to a harsh authority, the Germans, and in particular the legal bureaucracy, went even further. Since government was under all circumstances a grim business and the only alternative was a resumption of the chaos (humiliating de-feat, followed by left- and right-wing attempts to assume power, fol-lowed by hyperinflation that wiped out all the hard-earned savings of the middle classes, followed by a deceptive tranquility, followed by the financial crises of the late 1920s, dramatically increased un-employment, and ugly street-fighting), there was little purpose in fighting destiny, that is the will of the Führer. Some legal technicali-ties had to be taken care of, but as we know these presented no insurmountable obstacle. The German civil servants did their job and the result was that some citizens, defined as unworthy, were systematically deprived of all legal protection until it seemed only logical that they had to die naked, shot in the back or gassed like cattle.

The question of the role of group pressure in the process leading to the extermination of the Jews (and other vulnerable minorities such as the Sinti and the Roma) has been discussed intensively in the literature on the "Final Solution." There are two basic positions, that of Browning (1992), who argues that group pressure was deci-sive in convincing ordinary Germans to participate in the crimes against humanity, and that of Goldhagen (1996), who argues that it was not (for an overview of the German debate related to Goldhagen's book, see Schoeps, 1996). Individuals had a choice, and the only reason they did not disobey was that they had become fanatical Nazis, ready to kill for their beliefs.

I tend to side with Browning on this issue, only adding that group pressure was not confined to those situations in which Jews were killed, it existed in all of Nazi society, independent of the particular activity. In a sense the whole society was defined by it. That the people selected for elimination or gassing happened to be Jews (or Roma and Sinti, or the mentally ill, as in the aborted euthanasia campaign in which poison gas intended for insects was first systematically used against humans) was an historical coincidence. I believe it to be a gross mistake to try to find a metaphysical answer to the question, "Why the Jews?" The point is that any outsiders defined as not belonging to the "in-group" might have been selected for extermination as well.

What needs to be explained is not the particular choice of victim, which was probably a result of Hitler's personal idiosyncrasies (Flood, 1989) and his political schooling in a pre-First World War Vienna that was much more aggressively anti-Semitic than Germany at the time (Pulzer, 1988). If the strength of anti-Semitic feelings is the main criterion, Poland would be an even more likely candidate, as anti-Semitism there was backed up by a strong religious tradition. The question one should be asking is why most Germans, although they did not share Hitler's fanatical hatred of the Jews, went along with the policy of open discrimination that led to extermination.

Here group pressure played a decisive role. The Germans, for some historical reason, were far more sensitive to such group pressure than, for instance, the Poles or Austrians, who have traditionally had a much more individualistic culture. The explosive mixture of unbridled, almost anarchic anti-Semitism and the German tendency to surrender to group pressure explains the Holocaust. The decisive point in the German case was a fear of liberty, a strong tradition of obedience, and a tendency to surrender to an imagined destiny, a characteristic particularly typical of the middle classes. This was the group that voted overwhelmingly for Hitler, not for rational reasons as suggested by Brustein, but for emotional reasons they were unable to control. External events such as the humiliating defeat, followed by a sudden collapse of authority, unbridled political freedom, economic chaos, and illusory stability functioned as catalytic factors. Having chosen their destiny, they followed it to the bitter end. This unlimited trust in their leader and the willingness to follow him into death which was so widespread in the German population were the most prominent manifestations of the willingness to surrender to the extremely strong group pressure that was so characteristic of the Hitler years.

But cultural traits alone do not explain the strong group pressures of the Nazi regime. The very policy of isolating Germany from other nations and of expelling "aliens" had the effect of eliminating those "intersecting" loyalties and memberships of different circles which Simmel cites as a prerequisite of modern individuality. A good example is the theoretical physics that at the time had grown into a fertile international enterprise, creating a professional community beyond the narrow borders of nationality, race and religious creed (Moore, 1966; White and Gribbin, 1997). Hitler's policy of expelling Jews who held prominent positions and the meek response of their German colleagues effectively isolated German scientists from the rest of the world. Their ties were now exclusively to German colleagues, which made them even more vulnerable to group pressure. Hitler effectively transformed Germany into a pre-modern province in which individuals were more or less tied to their work, their families, and their close colleagues.

This was the society that the Allies occupied in the spring and summer of 1945. The question is, what happened in East Germany? We know more or less what happened in West Germany which, although it no doubt retains some provincialism, modernized culturally with remarkable speed. International contacts in science, business and the arts were soon resumed. West Germany became the "Mercedes nation" of Europe (*The Economist*, 1994) and the West Germans began to use their *Deutschmark*, earned through the export of superior and highly mechanized goods, to import trendy items from other countries and to tour the world. Cultural exchange programs were inaugurated with many countries (although the USA seems to have been more receptive to Germans after the Second World War than Europe, where memories of the politics of the Third Reich only abated very slowly). Another important factor was the change in demography. Germany today is a culturally mixed population. Millions of *Gastarbeiter* from the poorer parts of Europe (particularly Turkey, Yugoslavia, Greece and Italy) settled down in Germany after the war, in effect transforming it into a multicultural society.

All the social changes which contributed to cultural modernization and liberated the individual from the strong group pressure
characteristic of the Hitler years would not have come about, though,
if the political leadership of West Germany, in approaching the problem of coping with the past, had not dealt with the question of group
pressure and ways of reducing its most disastrous effects (Herf, 1997).
East German leaders do not appear to have considered this aspect.
Their analysis of what had gone wrong in the Weimar Republic was
economic rather than cultural. They believed that the Germans had
voted for the Nazis because of high unemployment and the peren-
nial crises of capitalism. By eliminating the causes of these social
ills, that is by expropriating private property and introducing state
planning of the economy, the possibility of a Nazi revival would be
eliminated once and for all. The problem of group pressure, underlying authoritarian traits, and the explosive combination of the two
only became visible after unification.

The Preference for a Group-oriented Lifestyle

The debate among German social scientists on the economic and
cultural transformation that took place in East Germany after reunification (see Giesen, 1991; Glaessner, 1992; Reissig, 1993; Joas and
Kohli, 1994; Gissendanner, 1996; Wiesenthal, 1996) contains surprisingly little mention of the issue of the strong group orientation
(Lay and Potting, 1995) which is possibly the most defining cultural
pattern among East Germans. Christiane F, a psychologist educated
in the GDR, describes the "differences in general behavior: the greater
distance in Western behavior—one doesn't hang the heart on the
tongue." She laments the "competitive thinking that destroys public
ownership of companies and drives an individualism that gets stronger all the time," and complains that "a firm standpoint is not required any more" (Grell and Wolf, 1992: 84). Susanne Rippl, in her
analysis of the strength of group membership among East and West
Germans, notes that for the former "the degree of social categoriza-
tion as an element of 'exclusive identity' ...is significantly stronger—they evidently identify more strongly with their 'old' identity
than do West Germans" (Rippl, 1997: 181).

The preference for a communal life built around unquestionable
truths is not something the East Germans try to hide. A young and
very successful East German movie star confessed in an interview

that she felt a vague dissatisfaction with her present life. The firm principles on which her life in the GDR had been built and the feeling that people were in it together had gone and had left a strong feeling of emptiness or lack of meaning (Paul, 1999). More generally, East Germans are convinced that their attachment to groups is more natural than the individualistic lifestyles of the West Germans and are proof that the GDR was the more "humane" of the two systems. "It was, in one way or another, more humane before" (Matussek, 1999b: 50) is a phrase one often hears among former GDR citizens. What they mean is that social relationships were much closer. In the West people tend to collect acquaintances in various social contexts or to build personal networks based upon "weak ties" (Granovetter, 1973) rather than finding it natural to share the destiny of one particular group only. Carla and Volker, two East German pupils from Thüringen. expressed their point of view in an interview with a West German magazine. According to Carla, "the mentalities of Ossies and Wessies are different. Among Ossies, the collective feeling of togetherness is still present to some degree. Among Wessies everyone is on his own." Volker, who had "already met many from the West," felt "these Wessies are mostly very distant. And it is very difficult to get close to them" (*Der Spiegel*, 1999: 28).

This strong feeling of cultural alienation from the West German lifestyle has been recorded by East German researchers, although their results do not seem to impress the social science establishment which is dominated by West Germans.

Thus Katarina Belwe, in an early article published in BISS PUBLIC on the issue of the "psychosocial well-being of the East Germans," refers to studies done by a young East German sociologist, Michael Kruse, immediately after reunification. Kruse found that:

> the adoption of a Federal German identity...emerged hesitantly. Having interviewed and observed youth from East Berlin over a period of three months, he argued that "instead of the Wall of concrete...a new Wall has emerged, which is not easy to surmount. The young who have been educated to a collective consciousness, don't feel good in the new society. Because of a strongly formed group feeling, they fear that they will have fewer chances in an "elbow society." (Belwe, 1992: 14).

This is the main reason why the mutual curiosity about other lifestyles which emerged after the fall of the Wall lasted only briefly.

> Many young East Berliners today react with estrangement and insecurity to the strong need of West German youth to stand apart from the mass. They often feel inferior,

which has a negative effect upon their feeling of self-worth. This feeling of being worth less than the West Berlin youth, the East Berlin youth counter with the phrase: "We want to be among ourselves again." Kruse also found that this feeling applied to "both Wessies and foreigners." (Belwe, 1992: 14)

East German youth see both categories as strangers to be avoided as far as possible because they seem to value individuality in a way unknown to and disapproved of by East Germans.

Whereas most East Germans have no difficulty in recognizing their dependence upon groups they are more reluctant to concede the negative aspects of such strong group dependence—pressure to conform, obedience, cultural stereotypes, ethnic prejudice, and so on (Portes and Rumbaut, 1996; Portes, 1999). In those cases in which the strongly conformist aspect of East German society has been acknowledged, for instance in the school system, the criticism has met with angry and abusive counter-arguments, not only from teachers but from parents as well (Gruner, 1990).

What is interesting is that West Germans also seem to have great difficulty in talking about the preference among East Germans for a collective lifestyle. To do so appears to remind them of a period in German history that is still an unhealed wound. It is striking that both West and East German social researchers rarely attempt to explore the historical roots of the cultural and political alienation of most East Germans from the West German system (Misselwitz, 1999). Instead the prevailing tendency is to view the more immediate past—the GDR dictatorship–as the main reason for the cultural differences in reunited Germany, as if the GDR had appeared out of nowhere.

All these factors suggest that we are dealing with strong emotions related to a common historical experience—the Nazi past. This hypothesis is borne out in the way Christian Pfeiffer's criticism of the collectivist methods of upbringing practiced by East Germans have been received in the German *Öffentlichkeit*. In West Germany, the most common reaction among researchers and teachers I talked to in the spring of 1999 was to avoid the matter. Their reluctance to tackle it was also reflected in the limited debate which has taken place in the mass media, for instance in the leading intellectual magazine, *Die Zeit*.

The general consensus seems to be that Pfeiffer has said far too much already. He has brought up an issue with which most West Germans have coped pragmatically, but not emotionally. With its associations with the Nazi past, it is an awkward issue which most

West Germans would prefer not to debate publicly (Bar-On, 1996; Rosenthal, 1997).

But whereas most West Germans express feelings of shame or guilt about the past—a shame which in some ways seems to increase as the present generation is confronted with events which are almost incomprehensible to them—Pfeiffer's work on the dangers of the collective exercise of power over the individual has elicited among East Germans feelings less of shame or guilt than of rage and a need to suppress once and for all views which are considered to be deviant and outrageous. This very reaction confirms his contention that there was a dark side to the group-oriented lifestyle that should be examined.

At a public lecture in Magdeburg in the spring of 1999 the audience was, according to a reporter in "a lynching mood." Pfeiffer's thesis was rejected outright by every speaker. After the lecture, an elderly lady approached the reporter and told him that she thought Pfeiffer had a valid point. "But I beg you not to write down my name, for this they stone you here." A young woman was somewhat braver. She gave the reporter her full name—Simone Mehlhase—adding that she was twenty-two years old and had been born in Magdeburg. She was able to be more honest because she no longer lived there and was merely visiting her family.

"When she was eighteen she had moved to Hanover to study and had had, she said, great difficulties in the beginning. 'I lacked personal independence.'" She doubted whether Pfeiffer's thesis explained all the hostility against strangers but had no doubt that the GDR upbringing was harmful. If "she had had children herself she wouldn't trust any kindergarten or school teacher from East Germany. 'No, I am positive about that'" (Kohlhoff, 1999).

Group Stereotypes

According to social psychological theory, a strong group-oriented identity will lead to a tendency to stereotype both oneself and the other. Stereotyping can be seen as a form of depersonalization in which both the individual and the other are judged in terms of their group membership and not by their personal worth. How does this work in the German case? How strong are the stereotypes of East and West Germans about their own group and the other group? An empirical investigation of this issue, done in the mid-nineteen-nineties, arrived at the following results:

Table 7.1
Auto- and Hetero-Stereotypes in East and West Germany

| | West German images | | East German images | |
	West Germans	East Germans	West Germans	East Germans
greedy	2.90	1.93	3.20	1.09
inconsiderate	2.85	1.75	3.29	1.09
egotistical	3.36	2.36	3.75	1.59
cunning	2.63	2.07	3.62	1.49
power hungry	3.13	1.89	3.81	1.27
helpful	2.51	3.08	2.28	3.94
conscientious	3.21	2.65	3.17	3.77
honest	2.53	2.87	2.45	3.67
humble	1.89	2.54	1.38	3.57
trustworthy	3.25	2.79	3.05	3.91
sympathetic	2.82	2.78	2.77	3.42

Range: 0 = "not at all"
      5 = "very much"
   2,5 = "average"

Source: Schmitt & Montada, 1999.

The most striking pattern that emerges from these figures is that negative stereotyping by East Germans of West Germans is significantly more pronounced than negative stereotyping of West Germans by East Germans. This works in reverse too, the positive stereotypes the East Germans have of themselves are more pronounced than the positive stereotypes the West Germans have of themselves.

> The relative devaluation of the other part of the population is more pronounced in East Germany than it is in West Germany ... the West Germans see themselves in a more critical light and, in their evaluation of the 'East Germans', there is a balance between positive and negative qualities. (Schmitt and Montada, 1999: 38)

East Germans generally regard West Germans as having only negative traits, while they monopolize all the positive traits for themselves. It is indeed thought provoking that they are unable to find even one area in which they perceive West Germans to be admirable.

The Maladjusted Personality

Although East German group behavior is clearly under-researched, there is a wealth of studies by both East and West Germans about the effects of the collective lifestyle upon individual coping strategies. The main thesis is that the lack of individuality in the GDR predisposes East Germans to massive adaptive failures. Schluchter suggests that:

> the authoritarian-technocratic party and state socialism of the GDR did not allow for a distinction between the role of the economic citizen and that of the political citizen and did not demand of the individual the ability to balance self and collective orientation, self interest and the common good. Instead of being expected to take personal responsibility, the individual was treated as an irresponsible child, "compensated" by the achievements of the socialist welfare state. The longevity of this supervisory and tutelary state resulted in the emergence of certain GDR-specific emotional (and cognitive) habits which also influenced those who did not identify with this social order. These habits have continued since the restructuring of the institutions. (Schluchter, 1996: 23)

The main question being asked is whether East Germans are emotionally and cognitively prepared to adapt as individuals to modern, functionally differentiated and highly individualistic societies. The issue of why they are still so addicted to a group-oriented lifestyle is not touched upon at all. The tacit assumption seems to be that the question is irrelevant. Pollack, who believes most East Germans to be much more adaptable than most of his West German colleagues assume (Pollack, 1999), has some interesting explanations for this preference but, like most East Germans, he attributes it to life in the GDR. The strong cultural continuity with Nazi German is left out of the equation.

In an early article Pollack argues that one of the main weaknesses of the GDR, and a possible reason for its collapse, was that it was over organized, It was an "organizational society" which left little space for originality. As such it endowed its member with certain ways of thinking that do not fit the requirements of West German society where individuals are expected to take the initiative. "Those who fell outside what could be organized and tested immediately faced the danger of being criminalized. Only those who clearly said 'yes' belonged." (Pollack, 1990: 294). He does not comment upon the obvious similarity between the GDR and Nazi Germany in this respect.

Most researchers avoid these sensitive issues though and focus upon the theory of the maladjusted personality. The inability to fit into a highly competitive society is seen as the root of strong cultural alienation. Belwe, referring to the results of Kruse's study, nevertheless believes that the main problem lies elsewhere.

The East Germans had to adapt, but they did not have to force themselves to the front; they had to stay together but did not permanently have to expose themselves to competition; they had to be modest in order to be half satisfied, but they did not have to run like mad in order to feel "in." (Belwe, 1992: 12)

Woderich focuses on the strong conformist traits of East Germans to explain the intellectual mediocrity of many of his former colleagues. The prevailing norm was "the wish not to be seen, the search for the protection of the anonymous middle." Pressure from without was not important here, it was:

the generally prevailing patterns of socialization which reduced the ability to expose and articulate individual interests, leanings and needs; the prevailing normality in the manner of thinking and everyday consciousness makes these types of strivings and impulses appear uncomfortable. (Woderich, 1992a: 86-7)

Meulemann argues that a particular kind of morality evolved in East Germany which focused on conventional and conformist traits. "Work, a sense of order, diligence, punctuality and obedience became more important than curiosity, individuality, creativity; conventional values that could be read from behavior, were more important than values such as autonomy" (Meulemann, 1998: 13). Similarly, Schluchter argues that in the GDR:

a great deal of time was spent maintaining solidarity in the work place. This was described as an informalization of work relations: Personalization dominated over reification. In ethnological terms one could say that what emerged were not "hot" but "cold" cultures, diffuse but not functionally specific ones, where the focus was on group morality as a particularistic inside morality, but not individual morality as a universal, professional morality. Regardless of all political forces, regardless of the pressure to perform (implementing the plan), regardless of all criticism of sometimes indecent working conditions, regardless of all fluctuation, what defined the individual lifestyle was not the profession and professional ethics but belonging to a work place. This influenced personalities that were characterized by a collective and not a self-orientation, entitlement and not achievement, localism and not cosmopolitanism. (Schluchter, 1996: 35-6)

Lenhardt and Stock (1997) argue that the primary objective of education in the GDR was not to educate citizens about equal rights. Individuals were primarily defined as members of a work force. Hence the dominant view of the community was that it consisted of producers not of citizens who should think critically. A teacher was not seen as an autonomous professional but as an expert hired by the state to perform a certain function. Moreover, unlike in West Germany, where the main principle of the educational system is freedom of choice in education and, in principle, unlimited access to higher education, only a carefully selected élite was allowed to enter higher education in the GDR. Whereas students or pupils in the GDR were mainly defined paternalistically as "talents" that the state chose to support, pupils/students in the Federal Republic were seen as endowed with certain inalienable rights which were protected by the constitution.

Beier emphasizes the degree to which life in the GDR was regulated from childhood by the state.

> Already a look at the numbers shows that life trajectories in the GDR as a rule moved along fixed paths. Eighty percent of the children entered crèches, 98 percent of the children when they later started school became "young pioneers." Then followed the *Freie Deutsche Jugend* (FDJ) of which about three-quarters of the youth were members and the "transitional ritual" *Judenweihe* in which 98 percent of all 14-year-olds participated. The phase of education was subjected to a strict time plan and the transition into the workforce was to a large degree planned ahead. Because of this and a more regimented life the youth had a "modernization gap" at the socio-cultural level, where there was little time for crises of maturity or the search for identity. "This can be seen in two quite different biographical patterns in the two Germanies. In West Germany the main biographical patterns follows the idea of a 'moratorium' or an extended search for identity"(Erikson, 1968). For this reason the period of education is more open and is characterized by unplanned extensions and there are often "delays in this status passage," with the result that marriage and children are normally postponed indefinitely (many young people do not marry at all but live as singles). In West Germany, women rarely married before they were thirty. In East Germany the average age for women was twenty-three. It was thus logical that most women had their children between the ages of twenty and twenty-five. From then on, to use the phrase of the demographers, the "generative phase" was as a rule completed. (Beier, 1995: 11-12)

One of the most important functions of schools was to teach individuals to submit to the power of the collective (Anweiler, 1988). According to Christa Wolf, who worked as a teacher, this was an area in which the GDR did indeed succeed. If children learned one thing in school it was "not to dance outside the rows ... to express the opinions that were expected if they wanted to have a life without the problems which obsessed their parents" (Wolf, 1990a: 9). This often led to a highly authoritarian style of teaching that reduced pupils to small soldiers who had learned the most important lesson—to obey and to conform. In a study done in the early 1980s, the Academy of Pedagogical Sciences found that "about half of those asked said that their most important experience of being a pupil, was the insight that one was in a subordinate position to the teacher, who did not allow criticism, and that the individual had no influence whatsoever upon the demands and decisions of the teacher" (Meier et al, 1983: 41).

This strong authoritarianism meant that teachers had little interest in developing more modern, student-centered teaching methods. "The main reason for lack of discipline or motivation was that the teaching was boring. The teaching was monotonous, dooming the individual to passivity...it resulted in aversion and sometimes also resistance" (Meier et al, 1983: 45).

The focus on group conformity and obedience as the main principle governing East German schools was expressed in a favorite slogan, *von ich zu wir* ("from I [want] to we [want]"). Studies done immediately before and after unification show that this resulted in a significantly stronger need for social recognition among East German students than among West German students.

The differences between East and West German students are extraordinarily great and moreover seem to have changed very little since reunification. East German students have a much stronger need to gain social recognition in the general sense (respect and authority). When it comes to limited authority within a given profession the difference is still there but is much smaller. Bräuer and Häublein conclude that the greater need for social recognition might be ex-

Table 7.2
The Need for Social Recognition

	Very important/important	Hardly/not at all important
"To be respected by others"		
GDR students 1989	71 %	5 %
GDR students 1990	70 %	8 %
FRG students 1990	34 %	24 %
"To exercise authority over others"		
GDR students 1989	64 %	9 %
GDR students 1990	57 %	12 %
FRG students 1990	25 %	38 %
"To be a recognized authority in one's profession"		
GDR students 1989	87 %	4 %
GDR students 1990	90 %	7 %
FRG students 1990	71 %	9 %

Source: Brämer and Häublein, 1990: 9

plained by "higher social ambitions," possibly reflecting the higher degree of self-reproduction among the East German intelligentsia. "[B]ut it can also be interpreted as a sign of low self-esteem. When individual worth is dependent upon the opinions of others, the opinions of others may be internalized and become the self image" (Brämer and Häublein, 1990: 8-9).

Ingrid Stratemann (1992), in a psychological study of character traits seen from a management point of view, distinguishes between "external" and "internal" attribution of causes of individual behavior. In the latter case, the individual sees himself or herself as the prime cause of or as responsible for life choices, whereas in the former, the individual sees himself or herself as a mere object of circumstances outside his or her control. In the GDR the former pattern seems to have dominated because of the centralized command structures which offered few opportunities for individual career plans among any employees, including the top managers. The result, according to Stratemann, was a "weak decision-making ability" and an attitude that any problem that arose had to be "considered" rather than dealt with practically. As an example she cites the case of a production manager who, having correctly registered that some machines were out of production, failed to take any initiative to replace them or have them repaired.

The most striking difference between employees in East and West Germany according to Stratemann is the absence among the former of a service ethic in relation to customers. "The most obvious problem was that job applicants from the new federal states tended to be introverted. In their immediate social interaction this is expressed in a particular personal modesty, less likelihood of initiating and continuing a conversation, and shyness (Stratemann, 1990: 23). Stratemann observes that a little training in personal appearance produced a significant change in behavior. Peter Becker agrees to some extent. When he compared East and West Germans, he found that:

the consistent result was that the behavior of East Germans is more controlled than that of West Germans. East Germans emphasize the importance of order and of following instructions...East Germans are more rule-oriented, that is rules have a stronger binding force for them. For instance they prefer strict speed limits, have little understanding of those who park in non-parking areas, and condemn infidelity more strongly ... Germans who have been socialized in the GDR are less spontaneous than West Germans: they feel they have to keep their behavior under control ... they are ... less liberated and are less likely to show enthusiasm. They get less pleasure out of doing crazy things. (Becker, 1992: 33)

Because West Germans are more spontaneous "it is easier for them to change their plans; in difficult situations it is easier for them to find a solution; they get more pleasure out of doing several things at once." East Germans prefer "assignments that are clearly specified, where I cannot make mistakes"; " I prefer to work in a collective, rather than in a place where everything depends on me." Becker suggests that the "greater enjoyment of improvisation and autonomy" among West Germans was furthered by a society where these values were "systematically supported and 'rewarded' in school, family, work and politics, whereas the East German were raised to be more cautious in this respect" (Becker, 1992: 34).

Becker's theory of a more rigid, controlled and cautious personality has been confirmed by a large psychological study, *Denken in Deutschland* (Thinking in Germany) (Strohschneider, 1996) on problem-solving methods among East and West Germans. Exposing the two groups to the so-called MANUTEX-test, which was developed to measure different "problem-solving styles,'" Badke-, Schaub and Buerscheuber concluded that East Germans are better at solving problems where the point of departure is certain fixed rules or where the problem solver is given sufficient time to think things over. In situations in which speed is required or where rules are unclear or tend to change, typically in crisis situations, the West Germans were the better problem solvers. Generally East Germans were insecure without a great deal of information—they wanted to make sure they were on the right track and they were markedly "cautious." By contrast West Germans adapted the amount of information needed to the situation and concentrated their attention and energy on formulating the problem and on any crises that occurred. "With only a few risk-oriented interventions they arrived faster at a positive result" (Badke-, Schaub and Buerschaper, 1996: 120).

Given these highly significant differences in socialization patterns and dominant personality traits in the two Germanies, it is not surprising that Katarina Belwe, in the article mentioned above, concluded that German reunification represented something of a culture shock for East Germans.

> The rapid reunification has...proved to be a fall from one world into another. Individuals have lost their points of orientation. Life-long habits have been broken. Social structures have collapsed. (Belwe, 1992: 7)

She points particularly to the:

considerable discrepancy between the behavioral repertoire of the ex-GDR citizens and the new demands... "the realities of socialism" produced a particular way of doing things that cannot simply be discarded, especially between today and tomorrow ... the mental demands that the pluralist democracy and the market economy lay on the actors are totally different from those that were acquired in the GDR. East Germans have the reputation of being norm-oriented, loyal to principles, and reliable. Compared with West Germans they are anxious, less spontaneous and almost hidebound...apart from that they are thin skinned, extremely vulnerable, have difficulty in handling conflicts... and have a tendency towards collective resentment. (Belwe, 1992: 9-10)

This impressively insightful summary of East German traits revealed by German reunification and the accompanying difficulties of adaptation omits one factor though, namely the preference for a group-oriented life style. Too great a focus on the lack of individual preparedness for a highly individualized society tends to exaggerate individual problems of adaptation and ignore the importance of the group. Thus one could argue that the most important trait of East Germans was their ability to separate the question of individual adaptation to the system from the question of identifying with the system. "The best thing about the GDR was ... that one was against it" (Dahn, 1999: 104).

Most East Germans had adapted themselves very well to a system they did not particularly like, so why should they not do so again after reunification? There are indeed clear indications that they did. As several studies on the transitions that took place on the labor market indicate, the East Germans turned out to be much more "flexible" then the image of the rigid, cautious and unspontaneous automatons suggested by psychological studies seems to indicate. "For almost three-fifths of the work force, incorporation into the West fundamentally disrupted security and stability." The huge number of people who had to move around from job to job or to find a new source of income without a steady, full-time occupation, indicates that the East Germans faced the new and tougher demands with a surprisingly high degree of stoicism. Although many workers no doubt felt "dazed and lost in the strange capitalist world,'" many more succeeded in getting a foot into the new system and although they experienced difficulties they were determined to make it. "For those fortunate enough to hang on, work became more demanding. Tough competition called for greater effort so that going through the motions no longer sufficed. Succeeding in a merciless market, required new skills, pride in performance and an ethic of responsibility."(Jarauch, 1994:195).

Cultural and Political Alienation

A curious anomaly of the East German situation is that it is the highly educated who were most alienated from the new system despite the fact that they fared relatively well on the labor market. One reason why education turned out not to be a handicap was suggested to me by Martin Diewald of the Max Planck Institute for Human Development, who pointed out the high premium German employers traditionally place on educational qualifications over mere work experience. This cultural pattern explains the finding of the research group that the most successful transitions were made among individuals with professional and vocational certificates (in that order), whereas unskilled workers had great difficulty finding jobs with West German employers for whom a vocational degree is a guarantee of pride in workmanship and the quality on which West German industry has traditionally built up its international reputation and competitive strategies (Nelson, 1994; Porter, 1990).

A possible reason for the alienation of the educated classes could be that East Germans learned to look upon themselves primarily as a work force in a productive community and that any attempt to escape from this community—whether by refusing to work or trying to emigrate—was as severely punished, not only by the state but by the collective of which the individual was a part and where he or she belonged. Irene Runge has suggested to me that the shame many East Germans felt at not being part of the work force destroyed friendships overnight, even some that had existed for a lifetime.

To get to the root of the matter, we have to focus upon the political schizophrenia of the East Germans who found themselves working for a system from which they were basically estranged. As they soon found the new system wanting in terms of at least some of their needs, in particular the strong role played by the collective, they disengaged emotionally. Because they no longer had to simulate loyalty or keep their disagreement and dissatisfaction secret their degree of identification with the West German political declined dramatically after 1990 and the original euphoria of having got rid of the hated GDR.

By 1998, only 13 percent of East Germans expressed satisfaction with the democratic institutions in the Federal Republic and only 17 percent saw themselves as fully equal citizens. Although only 11 percent wanted the old GDR back, 65 percent wanted neither the GDR nor the Federal Republic.

> It is thus a fact that political attitudes in East Germany have in no way developed in the direction of a growing trust in democracy, the constitutional state and the given economic order. Both a return among a section of the East Germans to basic socialist values and an orientation towards nationalistic resentments among another section are symptomatic of a growing alienation, a skepticism about the ideals expressed publicly [by most West Germans]. (Misselwitz, 1999: 26)

Since most East Germans certainly did not identify with the socialist system as such, one wonders what it is they see in retrospect as the most positive aspect of GDR society. It is here that the question of the preference for a group-oriented life style comes into play. What both East Germans leaning to the Marxist Left and those tending to the nationalist Right seem to miss most is life in the shadow of the group—the aspect that the GDR took over almost unchanged from Nazi Germany.

Second-Class Citizens

This preference for the group is rarely taken into account in explaining why East Germans often refer to themselves as second-class citizens, a description which makes no sense, given that economic development in reunited Germany has privileged East Germans to an extraordinary degree. In 1991 the average income of East German households was 45 percent of that of West German households. Three years later this income gap had been reduced dramatically with East German incomes rising to 74 percent of those of West Germans (Geissler, 1996: 54). If we use a different measurement of income level, namely financial surplus, or what remains of a household income at the end of the month after all regular expenses (taxes, installments, living costs, and so on) have been deducted, we find an even higher degree of economic equality. In 1991 the financial surplus of East German households was about 60 percent of West German households (304 DM compared to 508 DM), in 1994 it had risen to 84 percent (464 DM compared to 551 DM). "The frequently repeated argument that the increase in the cost of living eats up the increase in income in East Germany is thus not true" (Gensicke, 1995: 291).

Other economic facts consistently tell the story of a massive equalization in incomes, living standards and consumption patterns in the

1990s. Thus, whereas in 1988 66 percent of East German house-holds owned a washing machine, 43 percent owned a freezer, 4 per-cent owned a telephone, 52 percent owned a color television, and 52 percent owned a car, the corresponding figures for 1993 were 91 percent, 70 percent, 49 percent, 92 percent and 66 percent, com-pared with 88 percent, 80 percent, 97 percent, 95 percent, and 74 percent for West German households (Geissler, 1996: 51). The only significant difference after only three years of reunification was that there was still limited access to private telephones, which can be explained by the extremely low starting point (in fact, the growth rate in telephone ownership in East Germany over three years was more than 1000 percent).

Geissler points out that "the increase in incomes that took place in the new federal states in the first years after reunification is without comparison in the history of the Bonn Republic." Although there might still be some public employees who do not earn the same salaries as their counterparts in the Federal Republic, one should also note the "very rapid raise in incomes from one-third in 1989" to an expected "90 percent of the western level in 1996" (Geissler, 1996: 54). In some areas, particularly pensions, the average East German today receives a higher monthly income than the average West German, mainly because East German women were much more part of the regular labor force. "East German pension payments went up from 55.6 percent of the West German level in 1990 to 110 per-cent in July 1998" (Schwitzler, 1999: 33).

Whatever differences remain in income levels, they are insignifi-cant compared to what they were before reunification, a fact which is partially acknowledged by most East Germans. In 1992, 52 per-cent of them thought that their general situation had improved since reunification while only 18 percent thought it had deterio-rated. Forty-six percent said they were doing better economically, while 22 percent felt they were worse off than they had been (Gensicke, 1995: 292). In 1995, 50 percent of East Germans stated that life was better or much better for them personally then it had been in the GDR while 23 percent felt things were worse or much worse. Nevertheless, in 1995, 72 percent of East Germans regarded themselves as second-class citizens (*Der Spiegel*, 1995a: 46). In 1998 the corresponding figure was 83 percent (Misselwitz, 1999: 26.

In the *Spiegel* survey, the image of the second-class citizen is explained as the result of a combination of economic envy and wounded pride. The East Germans feel this "not only because things are going better, but also because they believe that they do not get the recognition they deserve from the West Germans." They have to defend themselves against the broadly accepted view in the old Federal states that they are accustomed to a much more leisurely pace of work. "Sixty percent disagree with that view" and "they are even more firm in rejecting the opinion that productivity in the GDR was low 'because of a lack of will to achieve.' Only 12 percent agree with that statement, while 87 percent believe that the low productivity 'can be explained by bad working conditions, for instance lack of material and old machines.' Moreover they see themselves as hindered in proving their efficiency. Since *die Wende* 'many more firms in the former GDR have been closed than was necessary.' Nine-two percent agree with that statement" (*Der Spiegel*, 1995a: 49).

The fact is that research on productivity in the GDR indicates strongly that East German workers are accustomed to not putting much energy into their work. A study done in 1991 revealed that industrial work in the GDR was characterized by "avoidance of responsibility" and "wide-spread laxity concerning working hours, use of materials, keeping appointments, quality of work." The explanation was that workers had problems with the centralized command economy; "that any effort...was destroyed by the plan" (Voskamp and Wittke, 1991: 177; cit. Roesler, 1997: 3). The lack of materials and problems with machines not only led to work stoppages and low morale, they also legitimated a work style characterized by "frequent breaks from work and a relaxed pace" (Rottenburg, 1991: 311).

Managers were powerless to interfere, partly because the system needed the workers during critical periods (the well-known "storming periods" when the monthly quotas had to be fulfilled), but mainly because the group norms in the work collectives were extraordinarily strong. "Who could pressure something out of the worker...the workers' control over the points and zones of production could not be broken up either by disciplinary measures or by offering individual wage increases" (Lüdtke, 1994: 196).

It was almost impossible to differentiate between workers and pay them according to their individual productivity. In the GDR "no one came home without a reward for special achievements" (Rottenburg, 1991: 115). The pursuit of individual ambitions and goals was seen as deviant behavior which did not fit into the group norms. Instead work increasingly became associated with a "social place and an instrument for the distributions of social benefits" (Voskamp and Wittke, 1991: 117, cit. Roesler, 1997: 3).

The Colonization Thesis

What is interesting is not that East German workers, largely because of the strength of the group, were able effectively to withstand the efforts of managers to increase the pace of work, discipline, and overall productivity, but that they deny that this was so. Although low productivity undoubtedly contributed to the mass closure of East German factories which went bankrupt long before it was possible to restructure and adapt them to Western markets (Christ and Neubauer, 1991; *Die Wirtschaft*, 1993) another factor, and one recognized by most Western economists, was that they were hugely overstaffed by Western standards and so were unable to pay the enormous pay increases demanded by the need to equalize incomes.

Despite the evidence, though, the "colonization" thesis—that industries were more or less willfully destroyed by West German capital, assisted by the conservative government under Kohl--has wide currency in both the East and the West. East Germans I have spoken to frequently argue that the reason so many factories in East Germany were closed was the fear of competition. Western intellectuals, whose sympathies lie with the antifascist, workers' and peasants' state, tend to see it as a kind of revenge against the ideological enemy and an attempt to prove once and for all that socialism has not worked and never will.

Although these and similar motives were no doubt present and, in specific cases, probably influenced the policy of Treuhand, the gigantic holding company that took over ownership of all publicly owned East German firms and privatized them or closed them down (Kampe, 1994; Köhler, 1994), the use of the term "colonization" is wildly exaggerated and analytically misplaced. A more appropriate way of looking at the situation would be to see it as a Darwinian struggle, with East German firms fighting for survival and failing the test. Christ and Neubauer (1991) contend that it is difficult to see how such a situation could have been avoided. As soon as the political decision was made to reunify the two countries economically and as a consequence of that to equalize incomes and living standards rapidly, East German industry, given its much lower productivity, was doomed to go under.

The East Germans, although they do not care to admit it, are of course aware of the fact that the rapid equalization could not have taken place without massive transfers of financial assistance from West to East. This awareness emerges clearly in an analysis done by Gensicke in which he compares two types of evaluations of the economic situation—the personal and the general. Between 1991 and 1994, an average of 15 percent of East Germans thought that their personal economic situation was bad. By contrast, an average of 60 percent thought that the general situation had improved (Gensicke, 1995: 287).

According to Gensicke economic statistics normally explain such discrepancies by pointing to the "media effect," since Western media tend for various reasons to overemphasize bad news. In this case, though, the "media effect" is clearly inadequate as an explanation for the dramatic gap between the two evaluations. "Such huge differences between personal and general evaluations of the situation ...have never before been observed in Western societies. In East Germany the discrepancy...since 1991 has been a minimum of 39 percent and maximum of 51 percent." Gensicke suggests that the reason is the "discrepancy between the weak economy in the new federal states and the enormous amounts of money streaming into them from the West...the net transfer of capital to the new federal states in 1993 varied, according to different calculations, between 150 to 180 billion DM" (Gensicke, 1995: 250).

Although the East Germans are no doubt aware of the source of the money, they prefer to pretend that the transfer does not exist and that it is they who are being robbed of their resources. This myth that capital is being transferred out of the country is the economic core of the "colonization" thesis. It is particularly evident in Daniela Dahn's summary of East German thinking about the economic results of unification in 1991.

> The East Germans have from their daily experiences the feeling that they are being cheated. During the economic union their savings accounts were reduced to half and they have to pay the drastically higher living costs since their wages are only the half of those in West Germany. (Dahn, 1999:63)

Since there are no factual grounds for these complaints, surely most East Germans must have noticed that not only are they able to buy things that were previously out of reach like color television sets and Western cars, they can now afford to pay for their own vacations? In an article originally published in 1988 Jens Reich makes the interesting point that East Germans had often felt humiliated when they traveled abroad, because they could not afford the same things as West Germans. When they visited their relatives in the West they were totally dependent upon them financially. The only people who were allowed to visit Western countries without special permission were retired persons and they were only permitted to take out 15 DM a year!

Even when relatives met on neutral ground, one of the socialist countries for instance, the same infuriating pattern of economic dependence was present. Reich describes the emotions induced by the sheer volume of wealth of the West Germans. Even if an East German saved for a year in preparation for the encounter, he could not take out more than 400 East German Mark. "With this he cannot pay for a hotel room and, when he visits a restaurant he has to stick to the entrée soup." If he wants to share a table at a restaurant with his West German relatives or acquaintances he must allow them to pay the bill. This leads, Reich points out, to a diminished self esteem which may result in aggression arising from a sense of humiliation at having to assume the role of a beggar (Reich, 1993:56).

The "colonization" thesis also does not take into account that another reason for the low productivity in the GDR could have been the group-oriented lifestyle which might also explain why productivity in East Germany is still only 60 percent of that of West Germany (although the wages are practically equal) and it might be a major reason why interest among West German firms in rebuilding East Germany industry has not been as high as was originally expected (Kupferberg, 1996b).

The Communications Wall

Theoretically it is easy to explain the communications wall between East and West Germans in purely "anthropological" terms. Since we are dealing with two groups socialized in different systems or cultural environments, we should expect problems of "intercultural communication." What is missing from such an apparently "neutral" or "objective" stance is the historical dimension. The interesting point about East and West Germany is not only that individuals from these cultures prefer different lifestyles but that the cultural differences have their origins in different ways of coping with German history and identity. If we compare the development that has taken place in the two Germanies with Simmel's theory of cultural modernization and socio-psychological experiments on the reactions of individuals faced with strong group pressure, we conclude that the main cultural difference between East and West Germans can be explained in terms of the quantity and quality of group membership. East Germans have experienced life in the shadow of the strong influence of the group, which strikingly resembles the artificial, laboratory-controlled conditions created by social psychologists. Viewed as a human laboratory, the GDR proves without doubt that groups, if we allow them to, can effectively eliminate individuality and that a strong identification with the group destroys critical thinking.

The situation in West Germany, on the other hand, demonstrates the validity of Simmel's opposing sociological thesis—that group membership can create independence, provided the monopoly of one or a few groups is broken. West German culture is clearly influenced by the sociological observation that individual membership of different, more or less overlapping groups weakens the power of the group over the individual and encourages the process of individualization. Simmel arrived at his conclusions by studying Kant's moral teaching and observing closely the buzzing life in turn-of-the-century Berlin where he lived at the corner of Unter den Linden and Friedrichsstrasse,

A particular aspect of the communications divide in reunited Germany is the complaint by West Germans that it is difficult to crack the East German "code" of communication. "What the battle was about I don't know. I could not understand it because I am a West German," wrote one reader describing the frustration of trying to understand two colleagues who were quarrelling over an article written by one of them which the other thought was scandalous. West Germans consider East Germans as difficult to comprehend as the Japanese.

When they are among their own and I happen to be there, I sometimes feel as though I am present at a meeting of a sect." Communication takes place "through a secret system of signs, a fine-spun net of rituals and microscopically small signals. One is reluctant to say what one thinks. And one doesn't want to write it either. A slight cough at a particular place in a particular clause can have an infinity of meanings. For us West Germans many East Germans have something mysterious, something unfathomable about them. They talk like us, but they almost never reveal anything about themselves. (Martenstein, 1999: 10)

Why should this be? Martenstein's own explanation, that in East Germany "in the course of decades and under the pressure of the dictatorship a culture developed where one wrote between the lines and talked between the lines" (Martenstein, 1999: 10) takes no account of the fact that this tendency did not emerge only after 1945. The GDR was an extension of the totalitarian regime which had ruled all of Germany from 1933 to 1945. Nazi Germany as a society was characterized to an extraordinary degree by the power of the group over the individual. The totalitarianism of the GDR was no doubt milder and more humane, but the cultural system of repressing individual thought, which had been perfected by the Nazis, was not touched in its essence. On the contrary it was incorporated into the communist system and remained in place until the regime collapsed in 1989. What we see today is the aftermath of the same cultural system, working within individuals who were socialized into thinking collectively.

This again confirms my hypothesis that the GDR can, to some extent, be described as an extended version of the laboratory experiments conducted by American social psychologists such as Sherif from the early nineteen-thirties onwards (the influence of the Nazi experience is obvious). Sherif's early experiments indicated that group pressure in an ambivalent situation has the effect of making individuals orient themselves towards the current consensus within the group, using the group as an instrument to help them cope with inner doubts and insecurity. Ash's experiments in the 1950s demonstrated an even more disturbing fact—that even in cases that were cognitively unambiguous, individuals still tended to conform to the consensus of the group, mainly because they feared being ostracized. This tendency contributes to the communications difficulties between East and West Germans in reunited Germany, indicating that the unmastered past has many unexpected faces.

8

Xenophobia and Right-Wing Extremism

Xenophobia as Everyday Reality

The peaceful end to the Marxist experiment in the East Germany and the overwhelming wish of East Germans to live in a reunited, democratic Germany was, by and large, accepted as a welcome event in West Germany, where a large majority at first supported the idea of reunification, although some were hesitant about the huge economic burden it represented (Jarauch, 1994). This goodwill diminished rapidly, though, as the West Germans began to discover some of the less endearing traits of their "brothers and sisters" such as unhealthy eating habits, wasted resources, lack of taste in choice of clothing, self-pity, inertia, excessive demands, and so on (Bittermann, 1993). The greatest gap, though, between East and West Germans can be found in their attitudes towards *Ausländer* (foreigners), and in the shameless assaults by youths on these *Ausländer* which often take place in broad daylight and sometimes in the presence of a passive audience (Böhm, 1993).

Xenophobia and right-wing extremist attacks are of course also a reality in West Germany. There is though, as Toralf Staud points out, an important difference: "In East Germany xenophobia is the norm" (Staud, 1999: 9). What is so particular about "hostility against foreigners in the new federal states" is that it has been so "obvious in its prevalence, its virulence, and its danger" (Watts, 1996: 7). Bergmann emphasizes that "young people in Eastern Germany...lead the statistics in Europe in regard to xenophobia" (Bergmann, 1997: 27). Above all, one finds in East Germany a type of shameless racism, that would be unthinkable in West Germany: "In East Germany right-wing extremist violence is a part of everyday life. The politicians look the other way" (Böhm, 1998: 1). Woderich emphasizes that "if we look at the general value statements, there is not a big difference ...between East and West Germans, but when it comes to their willingness to share a room with a foreigner, the degree of willingness among West German students is much higher than among their comrades from the new federal states" (Woderich, 1991a: 129-130).

Soon after reunification there was a series of assaults on refugees seeking asylum in both East and West Germany. There was one small, but decisive difference though: In East Germany the attacks took place in broad daylight and sometimes with the open support of the local population:

> In Rostock-Lichtenhagen the young hooligans really did believe they were simply carrying out the wishes of a large number of spectators; that they were so doing was obvious from the applause and approval of the latter. There has been nothing comparable to this in the old *Länder*. Here, the arson attacks have so far been staged under cover of night, with a getaway car at the ready. (Krell et al., 1996: 158)

This pattern had not changed radically ten years after the fall of the Wall. In the new federal state it is commonplace that

> right-wing youth express their inclinations openly. They walk around dressed in heavy boots, black jackets and other symbols. They meet with almost no opposition. Right-wing extremists dominate the public spaces. In large parts of the country they control public opinion. Foreigners were driven out of Magdeburg during daylight. During the pogrom-like debaucheries in Hoyerswerda curious spectators watched. In West Germany it happens differently: Right-wing extremist hate crimes are mostly executed anonymously under cover of darkness, as in Solingen and Mölln. (Staud, 1999: 9)

The decisive difference then between East and West Germany is that in the one xenophobia and violent assaults on foreigners are part of everyday life while in the other they are regarded as intolerable and a radical break with decent and civilized behavior. What is so striking about East Germany today is that nobody really seems to care that these incidents are taken place. According to Andrea Böhm, it is official policy that

> foreigners in the new federal states at present can only live a 'confined life,' as the civil servant in charge of *Ausländerfragen im Brandenburg* expressed it. To live a "confined life" means to avoid public transport...particularly at night. Gas stations, youth clubs and restaurants are taboo. To live a "confined life" means no longer visiting a swimming pool with one's children. Owners of *Döhnerstores* [mobile shops or small restaurants serving Turkish meals] need good fire insurance and an escort at night. Most of them have reluctantly become used to this new reality. So has society. (Böhm, 1998: 1)

Böhm cites three characteristics of East German xenophobia. The first is its frequency and normality. "One also finds right-wing extremism in the West. But there it is not embedded in a right-wing extremist everyday culture. To be right wing, nationalist and hostile to foreigners is the norm for many young East Germans today."

The problem cannot be solved by the police and legal authorities alone.

> The latter do not take their task seriously. By means of raids one can prevent criminal offences, punishment can deter other perpetrators. But one cannot create a public spirit, tolerance and respect for the value of human life in this manner. For this one needs a democratic civil society. (Böhm, 1998: 1)

This introduces the third and decisive problem, namely the absence of a civic spirit or ethos regulating how conflicts are to be solved. "A democratic civil society competent to cope with conflicts, does not exist in East Germany" (Böhm, 1998: 1). Toralf Staud fully agrees with this analysis.

> A positive evaluation of civil rights, a conscious liberal disposition, a feeling of responsibility for the rights of others—all those things that evolved in West Germany in fifty years—are lacking in East Germany. This lack is something the state cannot compensate for, no matter how large a police force it sets up. (Staud, 1999: 9)

Staud's hypothesis is verified by statistics. The extent of right-wing extremist violence is significantly greater in the new federal states. Between 1.5 and 2 incidents per 100,000—the lowest figures recorded—were registered in Thüringen and Sachsen. The highest figures were more than 3.5 per 100,000 (Brandenburg and Mecklenburg-Vorpommern). The figure for Sachsen-Anhalt was 2.5 per 100,000. By contrast the highest figure for the old federal states was around 1 per 100,000 (Hamburg and Schleswig-Holstein). The lowest figures were under 0.5 per 100,000 (Hessen, Bayern, Rheinland Pfalz, Saarland). Nordrhein-Westphalen, Bremen and Niedersachsen were placed in between—somewhat over 0.5 per 100,000 (Gaschke, 1998: 3).

Since the number of foreigners or immigrants is significantly smaller in the new federal states, the risk that a foreigner will be assaulted and subject to right-wing violence is far higher than the above figures indicate. According to calculations by the West German criminologist Christian Pfeiffer the statistical probability "that a foreigner will be a victim of violent assault is 25 times higher in East Germany. The number of xenophobic deeds in relation to the population is four times higher. Xenophobia is twice as high, and not only today. This number was already mentioned in 1990. Neither unemployment, nor imported radicalism from the West can thus be used as an explanation. There must be internal reasons" (Kohlhoff, 1999).

The Theory

Traditionally, according to Minkenberg, two main approaches can be found in the literature on xenophobia and right-wing extremism: "One approach, which is associated with the work of Theodor Adorno, emphasizes the personality of supporters of the extreme right: in particular intolerance, rigid thinking, authoritarianism" (Minkenberg, 1994: 172). The working class in particular is regarded as harboring a potentially fascist and anti-Semitic mind-set (Adorno et al., 1964). The other approach builds upon Lipset's theory and interprets fascism as a kind of rebellion of the middle classes (Lipset, 1983). Here the focus is upon factors like status polarization, marginality, or deprivation and protest both against "capitalism and socialism, big business and big unions" (cit. Minkenberg, 1994: 172).

There is a third approach which focuses less upon the specific causes of right-wing extremism and xenophobia than on those factors that might prevent this pathological phenomenon from growing out of control. Thus Scheuch and Klingemann assume that

> the potential for right-wing movements exists in all industrialized societies and should be understood as a "normal" pathological condition. In all fast-growing modernizing countries there will be some people or whole social groups that cannot cope with economic and cultural development in their society and that react to pressures of readjustment with rigidity or closed-mindedness. (Minkenberg, 1994: 172)

If this is indeed the case, the social sciences must reach beyond merely understanding why this phenomenon occurs, they must also try to find an answer to how society can cope with it and ensure that it does not get out of control. Everett Hughes suggests this control, or containment, approach in his classic essay "Good people and dirty work." He contends that the main problem for the social sciences in relation to what happened in Nazi Germany is not to explain the existence of racial hatred but rather to deal with the frightening fact that ordinary, civilized citizens consented to participating in a state initiated racist policy which moved from systematic ethnic and racial discrimination to physical extermination. "How could such dirty work be done among and, in a sense by, the millions of ordinary, civilized German people?" (Hughes, 1964: 24-25)

He points out that the "essential underlying sentiments on racial matters in Germany were not different in kind from those prevailing throughout the western world, especially the Anglo-Saxon countries" (Hughes, 1964: 26). Similar sentiments exist more or less secretly in all civilized countries and it takes very little to bring them out of hiding. "It would not take a very great turn of events to increase the number of such people, and to bring them to the surface" (Hughes, 1964: 34). The fact that most Western countries, despite the existence of similar racist views, were able during the period between the wars to contain them and effectively prevent them from influencing the public climate in any significant way can, according to Hughes, be explained primarily by the existence of a strong civic spirit, embedded in the ethical values and norms of the broad population but also expressed in the way in which political institutions function in practice. "It is a matter of checks and balances, what we might call the social and moral constitution of society" (Hughes, 1964: 35).

Hughes's thesis has been confirmed by Friedländer's recent detailed and frightening study on the way in which the anti-Semitic policies of the Nazi regime functioned in practice and how Germans responded to them (Friedländer, 1997). He demonstrates how most Germans quickly adapted themselves to the Nuremberg laws, how there were almost no protests when Jewish professionals were fired just because they were Jews, and how terrified some Aryan Germans were at the thought that there might be a drop of Jewish blood in their veins. Instead of a storm of protest or silent sabotage, Hitler's openly racist policies were greeted with acquiescence, passivity and pragmatic adaptation, precisely as Szilard had predicted when he shared living quarters with German academic colleagues from the Kaiser Wilhelm Institute in Berlin in the early nineteen-thirties. These colleagues were far from being fanatical anti-Semites, they simply cared much more about their personal careers than about any injustices that might be done to their colleagues. Contrary to Goldhagen's thesis that all Germans somehow shared Hitler's most fanatical views about the Jews (Goldhagen, 1996) Friedländer's book suggests a far simpler reason—German society had no moral backbone, or at least not one strong enough to resist the onslaught of an openly immoral policy.

The most important conclusion to be drawn from Nazi Germany is that right-wing extremism can be caused by anything from an unhappy childhood to frustrated career ambitions, a lack of belief in the future, or bad role models. It would be utopian to believe that a modern society could eliminate all possible causes of racist feelings and world-views. The main task of the social sciences is to identify those factors that normally inhibit racism from becoming a strong power in society.

Hughes's approach, according to Hagan et al., is very close to modern control theory. "This reformulation parries the question commonly asked in psychologically oriented theories of crime and deviance, 'Why do they do it?' with the question provocatively posed by modern control theory: 'How is it that more of us do not get involved?'"(Hagan et al., 1995: 1031). According to the psychotherapist Ute Benz, "the young notice when the grownups themselves damage the fundamental democratic substance" (Böhm, 1998: 1). This happens both at home, where "those bloody foreigners who are stealing our jobs" are railed at, but also and in particular in contact with schools and public authorities which often demonstrate a shocking passivity:

> The teacher tolerates the swastikas on his pupils' leather jackets, because he does not want to get into an argument. The social worker listens to the "Turks get out" songs in the youth club because she doesn't want to quarrel with "her youth." The mayor does not order anti-Semitic graffiti to be removed because "that is not his business." All three have in common that they can identify on at least one point with the youth: they are furious about the foreigners. It is not right-wing extremism but hostility towards foreigners that has the support of the majority in the new federal states. This majority already existed in the GDR. Today it runs through the adherents of the CDU, the SPD, the PDS and the Greens. (Böhm, 1998: 38)

Youth with no Future

German right-wing extremism is often explained as a basically socioeconomic phenomenon. With the high unemployment rate (sometimes in combination with unimaginative infrastructure) leaving little hope for the future, the neo-Nazis offer a touch of adventure to underprivileged youths facing a dull, predictable future. Thus Susanne Gaschke sees the right-wing street terror in the small industrial town of Eberswalde north of Berlin as understandable in a situation in which "there are 15,000 Plattenbau [prefabricated apartments] with all their problems—25 percent unemployment and a violent architecture." Attacking foreigners because of the color of their skin is seen as a more or less rational response, a protest against the desperate situation in which East German youth feel they have been placed since reunification.

The concept of a correlation between underprivileged groups and authoritarian political views and movements is not new, such a correlation is emphasizcd by both Adorno and by Lipset, although their explanations are somewhat different. Recent studies in Germany confirm its existence. According to Schubert,

> the influence of education and family background is ... noticeable; young people with higher education (college and college preparatory high school) have a more positive view of foreigners than their less educated contemporaries. This holds true for young people whose parents have college degrees. (Schubert, 1997: 146)

A study recently completed in Bielefeld confirms this general pattern:

> As in many other studies on right-wing extremism, the data from Bielefeld confirms the correlation between low educational level and low educational and vocational aspirations on the one hand and xenophobic, right-wing extremist views on the other. The correlation is as a rule somewhat stronger than that between social background and xenophobia/right-wing extremism, but to a large degree follow the same pattern. (Hopf, 1994: 203)

These links can be interpreted in many different ways. One is that higher education brings greater knowledge, which might contribute to the elimination of prejudice against foreigners and minorities. Another is that higher education removes the individual from environments in which newly arrived immigrants are most likely to congregate, and a third is that higher education protects the individual from having to compete with immigrants for jobs or social welfare. Turning this logic around, one would expect underprivileged groups to be over represented among right-wing factions everywhere, not only in East or West Germany. This assumption is confirmed in literature such as Helmut Willems's seminal work, *Fremdenfeindliche Gewalt: Einstellungen, Täter, Konflikteskalation*. Willems and those who have worked in this tradition (Björgo, 1993; Weaver, 1995; Bergmann, 1997) have identified a scale of young right-wing radical criminals. They include hangers-on who are not particularly xenophobic but participate largely because they enjoy the company; criminal thugs who are also not strongly xenophobic but need a way to compensate for previous failures and to increase their self-esteem; xenophobic types who feel they are suffering systematic disadvantages because of the presence of foreigners and therefore want them out; and politically motivated youth with a strong ideological commitment to the neo-Nazi worldview.

The hangers-on rarely take the initiative in assaults on foreigners but allow themselves to be drawn into xenophobic group activities, mainly because they are afraid of being thrown out of the group. Björgo (1993) has arrived at similar conclusions in his studies on right-wing extremists in Scandinavia. There the criminal thugs are as a rule somewhat older and have had a series of negative experiences such as violence and alcohol in the family, dropping out of school, and a long criminal career. These thugs are "action oriented, aggressive, and inclined to violence." The violence is diffuse and is "by no means directed solely against 'foreigners'; it is aimed at any kind of victims—mostly people who rank as weak, or are perceived as such," which suggests that their xenophobia derives from a need to "compensate for experiences of failure and to firm up the individual's own identity" (Krell et al., 1996: 155).

Although the personal motives might be different, there are some common features that serve to create the bond that unites them and makes them perpetrate their ugly activities:

> These youths are rootless and disoriented...they have low self-esteem and are extremely insecure about economic and social competition. Rightist scenes and cliques provide them with adventure, acceptance, direction, and security. Through special clothes, hairstyles, symbols, and slogans, these youth find empowerment in the group's identity. Xenophobic violence, usually accompanied by heavy drinking, provides excitement in an otherwise tedious daily life. In the world of many offenders, they are *Geil auf Gewalt*, or "turned on by violence," and engage in such violence "just for the fun of it." (Weaver, 1995: 146)

Willems's theory is by and large confirmed by statistical investigations in Germany which prove, not unexpectedly, that there is a strong over representation of young people, men and the more poorly educated. Bergmann cites a study done by the German Ministry of the Interior which reached the following conclusion:

> According to an analysis of 758 convictions of participants in right-wing extremist acts of violence since 1991, 78 percent of the offenders were between 14 and 20 years old,

only three percent were over 30 and only one percent were women. In an evaluation of the education and career level of offenders, most were found to have little education, that is 78 percent attended *Hauptschule*...10 percent attended *Realschule*...and half of them were still in school or job training; approximately 29 percent had not completed any vocational training whatsoever or had quit such a program at least once. (Bergmann, 1997: 32)

According to Krell et al. a significant proportion of right-wing offenders had earlier been registered by the authorities as deviants or criminals. "Previous police records for non-political offences exist for 47 percent of them, rising to 63 percent for those over 25 years of age" (Krell et al., 1996: 155). Somewhat surprisingly though, they find that unemployment is not one of the factors that distinguish this group from other youth groups.

In their own analysis of violent right-wing offenders between 1991 and 1994, the *Verfassungsschutz* [a section of the police that controls groups and individuals who are suspected of using illegal means to change the West German constitution] concludes that 22 percent were unemployed, but that this was basically a result of the age structure of the group, many of whom were in the gray zone between leaving school and finding a job. (Krell et al., 1996: 167)

This does not support the common belief, expressed in most mass media analyses, that the extent and virulence of right-wing extremism is "understandable" because of the high unemployment rate and feelings of insecurity about an uncertain future. On the contrary, Böhm emphasizes that many of the violent offenders have work or are in job training (Böhm, 1998: 1). When it comes to membership of right-wing organizations, it is interesting that the leader of the NPD, Hans Günter Eisenecker—a lawyer from Hamburg who moved to East Germany in 1992—in a conversation with a journalist from *Die Zeit* complains that "among members of the NPD there are almost no unemployed," and that "most of them therefore have to little time to campaign for the party" (Staud, 1998: 3).

This sounds very strange and does not at all fit the "obvious" truth that right-wing extremism in East Germany is primarily an effect of higher unemployment rates. It becomes even stranger, when we look at how youth in East Germany actually see the future. Here again we have become used to the "obvious" truth that they regard it as hopeless. However, investigations into their expectations indicate that they look upon the future with a high degree of optimism. This can be seen in Table 8.1.

Table 8.1
How East German Youths Rate the Possibility of Realizing Their Ambitions
Do you believe your career ambitions are feasible (percentages)?

	Yes, there is a strong possibility	Yes, but with difficulty	Not now, perhaps later	No chance ever
All	46.6	39.0	12.3	2.1
Pupils	28.4	57.7	10.0	4.0
Trainees	49.1	34.2	14.1	2.7
Students	41.7	45.0	11.4	1.9
Blue Collar	46.3	33.6	17.6	2.6
White Collar	58.3	33.9	7.5	0.4
Self-employed	57.5	34.4	8.1	0.0
Unemployed	23.8	48.7	20.1	7.5
16 – 19	39.1	45.0	12.3	3.5
20 – 24	51.2	35.8	11.5	1.5
25 – 29	47.0	38.3	12.9	1.8
Men	49.1	36.8	12.5	1.6
Women	41.9	43.4	11.6	3.1

Source: Beyer, 1996: 31

Almost all categories of youth rate the expectation of finding a job within their chosen area as very high. Even among the unemployed, not even ten percent see the future as hopeless. Women are almost twice as pessimistic as men with 3.1 percent of them viewing the future as hopeless, compared with 1.6 percent of the men. Nevertheless, 99 percent of all right-wing extremist crimes are committed by men.

Beyer's concludes that the study totally rebuts the media image of East Germans youths as anxious and pessimistic. On the contrary, they

> present themselves as a generation with great optimism and as oriented towards the future. In spite of many problems that the transformation brought for most young East Germans and their families, they have more self-esteem and are convinced that they will be able to realize their life goals better than they could have under the GDR's socialist system. They do not see any insurmountable barriers to coping with the new freedoms, taking the initiative, and using the opportunity to take their occupations and careers in their own hands. This strong feeling of self-esteem is expressed in many ways and fits into what Elisabeth Noelle Neumann calls the "fundamental order of the feeling of reunification which expresses joy in spite of the fact that the media picture gives a negative impression." (Beyer, 1996: 31)

We thus reach the surprising conclusion that mass unemployment is perhaps not the large and looming social problem in East Germany that is often taken for granted. What we tend to forget is that East Germany has gone through tremendous socioeconomic changes and that most East Germans have adapted surprisingly fast to the new system. If their parents have coped reasonably well with the enormous uncertainty why should the youth not expect to cope even better? Again, the figures tell the story of the enormity of the changes and the remarkable degree of adaptability of an East German population that was generally seen as lacking initiative:

> Half a year after accession, one-fifth of the workers (21 percent) had moved to a new position, partly by commuting westward (4 percent); one-sixth (16 percent) worked reduced hours; and the remainder were either unemployed (8 percent) or had retired prematurely (10 percent). For virtually everyone, unification disbanded work collectives, upset comfortable routines, and severed social ties. (Jarauch, 1994: 195)

The growing self-esteem among East Germans that has been noticeable since the mid-nineteen-nineties (*Der Spiegel*, 1995) should be seen against this background. They themselves were probably surprised at how well they managed the difficult transition and this—probably combined with a sense of the much greater economic leeway offered by rapidly rising incomes for all categories, employed or not—made them more aggressively assertive. Although optimistic, they were not necessarily satisfied. The system to which they had adapted was very far from their image of an ideal society. The degree of identification with the underlying values and priorities of the Federal Republic of Germany thus seems to have declined rather than increased over the years. "Eight years after unification...17 percent of the East Germans feel like federal citizens, while almost two-thirds cannot identify with the Federal republic" (Böhm, 1998: 1).

This hardly justifies the assumption that right-wing extremism is mainly a socioeconomic problem. On the contrary, comparative studies of the authoritarian personality, xenophobia and aggression indicate that authoritarian attitudes might very well go hand in hand with a high degree of confidence about the future. One might be authoritarian, nationalistic and xenophobic for quite other reasons than having had a problematic childhood, a criminal career, or being unemployed. But in order to grasp these other reasons, we have to move beyond the "deviance" paradigm that has dominated so much of the contemporary approach to the phenomenon of youthful xenophobia and right-wing extremism, particularly in the Scandinavian countries.

Table 8.2
Authoritarian Attitudes among East and West German Youth (14-20 years)

	Men		Women	
	West	East	West	East
authoritarian upbringing	2.1	2.3	2.2	2.2
xenophobia	2.4	2.7	2.3	2.4
authoritarianism	2.5	2.8	2.5	2.8
conventionalism	2.5	2.8	2.4	2.5
aggression	3.0	3.5	2.8	3.3
submissiveness	2.1	2.2	2.1	2.2

Source: Rippl and Seipel 1998: 273

Rippl and Spiegel tested the theory about the authoritarian personality on data collected in the early 1990s among school youths
between 14-20 years old. Taking into account demographic differences in terms of types of school and regions, they arrived at the
following results.

Some of the conclusions we can draw from the table are that the
level of authoritarianism and aggression is markedly higher among
both male and female youth in East Germany; that the higher degree
of xenophobia among East German youth is mainly a male phenomenon; that there is a clear tendency towards conventionalism,
particularly among young East German men, and that almost as many
West as East Germans experienced an authoritarian upbringing and
are submissive.

These data conflict with Hans-Joachim Maaz's assertion that methods of upbringing in East German families were significantly more
authoritarian than those in West Germany (Maaz, 1992). In a study
on pro- and antisocial motives among youths in East and West Germany Trommsdorff and Kornadt emphasize that the most important
difference seems to have been the role played by the state in the
upbringing of children and youth:

> The goal of child rearing was to achieve a socialist personality. The official educational
> programs were based on the assumption of a *tabula rasa* model of human
> development...according to which child rearing and education were considered a task of
> the state. Therefore, the family was largely deprived of its function of socializing the
> children. This was implemented by having infants enrolled in *Kinderkrippen* [the state
> controlled all day nurseries] as early as possible, usually on the second half of the first
> year. On average, about 80 percent of all infants were institutionalized in *Kinderkrippen*.
> (Trommsdorff and Kornadt, 1995: 40)

The marked differences in the levels of aggression of East and West German youths confirm, however, Hans-Joachim's thesis of the existence of a *Gefühlstau* (an emotionally blocked personality) among East German youths (and East Germans in general) because of the massive overkill of state-controlled socialization in relation to the role of the family. The fact that, at a very early age, their significant others were replaced by institutional representatives had the effect of making the upbringing of children in the GDR similar to that associated with the military:

> Any GDR citizen can, if we are to be honest, sing a song about how "discipline and order" were implemented. An atmosphere of drill to punctuality, cleanness and politeness ruled everywhere. To integrate and submit to the collective and to collective norms was always the supreme command and was implemented by a ruthless annihilation of individual peculiarities, possibilities and potentials. To sit still, to control oneself...to recognize the leadership of the adults without resistance and with gratitude, and practicing obedience were the foremost virtues and duties of the child. One can summarize the goal of state education in one point: To inhibit individuality and to destroy free will. This principle was ruthlessly implemented at all levels of state upbringing. (Maaz, 1992: 25)

This collectivist discipline and the subordination of the individual to the group started very early in the over institutionalized GDR where the main pedagogical principle from the very start was to teach the child that the individual is insignificant—what matters is the collective to which the individual must submit, learning not to "dance outside the rows" (Gruner, 1990: 9). An example of this—discovered by Christian Pfeiffer during his research into right-wing extremist violence in East Germany—was the strange ritual in East German *Kinderkrippen* of training infants to expose themselves publicly while sitting on chamber pots in rows at certain times of the day, as if to emphasize that even bodily needs can be shaped to fit the laws of collective life. Although this illustrates very graphically what Maaz and other East German intellectuals such as Christa Wolff were talking of in the early 1990s when they publicly condemned the disastrous effects of the official collectivist ideology upon human personality, the mood of the late 1990s appears not to have been very receptive to such an honest and self-critical reappraisal of the GDR. In East Germany today nobody seems to care about what the practice of socialism really meant.

The question of course is whether Pfeiffer's thesis—that these early patterns of child rearing can explain the present level of xenophobia and right-wing extremist violence in East Germany—is correct. At least one aspect of his explanation does seem plausible. One of the most significant differences between xenophobic youths in East and West Germany is that in East Germany violence is largely a group activity, they "hunt in packs," whereas the West German neo-Nazis who attack foreigners are inclined to be lone wolves. In 55 percent of the cases youths in Leipzig who had perpetrated violent acts had acted in groups, whereas in Stuttgart this was only the case in 22 percent of the cases. This does indeed suggest "how strong the impact of this 'group pressure' still is and that the collectivist rituals around disciplining the body which date from infancy do not disappear at once, in fact it is not very plausible that "the 'foul smell from the GDR' has already disappeared from the schools and the kindergartens" (Kohlhoff, 1999: 3).

Pfeiffer's thesis may indeed explain why youth violence in East Germany is, as a rule, perpetrated in groups, but it cannot explain the level of aggression. When East German skinheads attack, they attack to kill in the most brutal manner possible—as one of them expressed it, they like to hear the skull "crack" under their boots (Kramer, 1993). It also cannot explain the shocking absence of guilt or shame these perpetrators tend to exhibit in court; it is almost like seeing the Nuremburg Trials rolling across the screen once again—brutal criminals confessing or denying their crimes, but most of all rejecting any appeal from the court for signs of regret (Broder, 1994).

One explanation could of course be that we are dealing with criminals, persons with a history of deviancy dating back to childhood. They are mostly individuals from broken homes and failed schooling, the risk groups of any modern society, and for them politics is not the only motivation (this would explain why it is not only foreigners who are attacked but also the homeless and other vagrants). The problem with this explanation is that it does not address the problem of a general lack of empathy or the ability to identify with others among all categories of East German youth, regardless of family background and educational level. Although the goal in East German schools was to raise individuals with a "socialist personality"—which most educators in Western societies would associate with concern for the weak and vulnerable—data from Trommsforffs and Kornadt's brilliant study suggest that the youth generally have a less developed "social" self. This paradoxical conclusion has been arrived at independently by other researchers (Pollack, 1992; 1997; 1999) but nowhere as strikingly as in Trommsdorff's and Kornadt's study.

> Our findings revealed significantly less aggression inhibition in East German than in West German adolescents...East German females were more aggressive than West German females, East German males were more aggressive than West German males... East German youth showed significantly more aggressive reactions when frustrated than West German youth...we also found significant differences in aggression inhibition components. Results relating to emotional reactions inhibiting aggression showed that East German adolescents felt less shame and guilt than West German adolescents ... also, East German adolescents exhibited less inhibition of aggression than West German adolescents. (Trommsdorff and Kornadt, 1995: 47)

Independent measures of the degree of social versus antisocial tendencies also clearly indicated that East German youths were less altruistic than West German youths and that East German males in particular showed a lower degree of empathy (Trommsdorff and Kornadt, 1995: 47).

These results force us to rethink the content of the socialist socialization in the GDR. There was something in the pedagogical principles itself and particularly in the idea of a systematic collectivist child rearing controlled by the state that somehow undermined levels of empathy and thereby, indirectly, "normal" feelings of shame and guilt. Assuming that some level of empathy with other human beings is necessary in order to establish a degree of tolerance or at least to inhibit aggression against those who look different or appear unable to defend themselves, the absence of such empathy would indicate damage to the very substance of morality. At the same time we must ask ourselves the even more troubling question whether the socialist education in the GDR enforced by the state was so very different from the traditional upbringing of Germans—a tradition carried to its extreme during the Third Reich.

In this context it is interesting that Rytlewski (1989) emphasizes the curious coexistence of two political cultures in the GDR—the "staged public sphere based upon power," and a more traditional political culture, orienting itself towards attitudes and mindsets which existed during the *Kaiserreich* and National Socialism. What is strange is the degree of consensus that emerged between these two cultures:

> At the bottom of the acceptance by the majority of the [GDR] bureaucracy, with its total, political-social dominance lie...important sources of social and emotional history which have always been underestimated in investigations and evaluations of the social climate of the GDR. (Rytlewski, 1989:213; cit. Woderich, 1991b: 111)

One explanation of the paradox above is the "authoritarian state thinking and behavioral patterns which are rooted in the psyche" (Woderich, 1991a: 122). Another has to do with the very way in which the dominant communist/socialist political culture was presented, and in particular its strongly imaginary elements. What were the long-term effects upon the East German psyche of the fact that both parents and children were brought up in what Broder calls a "republic of simulators" (Broder, 1994) with respect to questions of empathy, feelings of shame and the inhibition of aggression? Pedagogical methods are one thing, but the school system never works in an historical and political vacuum. Which brings us back to the original question. What were the consequences of the GDR's lack of recognition of its own ties to Nazi Germany; the absence of the cultural and emotional "deNazification" of the society which, according to Hughes, is necessary to create the type of "moral constitution" that contains racist movements and keeps them from growing out of control?

Lack of Political Correctness or Lack of a Civic Ethos?

In the first years after reunification the wave of hatred and violence that swept over foreigners was not confined to Germany. Similar phenomena were observed in other countries, including Sweden and Norway—countries which prided themselves on their peaceful and tolerant populations. This coincidence obscured particular aspects of German history and the East German situation was more or less ignored when it was discovered that the phenomenon existed outside Germany as well. This probably explains why the most popular theory at the time (not surprisingly it was formulated by a Scandinavian) focused on politics. In the article "Terrorist Violence against Immigrants and Refugees in Scandinavia: Patterns and Motives" Björgo posits a new framework in which "a polarized political situation in which immigrants and immigrant politics are hotly debated" (Björgo, 1993: 43) becomes an autonomous and even predominant factor. In a follow-up article published in 1996 in the Scandinavian *Journal of Peace Research*, three German writers expand the model into a German context, emphasizing that

the causes of this violence lie—in addition to the specific individual and family context of the offenders – in overall social conditions and developments: the anomie following on the collapse of the former GDR; existing or impending modernization-induced losses in both parts of Germany; the dominance culture; general crisis of civilization; and problems related to masculinity. (Krell et al., 1996: 165)

With so many trends in the contemporary world going in the wrong direction simultaneously, one would think that virulent extremism and widespread xenophobia would present a potent danger to democracy everywhere, which is certainly not the case. The political system is still functioning satisfactorily, the moral constitution might be damaged, but it is still strong enough to keep developments under control in most countries in both Eastern and Western Europe. In the Federal Republic there was indeed a period in 1991 when the political élite and the authorities seemed to have lost control over the situation. The break down of communism combined with the very liberal asylum laws that are or were unique to West Germany, had led to an uncontrolled immigration to reunited Germany and politicians felt under pressure to do something to reassert state authority. This factor alone would hardly have evolved into an uncontrollable situation had it not been for two further factors—both of them unique to the situation in East Germany. Werner Bergmann describes them:

> Because of the extensive break down of police authority, especially in rural areas, and the reorganization of the judicial system, conditions served to encourage violent, right-wing extremist criminals because the risk of getting apprehended and convicted was relatively low. In addition the setting up of accommodation for asylum seekers in overwhelmed eastern communities led to local conflicts that seemed to legitimize the violent actions of young people against these homes. (Bergmann, 1997: 3)

The wave of right-wing extremist violence in both parts of Germany that resulted from this momentary loss of control soon came to an end though, mainly because a shocked public reacted immediately and demanded a clear political stand from the government and tough legal action against the offenders, and the results were soon visible. By late 1992,

> the opportunity structure had changed...since then the overwhelming majority of Germans and the public have expressed clear opposition to violence against foreigners. Bans on organizations, coordinated investigations, searches and seizures, countless criminal proceedings, and high sentences for xenophobic crimes have had a perceptible impact upon the right-wing scene. The number of serious acts of violence and other forms of extremist violations of law thus decreased in 1993-1994. (Bergmann, 1997: 33)

This general statement applies mainly to West Germany. In East Germany the intensified activities of the police force and legal authorities were transitory. They were not founded in a strong civic ethos so the main problem was not whether politicians and authorities demonstrated the necessary firmness and consistency, but whether there was a strong and living civic spirit which demanded that the authorities take responsibility. If the increasing use of force or harsh prison sentences are the only instruments which can keep xenophobia under control, society has a problem. It is one which must be focused upon and not be avoided as is often the case in Germany. The use of the Scandinavian formula is no doubt tempting, but it would be out of place in the German context. Clearly the problem cannot be reduced, as Krell suggests, to simply blaming the politicians. The German debate on issues of immigration and immigration control failed in two respects. The politicians did not distance themselves promptly enough or effectively enough from the violence and their debate on the issues of asylum failed to ameliorate hostility towards foreigners (Krell et al., 1996: 166).

The biggest problem with this analysis is that it suggests that political correctness rather than a strong civic ethos is the best way to keep racist feelings and movements under control. Although the theory is widely popular among intellectuals, it has nevertheless been disproved by the GDR itself. If ever there was a state that consistently used the principle of political correctness it was the GDR. Political correctness, as I understand it, means advocating a strategy of not talking about an unpopular subject in the hope that it will then simply disappear. This is how the GDR coped with the fact that Nazi Germany was a product of German political culture and psyche and that is also how they coped with the fact that xenophobia and neo-Nazism became increasingly popular in the final years of the GDR.

According to Farin and Seiden-Pielen "there was always a neo-Nazi and right-wing extremist potential in the GDR...but it was only the...agony of GDR-society...in the eighties that made it virulent, active and aggressive" (Farin and Seiden-Pielen, 1992: 73). Until 1986 the GDR was indeed able to prevent it from asserting itself, but with the rapid decline of belief in the Marxist utopia, East German youths, accustomed to thinking in simple slogans and to seeing themselves marching together as victors of history, started looking for new ideas. In 1987 the Stasis observed a growing interest in National Socialist literature and recordings of speeches by Nazi leaders became increasingly popular, as did the celebration of Hitler's birthday. Anti-Semitic and National Socialist music and computer games began to be imported from the West. In 1988 there were approximately 1,000 registered "Faschos" and "Skinheads." In that year four youths from Halle were "brought to court for having brutally beaten a man from Mozambique." In their defense they said that "they only wanted to 'smack a nigger'" (Farin and Seiden-Pielen, 1992: 74).

In 1989 things deteriorated further and there were several reports of schools celebrating Hitler's centenary. As the GDR was about to celebrate its own 40th anniversary in October and did not want to have any rival celebrations, particularly not of that kind, it was decided that radical action must be taken. Although fascism had officially been rooted out forty years before, the order was given to root it out again. The security forces did what they could to implement the orders and by the end of October more then 400 people had been arrested. It became obvious that the problem could not be solved by repression so the line was changed to avoid confronting it:

> they are only hooligans, and in these cases there is no political background, no ideology, no racist motives, the fact that it was an African who was beaten is pure coincidence. They were drunk and he happened to run by and stare provocatively at them. In the courts, too, political motives were no longer mentioned, even when the perpetrators expanded upon their right-wing extremist worldview during the trial. (Farin and Seidel-Pielen, 1992: 84)

Thus ended the GDR's experiment with the politically correct approach to rooting out fascism. Having first decided not to talk about the past, they ended up not wanting to talk about the present either. The problem with many analyses of right-wing extremism in Germany—and that of Krell et al. is far from the worst—is that they are depressingly alike in that they share the same utopian view of reality that produced the politically correct syndrome reported by Farin and Seidel-Pielen. This is also why they ultimately chose to retreat from their own observations about the clear difference between right-wing extremist assaults in East and West Germany. After noting the difference, which they innocently refer to as a difference in "political culture" (no mention of a ghost named Hitler here), they hasten to minimize it or explain it away. Thus they tell us, as if they knew, that because there were no ordinary citizens present to applaud attacks on foreigners in broad daylight in West Germany, no conclusions can be drawn about the difference in civic ethos between the two parts of Germany. In fact the importance of this civic ethos is not even mentioned, because Krell et al. have already decided that what is needed is political correctness. "It doesn't mean that violence in the West has not been greeted with a silent applause. But until now it [the applause] has remained secret. It has not dared to express itself openly" (Krell et. al., 1996: 158).

For them the main role of democracy is to ensure that some thoughts are never uttered. We have to pretend that they do not exist, and that will solve the problem once and for all. Which suggests that the élites of the GDR might not be the only ones to have missed the most important lesson to be drawn from Nazi Germany.

The National Heritage and Xenophobia

The West German intelligentsia have often been excessively and unjustly critical about the way in which the Federal Republic coped with its past despite the fact that relative to other nations deeply involved in war crimes, it has been relatively willing to discuss and admit its moral responsibility for what happened in the Third Reich (Bergmann, 1995; Buruma, 1996). One of the effects of this relative openness has been a strong tendency among political leaders (Herf, 1997) and intellectuals (Mommsen, 1990) to distance themselves from large chunks of German history. What should be emphasized is that this self-critical endeavor does not only concern the Hitler years and the way in which different groups of Germans behaved during that period (Maier, 1988; Baldwin, 1990) it also aims to identify those aspects of German history and culture that made Hitler possible.

Because this history *de facto* led to a Hitler, there is precious little left on which to build up a national identity. Even the world "national" almost became taboo in German public debate because of its association with "National Socialism" (Mitscherlich and Runge, 1993; Bubis and Schäuble, 1996). In this context it is important to emphasize that "in the West there was public debate about the role played by patriotism and obedience during the Nazi era. The West German anti-authoritarian student movement of the late 1950s and the early 1970s focused very strongly on this aspect" (Rippl and Boehnke, 1995: 67). By contrast, there was no critical debate about that aspect of the past in the GDR, the only questions addressed were ideological ones of antifacism.

One of the results of this greater openness was that historians mercilessly undermined one national myth after another. One of the most important works in this context was a study in the early 1960s by Fritz Fischer on the military build-up under the last Kaiser (Fischer, 1986). In it Fischer documents the detailed plans of the German General Staff for conquering large parts of Europe in pursuit of their goal to become the unrivalled continental power. If this is so, it was not, as is often claimed, the Treaty of Versailles that was the catalyst for the historical dynamic that ended in the rise and fall of the Third Reich, but Germany's own plans for imperialist expansion. In that case the Germans must ask themselves what it was in their own history that made a Hitler possible. As Herf demonstrates brilliantly in his book on "Divided Memory," this was precisely the problem that concerned Adenauer, the first Chancellor of the Bonn Republic, when he speculated about what had gone wrong and what should be done. Adenauer's analysis, as presented by Herf, needs, however, to be backed up with extensive sociological documentation. The GDR and the way in which East Germans coped with "inner unification" certainly add credibility to Adenauer's insight into the German mind.

Among ordinary West Germans, national pride was surprisingly feeble compared with that in other West European nations (Scheuch, 1991). If there is a German patriotism it is not founded on the past but on a strong belief in the future based upon the visible progress made after the war—the strong economy (symbolized by the Deutschmark), and what Habermas calls *Verfassungspatriotismus* (the belief in a stable and constitutional democracy supported by a strong civic ethos). Almond and Verba in their comparison note the presence of a strong "civic culture" in West Germany, but not in East Germany (Minkenberg, 1994).

The GDR's attitude to nationalism was more ambiguous. Basically its interpretation of German history was purely socioeconomic. There were two opposing histories in Germany—that of the capitalists and the big landowners who were responsible for everything that was bad and reactionary (including Hitler), and that of the common people, the workers and farmers (and later also the professionals). This simple and soothing interpretation was the essence of the "theory of fascism" (Craig, 1991) and it had two consequences. Not only did the East Germans not have to ask themselves awkward questions about the Nazi past, they did not have to ask themselves what had made a Hitler possible in the first place and, in particular, they did not have to look more closely into cultural traditions and mindsets.

The paradox was thus that although the GDR saw itself as a radical break with the Nazi past, the very belief that there had been such a break allowed the traditional German character and culture, of which the Third Reich was the logical conclusion, to continue after the Nazi defeat. The GDR never made that cultural break because it thought it was irrelevant and because it knew better. The result was that typically German cultural traits coexisted with the militaristic, nationalistic and authoritarian xenophobic tradition which Hitler did not invent but simply carried to its extreme and, whereas in West Germany these traits more or less died out during the half century after the end of the Second World War, in East Germany they survived to a greater or lesser degree.

Schubert points out that "the East German political culture retained without doubt certain Prussian elements" and this is one of the reasons why the two political cultures that Rytlewski talked of could so easily coexist. "Authoritarian and antidemocratic patterns" such as "underclass authoritarianism and subaltern-petty bourgeois political and cultural traits (*Untertanengeist*)" could "easily be integrated into Stalinist and later bureaucratic socialism and thus linked to Prussia's traditional statism and paternalism." This in turn explains the return of these repressed cultural traditions after reunification.

> Tough behavioral patterns, many of them similar to right-wing authoritarianism, existed long before the dissolution of East Germany. In fact, the socialist state and society played a considerable role in (re)producing them, as evidenced by the existence of a right-wing youth scene, as well as suppressed xenophobia and nationalism in the private opinions of East Germans before unification. (Schubert, 1997: 152-3)

Weaver points out that:

> Public opinion data gathered on youth attitudes by GDR survey organizations in the summer of 1990 show that East German youth were particularly susceptible to exaggerated feelings of national identity months before unification and the first arrival of asylum seekers in eastern Germany. (Weaver, 1995: 151)

Ten years later, East German skinheads gladly allow themselves to be photographed by national magazines, holding the baseball bats they carry to crack open the skulls of foreigners they have hunted down. A typical example is Berndt, eighteen years old and an industrial mechanic. He explains to the journalist from *Die Zeit*. "I am right wing. That is national pride, to support one's country and fight its enemies. And I'll hammer the face of those who dare to dare to raise their voice" (Böhm, 1998: 1).

Weaver believes that the collapse of the GDR precipitated the right-wing movements because their members had lost their "honored role in society." Much of the youth infrastructure had been closed.

> Gyms, movie houses, and libraries, once founded and administered by the state have been drastically reduced because of budget cuts. Youth discothèques, camping trips, free vacations and athletic clubs have also been discontinued. The Free German Youth has been disbanded. (Weaver, 1995: 147)

> The ideological remnants of fascism still present in people's minds in the GDR were reinforced by the SED's brand of socialism. In its attempt to fortify the cultural identity of the GDR, the regime turned to promoting the country's Prussian heritage and values: hierarchical order, duty, discipline, hard work and cleanliness. Socialism, as practiced by the SED, strove for social uniformity and homogeneity. The "conflict-free" society of which the GDR boasted became a source of great pride: East German society was one in which every expression of individualism, pluralism and personal eccentricity was suppressed by social conformity. Foreigners, by virtue of their different skin colors, languages, and cultural traditions, disturbed the homogeneity and familiarity of the GDR's ordered society. If ever there was fertile ground for the resurgence of fascist thought, it was in the totalitarian society of the GDR. (Weaver, 1995: 152)

Böhm also emphasizes the importance of the "feeling of a homogenous *Volkcommunity* that it [GDR] mediated" (Böhm, 1998: 1). This experience of a strongly homogenous community was a direct heritage from Nazi Germany, and it never died out in the GDR, for the simple reason that the GDR never seriously asked itself questions about the obvious parallels between the nationalist utopia of a homogenous *Volk* and the Marxist utopia of a classless society (Greenfeld, 1992). These victors of history were more interested in abolishing capitalism than in finding a way to contain xenophobia, believing that by striving for a well-ordered and homogenous society they would automatically solve the problem. It is interesting that this theory of how to get rid of xenophobia was originally invented by an intellectual with a Jewish background, and the fact that some of the GDR's most dedicated citizens happened to be Jews should probably be seen in this context.

Today these people are in deep confusion, as the very foundation of their beliefs crumbles under them. "The shock of the collapse of the government in the Soviet Union as well as in the DDR has left many ideologically oriented Marxists personally and psychologically adrift" (Cohn, 1994: 78). Precisely because they did not want to recognize that there is no utopian solution to xenophobia or anti-Semitism but that these are diseases that Jews and other vulnerable minorities have to live with, they still cling to their Marxist illusions, trying to save what cannot be saved. Most of them are so occupied with saving their own careers and legitimizing their pasts that they have not even noticed the explosive rise of a xenophobic youth culture in the former GDR, nor have they begun to reflect upon the obvious similarities between what these youths are seeking and what the GDR provided.

Neo-Nazi intellectuals seem to be more far sighted in this respect, as they seek to establish their future political alliances in and outside East Germany. Hans-Günther Eisener, the chairman of NPD, is optimistic about the future precisely because of the type of Germans the Marxist utopia produced, or rather, preserved. "What is particularly important for East Germans is order, diligence, cleanliness. Values like liberty and tolerance hardly exist in their consciousness. The citizens still remember a society, where the collective meant more then the individual."

The journalist who interviewed Eisener notes that

> NPD consciously praises GDR's *soziale Errungenschaften*. In many respects NPD is not far from PDS when it demands a constitutional right to an apartment and promises that under its leadership apartments will never be object of capitalist speculation again. "Our demands for *Volkseigentum* regularly evoke enthusiasm," the NPD leader says. He is happy that after the war there was no reeducation, no "indoctrination." "The people are not yet estranged from their natural life interests." They are still far enough away from the capitalist system to be "able to judge it." Eisener has invited former functionaries of the GDR to enter the NPD. Proudly he speaks of contacts with the communist list in PDS, with China and North Korea – both nationalist and anticapitalist states. (Staud, 1998: 3)

This strong sense of membership of a homogenous *Volkgemeinschaft* that Böhm talks of was hardly a coincidence. It should be seen in the context of the longing for order, subordination to the collective, anti-capitalism and other strongly traditionalist, antimodern values that seem to exist in the East German population and out of which the widespread xenophobia and right-wing extremism has emerged. The much propagated theory of a radical break with fascism was one of many myths. In order to contain the xenophobia, it is important to stop pretending and to face the truth, however inconvenient that might be. If the GDR had an "historic mission" it was not to break with that part of German history that made Hitler possible, but to conserve the "cultural datedness" of the German nation upon which Hitler rose to power and then perfected. Both Marxism and Nazism are basically romantic utopias. What a modern society needs is a strong civic ethos, only then can it prevent different varieties of utopian totalitarianism from getting out of control.

9

When the World was Simple:
GDR Nostalgia—A Return to Innocence

1945 and 1989

How do East Germans view the past? Rosemarie Beier, perusing the comments written in guest books at an exhibition in East Berlin in 1993, titled "*Lebensstationen in Deutschland*," (Landmarks in Germany) noticed a conspicuous absence of self-critical reflections on life in the GDR. Almost all the comments expressed

> complaints about lost worlds and a movement backwards. There is an almost total absence of the sober, critical view of conditions as they really were that is sought by contemporary social thinkers ... it is terrifying that only a few visitors to the exhibition from the former GDR saw the end of their state as an opportunity for personal development. There is a striking discrepancy between the *Vergangenheitsaufarbeitung* [coming to grips with the past] sought in cultural journals and in books and the tasks that contributors to the guest books felt needed to be dealt with ... in the guest books there is a predominance of moods and opinions expressing anger over (assumed or actual) injustices. (Beier, 1995: 12-13)

Von Plato points to clear parallels between the way in which the transition from a totalitarian dictatorship to a democracy was experienced in 1945 and how it was experienced in 1989. Although West Germans today have largely forgotten it, their pitiful attempts to idealize Nazi Germany and emphasize their lack of moral responsibility for its crimes, their behavior is now being echoed by the East Germans. "Today one can more or less hear in the GDR similar statements to those that were heard after 1945: 'Not everything was bad,' 'I only did my duty.'...'My idealism was misused,' 'I don't have anything to blame myself for since I couldn't change anything anyhow'" (von Plato, 1995: 14).

171

One also hears complaints similar to those expressed after 1945 of having suffered enough. Then it was the war, the bombings, the dead soldiers and the starving civilians—as if people had not participated in bringing these miseries upon themselves—today the main claim for victim status is the accumulated costs of having lived in the wrong Germany and an eagerness to compensate for having lost opportunities to share in its consumer paradise: "We have suffered enough, while the West Germans were doing well." Or "We lost the war three times, first against the Allies, then because of the Soviet system and the Reparations in the time of the occupation and the GDR, and today we lose for a third time" (von Plato, 1995: 14-15).

GDR nostalgia is of course caused by many other things as well—there are elements of cultural alienation from a structure in which people do not feel at home, expressed in a lack of identification with the West German system; there are elements of a strong longing for a harmonious and well-ordered society firmly led from above (*Volksgemeinschaft*—a united national community) as expressed in the xenophobia and right-wing extremism; there are also worries among the educated middle classes about careers to be saved and personal choices to be legitimized. What lies at the root of GDR nostalgia, though, is something else—an attempt to return to that blissful state of moral innocence where everything seemed clear, where there were a few simple principles to hold on to, where one had no doubts about oneself and one's deeds, where everything one did was perfectly right, merely because others were doing the same or just doing what they were told.

Although it is a self-deceptive dream—the world is far too complex to fit into simple moral principles and people are expected to respond as morally responsible citizens—many East Germans are simply overwhelmed by the amount of moral work required of them and react by withdrawing into the closed and simple world of yesterday. "Accusations against former GDR-citizens in terms of how they behaved in a dictatorship, of collusion with the system, excessive adaptation or collaboration with the powerful" has the effect of "deepening the specific East German identity" (Fritze, 1995a: 58). The East Germans are "irritated" by these accusations which to them only reveal how little the West Germans understand what it means to live under a dictatorship (Fritze, 1995b). The problem is of course that the West Germans understand only too well, having groped with exactly these moral issues for the past fifty years.

A Good Idea Badly Executed

When, in 1948, the West German Allenbach Institute "asked West Germans to give their honest opinions about National Socialism, 58 percent agreed...that National Socialism was a fine idea in itself and that the problem was that the ideals had been distorted in practice"(Kupferberg, 1999: 166). This surprising affirmation among a majority of belief in the Nazi ideals was observed in a number of follow-up studies and it only began to decline in the mid-nineteen-fifties, ten years after the defeat of Nazi Germany (Scheuch, 1991). In 1995, *Der Spiegel* asked East Germans a similar question. An overwhelming majority, 79 percent, agreed with the statement "the idea of socialism is good, but the politicians were unable to realize it" (*Der Spiegel*, 1995a: 46). That socialism is indeed a much more popular idea in East Germany than in West Germany is indicated by the following table below.

There is a 30 to 39 percent difference in attitude between the two population. In West Germany it represents a minority view (although a substantial minority), in East Germany an overwhelming majority still believes in socialist ideals. This is very interesting. The question is how these figures are to be interpreted. If such a huge majority really believe that socialism is such a fine idea and that the only problem was the way in which it was put into practice (presumably by incompetent politicians), why did they not insist upon trying again? Why was there such massive pressure among the East German population for unification? And if they really believe that socialism is such a fine idea, why do they not vote in greater numbers for the PDS, which attracts only about 20 percent of the popular vote rather than the 70 percent that might have been expected.

This suggests that rather than expressing an ideological preference, the strong affirmation of socialism should be seen as an attempt by East Germans to cope with the fact that they collaborated

Table 9.1
Attitudes to the Socialist Idea in the New Federal States (NFS) and the Old Federal States (OFS)   (percentages)

		1991	1992	1994	1995
Socialism is a good idea that has	NFS	69	68	78	72
been badly executed	OFS	36	39	39	42

Source: Koch, 1998: 50

with an immoral system twice and should be ashamed of it, but are not. It is their way of defending themselves and avoiding unpleasant truths about themselves that might be raised in encounters with West Germans if and when the latter start asking unwelcome questions about moral collaboration with or adaptation to a totalitarian system. By contrast, the West German figure probably expresses a continuing ideological preference. While there are obvious similarities between National Socialism and Marxist socialism—both are totalitarian and utopian—social democracy, the type of socialism found in West Germany, is based upon a strong commitment to democracy and there is no shame in continuing to support it.

Those who supported the socialism of East Germany, however, cannot allow themselves the same luxury. The failure of (Marxist) socialism has left them feeling. A case in point is that of Gudrun (born in 1945) who became a committed Marxist almost by mistake. In August 1961, the night the borders were sealed and the building of the Wall began, she and her family were visiting friends in West Berlin. Gudrun would most certainly have preferred to stay in West Berlin, but her father decided otherwise. In the beginning of her story, told in December 1994, she admits that she (then sixteen years old) resisted the thought of returning to East Berlin. A year later she had changed her outlook completely and had become a glowing socialist, a *Rote Socke* (Red Sock—a derogatory term for members of the SED, the ruling party in the GDR), the only one in the family who identified with the GDR's socialist ideals.

She explains this conversion as a sudden love for the exploited. "What convinced me...was the idea as such, the social justice...and I actually expected the socialist idea, which I see today as utopian, to be feasible." At the end of the interview she reiterates her current viewpoint: "I sometimes wish...that what you learned in school, about Marx, crises, capitalism, everything, you could see it verified by events. I believe that capitalism in its current form will not sustain itself forever. But I also see that socialism, as it was conceived, was not possible, because the people are not like that. It doesn't work" (Aalborg-Interview).

Although Gudrun is skeptical now about the possibility of the practical realization of the socialist ideal, what is more important for her at present is not the ideological issue but the fact that she adopted the idea mainly for opportunistic reasons. In order not to risk destroying her own professional career chances in the GDR, she sided with the Marxist state against her own family. As Wolfgang Engler points out, this was far from unusual in the GDR, and often resulted in a particular kind of self-deception where the individual persuaded himself or herself that he or she was acting from conviction rather than opportunism. In this way people could protect themselves from an awareness of the immorality of their actions.

> If one makes an inner adaptation out of an external one [one has to] take into account conflicts, discords and separations, in order to protect one's personal capital from devaluing. And this often happened. Children, working in "sensitive" areas broke with their parents, who were not prepared to destroy their personal relationships with the western world; parents disowned their children, who had lost all hope and had determined to emigrate or escape; married couples and friends became estranged for this and similar reasons. (Engler, 1992: 30)

Today, many people who claim to have acted out of idealistic rather than opportunistic motives find themselves having to defend a position that is obviously immoral. What are they going to say to their parents, children, ex-husbands or ex-wives, or friends they deserted for selfish reasons while deceiving themselves that they did so for the sake of the poor and exploited? Gudrun's case, far from being unique, represents the tip of a moral iceberg that shatters the peace of mind of millions like her. One did not have to be an "idealist" or a "believer" to have been asked at least occasionally to betray, if not one's relatives or friends, then at least oneself and one's own integrity. One example was the *Jugend-Weihe* ritual (a coming of age ritual which has largely replaced the religious confirmation ceremony in East Germany) in which more than 90 percent of young East Germans participated, where the climax was the *Löbnis*, the public oath to remain loyal to the ideal of socialism (and attachment to the GDR). The figure would hardly have been so high, had parents not actively encouraged their children to participate, it was an open secret that many young people only pretended to believe in the ideal. Havel maintains that participation in a public lie was the moral price individuals in communist states were prepared to pay in order to be left in peace (Kupferberg, 1999: 32).

German reunification has brutally exposed the burning shame of having acted immorally and opportunistically and this shame lies at the heart of East German nostalgia. Like Gudrun, a large majority of East Germans who in one way or another acted in this way today find it easier to assert that they did what they did out of conviction.

This would explain the extraordinary explosion of true believers in the Marxist utopia. What should be stressed is that it is felt as a personal problem and that, as in Gudrun's case, people often react by attempting to return to a past where their behavior was considered an act of compassion and justice.

It also explains Gudrun's longing to return to a time when life was simple and individuals did not have to make moral choices but simply followed the group. For this reason she really wants to believe that at least some of what she was told in school was true. Like most East Germans who went through the school system she wants to be able to hold on to at least one thing that made the world simple and made opportunism or lack of moral responsibility look like a virtue. Although most East Germans have long outgrown such feelings, the sudden exposure of a mass of betrayals and dishonesty makes them long to return to their comfort zone. It is far easier to be among the righteous without having to take personal moral responsibility for your choices in life, than to have to defend everything you do both to yourself and to the world.

"Not Everything was Bad in the GDR"

In a book supplementing the exhibition *Tempolinsen und P2 - Alltagskultur der DDR* (Lentils and two-roomed apartments—the everyday culture of the GDR) Mario Stumpfe spotlights this longing for moral simplicity and clear, uncomplicated choice, as the core of GDR nostalgia: "For probably nine-tenths of the population, the GDR was a convenient and not very complex society. It offered simple templates for life which could be accepted or rejected. There was not much to interpret" (Ludwig, 1996: 142). Among the simplest of these templates was that the state was "antifascist" and that the Nazi criminals all lived on the other side of the border. In the GDR the citizens were morally pure as snow (as long as they behaved themselves and joined in the antifascist choir). This concept of a radical break between the GDR and Nazi Germany which, until unification, was shared by much of the West German public, was suddenly called into question as a number of well-known academic, cultural and political personalities in East Germany were revealed to have been cooperating with the Stasi as *Informelle Mitarbeiter* (ordinary citizens who volunteered to spy on their neighbors or colleagues). Many others who were under suspicion emphatically denied the charges, sometimes even when the evidence was beyond doubt.

The revelation of the staggering number of IM (about 150,000) and the fact that the Stasi kept files on millions of people removed at one stroke the moral protection of East Germany's antifascist image. Questions began to be asked about the similarities between Nazi Germany and the GDR.

In the self searching that followed the revelations important questions were raised about a theme the GDR had always evaded, namely whether moral responsibility had ever been assumed for what had taken place in Nazi Germany. The refusal to recognize that moral responsibility had been at the core of the GDR's collective identity. By maintaining that as a socialist state it had nothing to do with that past, it spared itself difficult moral questions such as what role citizens of the GDR or their families had played in Nazi Germany.

In order to prop up this image of innocence, East Germans began to maintain that "not everything was bad in the GDR." Although 70 percent of them agree that socialism as practiced was a badly executed version of a good idea, they believed it had many good points, particularly in comparison to its capitalist rival. Koch, in this context, speaks of a "selective retrospective upgrading of life in the GDR." Soon after the Wall came down most East Germans only considered the GDR superior to West Germany in three of nine categories. By the mid-nineteen-nineties they believed the GDR had been superior in seven of the nine (Koch, 1997: 99).

This swing is illustrated in the following table:

Table 9.2
The Superiority of the GDR (percentages)

	1990	1995
Science and Technology	2	6
Living Standards	2	8
Health System	18	57
Accommodation	27	53
General Education	28	64
Vocational Education	33	70
Protection against Crime	62	88
Social Security	65	92
Equal Opportunities for Women	67	87

Source: *Der Spiegel*, 1995: 43; Montada and Dieter, 1999: 42

Table 9.3
Changes in the Evaluation of the GDR between 1990 and 1995 (percentages)

	1990	1995
A tutelary state	73.4	40.4
Total control	72.6	42.0
Too much equality	44.8	30.8
The subjection of the population	46.7	18.4

Source: Schmitt and Montada, 1999: 41

The fact that distance began to lend enchantment to the view of the GDR is clearly illustrated by the following table in which the totalitarian political system is regarded with increasing affection.

Surely the mere passage of time cannot explain this dramatic decline in the way former citizens of the GDR remember the political system of their own state. Something else is at stake here. Koch (1997; 1998) somewhat generously calls it "selective memory" but it is more appropriate to call it pretence. The East Germans prefer to pretend that their state was not the same state that they had earlier found intolerable. Their collective memory had adjusted to the needs of the present in the same way that they had adjusted during the time of the GDR in order to cope with the Nazi past.

The reason their memories seem to have been better in 1990 was not simply that only a short time had elapsed but that they had not yet lost their view of themselves as being morally superior because they were antifascist. The realization that far from having broken radically with National Socialism, the GDR had perpetuated a totalitarian system was deeply disturbing. It could only be coped with by returning to a blissful state of moral innocence in which they convinced themselves that they had truly believed in the totalitarian practices of the state.

No Outsiders Allowed

Instead of starting a process of self-critical reflection about their own role in socialism and also about the obvious continuity between Nazi Germany and the GDR, most East Germans withdrew into themselves and recreated the state of innocence that had characterized the GDR. In order to remain in that state they had to make sure that outsiders did not interfere—this was one area in which they were in total agreement. So, in 1995, 97 percent of all East Germans agreed with the statement that "only those who lived in the GDR could participate in discussions about life there" (*Der Spiegel*, 1995a: 49). Since new ideas are often introduced by outsiders or strangers who, because of their outsider status have less to lose by telling the truth (Coser, 1968: 129) confining the discussion to the group is surely a kind of intellectual insurance against having to reflect self critically upon one's own history.

This consensus among East Germans confirms the enormous impact of the GDR's antifascist identity-construct upon their mentality. They had been collectively expiated from responsibility for or shame about Nazi crimes and had lived for the next fifty years under the illusion that they had nothing to reproach themselves about. They believed they had rooted out fascism once and for all from their part of Germany. Alas, the West Germans had not learned their lessons as well, so West Germany represented the threat of a possible return of the Nazis. The East Germans had to be vigilant and watch out for these "class enemies" who tried to sabotage the socialist, antifascist state wherever they could. These simple principles constituted the moral backbone of the GDR. Its citizens knew that it was a dictatorship but believed the dictatorship was necessary to keep the "class enemies" in place. They could not have imagined that they would one day be indicted for cooperating with this dictatorship.

The collapse of the GDR and the reunification of Germany had the unintended effect of forcing the East Germans to face a species of compatriot who had had ample time to ponder such difficult moral issues as what it means to live in a totalitarian dictatorship—the many compromises, large and small that had to be made—and (this was the crucial difference between the two Germanies) the knowledge that similar morally dubious behavior had once led to the murder of 6-million Jews. The West Germans could not and would not take these moral issues lightly. It shocked them to find that they meant almost nothing to the East Germans.

Wolf Biermann, a West German from Hamburg who had lived in the GDR for some twenty years under the illusion that he was living in the "better Germany," was shocked when shortly after the collapse of the GDR he found out that his close friend Sasha Anderson, who had posed as a dissident artist in the Prenslaer Berg milieu, had been informing on him. Even more shocking though was Sasha Anderson's reaction. He did not deny that he had been informing on

Biermann and other dissident artists for the Stasi and he showed no trace of remorse. He simply could not see that what he had done had been morally wrong.

This tragi-comedy repeated itself some years later when another cultural figure, Hanno Harnish, who had moved into Biermann's apartment on Chaussee-strasse after the latter had been deprived of his GDR citizenship, refused to move out when Biermann wanted his apartment back. It emerged that Harnish too had been an IM for the Stasi. Again this had no impact whatsoever upon Harnish's reputation or career. He had become an important figure in the PDS as well as in the cultural life of East Berlin, and there he firmly remained. On one occasion the two met in public when, after a concert Harnisch went up on stage and presented himself.

"I am Hanno Harnisch," he said, offering his hand. "Yes I know," Biermann said, refusing to take the hand, shouting instead, "You are a criminal, you are an informer." Shocked and enraged, Harnisch left the stage. Later Harnisch revealed to a reporter who inquired about the incident that his daughter, who had witnessed the scene, had asked him whether he was a criminal. This had so enraged Harnisch that he would have strangled Wolf Biermann then and there if the presence of the child had not made him restrain himself (Matussek, 1999: 122).

Although the Harnisch case was extreme, the widespread moral support and understanding he and others like him received in post-GDR East Germany (Mathiopolous, 1994) suggests that we are dealing with a more general problem. East Germans appear never to have asked themselves whether it was morally acceptable to reach an accommodation with the totalitarian GDR. This type of question only raises itself after a period of moral work. It involves the dual problem of moral complicity with both the Nazi and the GDR dictatorship that the East Germans are faced with today. The ruthless and systematic exposure of the lies and self-deception of the past has made individuals acutely aware of the fact that they did not act like adults but like innocent children, believing all they were told. Unless they are prepared to face the truth about themselves and move on, it is much easier to return to that childish state of innocence where everything was simple, clear and self-evident.

Most of the collective imagination and creativity of the East Germans since the collapse of the GDR has been dedicated to recapturing this innocence.

Victims of History

The main result of the enormous creative energy that the collective mind has put into this enterprise has been the emergence of the theory that the East Germans are victims of history. Daniela Dahn suggests that they have no reason to engage in a discussion about how the GDR coped with the Nazi past as long as they are still struggling to recoup their career losses (Dahn, 1999). Detlef Pollack believes it is reasonable that most East Germans do not want to have West Germans questioning them about the past as long as they are suffering from the socioeconomic inequalities of reunited Germany and as long as the industrial structure in East Germany remains so weak (Pollack, 1999). Alexander and Margrete Mitscherlich point out that this attitude is similar to that of many former Nazis in West Germany who felt that they had suffered enough and now wanted to enjoy life and hear nothing about the Nazi past (Mitscherlich and Mitscherlich, 1977).

It is certainly ironic that the antifascist GDR which, as recently as October 1989, had proudly insisted that its citizens were the "victors of history" is now seen in a different guise. What is even more ironic is that the new myth of being the victims of history has been taken over almost verbatim from the way West German ex-Nazis coped with the defeat of 1945. What the former Nazis had not learned or had not learned as well was the ability to pretend. For them the defeat of 1945 certainly was a defeat. But how can the survivors of a totalitarian political system and a badly functioning socialist economy be seen as victims? How can a reunification desired by an overwhelming majority of the population be termed colonization? How can the most rapid increase in income ever to take place in the history of post-war Germany be described as a "disappointment based upon too great expectations of the western system" (Pollack, 1999: 21)?

There is indeed something rotten in East Germany, but it is not West German democracy and capitalism that stinks. The stench comes from a country that for half a century pretended that it had coped with its Nazi past once and for all and succeeded to such a degree that that pretence became a way of life. This is the main reason why the management of the past in East Germany has hardly begun.

10

Conclusion

Nazi Germany, the GDR, and Inner Unification

For most of the world, the question of German unification was mainly a diplomatic and foreign policy issue (Zelikow and Rice, 1995; Heurlin, 1996; McAdams, 1997). The unexpected fall of the Wall in early November 1989 and the results of the first free elections in the GDR in March 1990 which, to the surprise of many, resulted in a massive majority for the Conservative parties which had been advocating immediate unification, were merely a background to what was seen as more important, namely the definitive end of the Cold War and the collapse of communism in Eastern Europe and the Soviet Union. For the Germans, and in particular the East Germans, this background was their reality and had direct repercussion upon their own lives.

Although most of the public debate in reunited Germany has tended to focus upon economic issues such as the collapse of East German industry, mass unemployment, career difficulties and differences in wages and living standards, the main thesis of this book has been that the internal divide between East and West Germans is cultural and is based upon different moral values in the two Germanies. The invisible wall that has replaced the previous, highly visible territorial division of the German nation is rooted in issues of the past—the Nazi past as well as the GDR past. The core problem is and remains the question of moral responsibility for the crimes of the Nazi years and ways in which to avoid a repetition.

As I have suggested the core moral lesson from Nazi Germany is that evil originates when there is an unfavorable balance between the individual and the group. I have focused upon the situation in which the group overpowers the individual. I do not exclude the possibility that an extreme imbalance in the other direction might also be harmful and lead to evil and catastrophe, but in the German case the main problem was clearly too much group-orientation.

In this summary I will comment upon the degree to which the conclusions I have reached make a difference. What have I learned from writing this book and what can other scholars working in similar fields learn from it? Let me start with a personal experience. In September 1999, I participated in a seminar in Berlin on the use of the comparative method in historical studies. Among those invited was Robert Brubaker, whose seminal study on national identity constructs in Germany and France, *Citizenship and Nationhood in France and Germany*, seems to have had a strong impact on academic debate in Germany about the issue of national identity (Giesen and Junge, 1998) and on the study of national identities in general. Brubaker argues that national identity cannot be seen independently from the question of how countries receive and ultimately adopt new citizens into the national community. The choice of either the principle of *jus solis* (citizenship by residence—used by most Western nations) or that of *jus sanguinis* (citizenship by ethnic heritage—used by Germany) as criteria of immigration policy indicates something deeper about the type of nation we are dealing with and how this nation constructs its identity (Brubaker, 1992).

Although some of the problems encountered by East Germans after reunification are indeed similar to the problems of cultural adaptation of immigrants (Schumann, 1991; Howard, 1995) the East Germans certainly do not look upon themselves, nor are they treated by their West German "brothers and sisters" as mere immigrants. On the contrary, they feel they have a solid claim upon the accumulated wealth and productivity of the German state, that it is their state (Schramm and Schlese, 1992). The problem is that most of this wealth and productivity has originated in the West German sector—the relative contribution of East Germany is embarrassingly small. Thus in the mid-1990s, although East Germans represented about 20 percent of the population and territory, their share of German exports amounted to one percent (*The Economist*, 1994).

If it were not for the regular transfer of hundreds of billions of Deutschmark from West to East every year, the East Germans would be as poor as the citizens in other previously communist counties in Central Europe. This economic dependence upon the richer and more productive part of Germany is a fact of life. Nevertheless, it creates deep resentment among East Germans, making them feel inferior to their compatriots (Gensicke, 1995; Koch, 1996, 1997, 1998). The hatred many East Germans feel for West Germans originates in this feeling of inferiority, which again is rooted in culture or psyche and not in economic fact.

All statistics indicate that the East Germans live as well as the West Germans—national solidarity does indeed work, and there are no signs at all that this solidarity is diminishing. The West Germans might grumble about higher taxes and cuts in public pensions resulting from the necessity to redistribute wealth from richer to poorer, but there is no political party in Germany which seriously suggests that the huge transfers from West to East should cease. This indicates that Brubaker's approach to nationhood and citizenship might not be an adequate way of delineating the moral problem of civil rights and civic ethos (Bernstein, 1996; Putnam, 1993) that is at the foundation of German inner unification.

Brubaker asks how a foreigner or immigrant becomes accepted as a citizen of a host country, acquiring all the rights and duties of such a citizen. The problem in reunited Germany is that many East Germans feel uncomfortable with or disagree with the fundamental understanding of West Germans of what a citizen of Germany is and what can be expected of him or her. The issue is thus not one of naturalization procedures but of how citizenship rights and duties (Marshal, 1950) are to be defined. What do we actually mean when we talk of free and responsible citizens (*mündige Bürger*) and how do we distinguish such a citizen from a mere loyal subject (Bloch, 1978)? This is a question of mindset, but mindsets do not emerge from nowhere, they are always rooted in national identity constructs or interpretations of the past.

Among the participants in the Berlin seminar was a young German Ph.D. student who argued that Brubaker had misconstrued his two cases and that historical events and social constraints rather than principles have determined how immigrants were received in the two countries. This anecdotal evidence is only one of many indicators that the past, and in particular those factors which led to the uninhibited racial policies of the Nazi regime (Dawidowicz, 1986;

Hilberg, 1992), still exerts an important influence on the question of national identity in Germany. Although the country might be reunited, the Germans still brood over the reasons for its division after the war —namely the crimes of Nazi Germany (Maier, 1988; Giordano, 1990; Baldwin, 1990; Buruma, 1996).

My most important personal discovery, which emerged after years of research (beginning in the late 1970s) into the East German character and its underlying identity construct, was that this concern was a typically West German phenomenon, it simply did not exist in East Germany where citizens were led to believe that there was little in their past to feel guilty about or ashamed of. East Germans, particularly members of the intelligentsia, basically saw themselves as Marxist resistance fighters. They identified with those communist leaders who had some resistance credentials to boast about. In this way, personal and collective guilt in East Germany was conveniently brushed off, and the Nazi past was projected upon West Germany. Not only were there no communists in government there (Simon, 1995), West Germany had restored the very system of private capitalism and liberal democracy which, according to Marxist theory, had brought the Nazis to power in the first place (Meuschel, 1992).

This unique historical and biographical aspect of East German national identity and its possible impact upon the psyche of East Germans after unification has rarely been the focus of studies of national identity. Nor does it feature largely in studies of the inner divide between "Ossies" and "Wessies." There is a tendency, particularly among sociologists, to reduce the problem of the divide between East and West Germans to a socioeconomic one, emphasizing the differences in status between them (Geissler, 1993; 1996) or arguing that the cultural differences between the two groups are less important than their experiences of social and economic discrimination (Pollack, 1997; 1999; Pollack and Pickel, 1998).

This effectively amounts to limiting the study of the divide between the two peoples to what happened in East Germany after the economic and monetary union in July 1990 effectively reunited their countries (Kocka, 1995). Although understandable from a pure professional point of view—after all most sociologists are socialized into thinking that the present is more important or at least of greater interest than the past —such narrow methodology nevertheless grossly underestimates the hold the past has upon the present in all nations, reunited Germany being no exception.

The way in which a nation copes with its past determines its present. National identity constructs shape national mentalities. This is no less true in Germany than it is elsewhere. What is peculiar to the German case, however, is the way the country was forced by pressure from the rest of the world to reconsider its own past after 1945. Sociologists and social scientists in general should pay more attention to the fact that this pressure was far stronger in West than in East Germany. Sociologists tend to reduce the current problems of the cultural adaptation of the East Germans to a question of social inequality, but an historical and biographical perspective seems to suggest that the real problem of German reunification is the different ways in which the two Germanies coped with the past after 1945 (von Plato, 1991; 1995).

Whereas the dominant identity construct of West Germany has tended to emphasize the importance of individual moral responsibility, the East German psyche has been shaped by a totally different construct, emphasizing loyalty. These radically different views of the role of citizens in modern societies manifest themselves in different personalities, attitudes and norms. In order to understand how these differences have come about and why they linger on a decade after the fall of the Wall, it is necessary to look more closely at the competing national identity constructs which emerged in the two Germanies after the end of the Second World War, shaping and legitimizing their different personalities and creating two widely divergent national cultures.

National identity constructs are consciously created and kept alive mainly by the intellectual and political élites of a nation (Brass, 1991; Anderson, 1991; Hobsbawm, 1991; Smith 1986). It is thus important to distinguish between character and identity constructs in order to understand the dual sources of the communication wall that divides reunited Germany (Veen, 1997; Geiger, 1987). The East German character is not "natural," it is the political product of the former élites. We are dealing with learned behavior or socialization patterns which were motivated and legitimized by a particular worldview and specifically a view of the ideal balance between the individual and the collective in a modern society, as defined by these élites.

After the humiliating collapse of the "workers' and peasants' state" the East German élites continued to play a crucial role in keeping the inner wall alive in reunited Germany for a variety of reasons.

Although they might be under-represented among the élites in Germany as a whole, in particular among managers and professors (Bürklin, 1996; Solga, 1998), they still hold a cultural hegemony over public opinion in East Germany (Reich, 1996). This is yet another reason why the past continues to have such an important impact upon the present. In order to understand why inner unification has become much more of an obstacle than most observers believed in the early nineteen-nineties, an historical approach seems long overdue. Sociology cannot continue to ignore the historical sources of the national identity constructs in the two Germanies as these explain so much about the competition between the different strata in East Germany both before and after unification.

In order to study this historical dimension, I have found it convenient to distinguish between national identity constructs and character. The survival of what have turned out to be typically "German" rather than solely "East German" cultural traits and character can only be understood in the historical context of an attempt to deal with the Nazi past in the GDR. I have emphasized two aspects – the pretence of a radical break with the past (antifascism) and the self-deceptive belief in the liberating role of the Marxist utopia (the workers' and peasants' state). Whereas the element of self-deception is found mainly among the educated middle classes, illusion has been a central element of the East German character, as important as the preference for a group-oriented lifestyle and the longing for a harmonious *Volksgemeinschaft*.

Although there is a burgeoning literature on national identity and identity constructs, there are very few contemporary studies on how they influence the psyche or the dominant cultural traits of a nation (for a recent attempt, see Hedetoft, 1995). This methodological issue can be formulated as a more general question: Where do national psyches come from and how do they change? What role do national identity constructs play in shaping the psyche of a nation? German literature on the subject (for an overview see in particular Woderich, 1991a, 1991b, 1992a; 1992b) suggests that changes do take place, but they are long term and slow. Although a great deal of inertia is involved, it is not overwhelming – nations do change their customs and lifestyles, particularly in times of crisis and transformation, as individuals are forced out of their previous habits of mind and everyday norms of behavior are reshaped to fit in with new situations.

There is no inherent logic in such a transformation though. Inertia can prove too powerful for the transforming forces of history. A case in point is that of the Weimar Republic which was rejected from the start by social forces unable to deal with the risks and challenges of a modern society (Gay, 1969; 1970). A more lasting transformation came about after 1945, mainly because the shock of the defeat of Nazi ideals which had shaped the German mind forced the Germans to readjust to a world intolerant of these ideals (Schoenbaum, 1986; Gress, 1995).

What is interesting in the German case is that this readjustment took not one but two forms. The division of Germany (and ultimately Europe) into two competing ideological, political and economic "camps" suggests that it was ultimately the difference in political analysis of what had gone wrong in Germany and how a repetition could be avoided that shaped post-war German and European politics, until the sudden and unexpected collapse of the GDR exposed the fallacy behind the antifascist construct which had legitimated the existence of a "socialist GDR" (Fulbrook, 1992, 1997; Craig, 1991; Meuschel, 1992).

In order to understand the differences between the East and West German character today, we therefore have to go back to the construct that propped up communist rule and the socialist system in East Germany between 1945 and 1989. Although it is today in disarray, many East German intellectuals, for historical reasons, have great difficulty abandoning their personal investment in it. This difficulty in turn both reinforces and feeds upon the strong resistance of ordinary East Germans to accepting a state built on the principle of individual independence rather than on that of the blind loyalty characteristic of communist states.

This too illustrates the close link between national identity constructs and the popular psyche. As Jeffrey Herf argues convincingly in *Divided Memory* there was a vital difference between the way in which the political élites in West and East Germany constructed the past. What should be emphasized though is that these different identity constructs also had a lasting impact upon the collective psyche and the personal self images of East Germans.

The inconvenient truth for all those who sympathized with the attempts of the GDR to present itself as the "better Germany" (among them many western academics and intellectuals) is that the Marxist, antifascist identity construct only simulated a clean break with the Nazi past. This habit of pretence and the accompanying erosion of personal initiative, moral responsibility and free choice has ingrained itself in the East German mind and can help us better understand the division that grew between East and West Germans after unification.

Reunification of course involves economic and sociological issues as well as political, legal, administrative and educational ones, but the overriding issue is the moral one of the Nazi past. Reunification has resurrected a number of questions in German history which remain unanswered. One is why anti-Semitism, which has existed for more than two thousand years in the most diverse cultural contexts, was carried to such extremes in Germany (Katz, 1994; Weinberg, 1986; Strauss and Kampe, 1985; Wistrich, 1991). How can one can explain why a highly cultivated people who had produced a Goethe and a Beethoven should have joined or voted for a party openly advocating the brutal racist and imperialist vision of an Adolf Hitler and employing the vulgar propaganda of a Goebbels (Gordon, 1984; Brustein, 1996)? Why is it that so many Germans who were not particularly anti-Semitic or pro-Nazi offered so little resistance to the Nazi takeover and its virulent anti-Semitism (Friedländer, 1997) and more or less willingly participated in what had by 1941/42 developed into an open policy of extermination (Goldhagen, 1996)?

One way of approaching the last issue, in which I am particularly interested, is to ask the related question of what the Germans actually learned from the Hitler era. How did the two Germanies emerging after the defeat of Nazi Germany in 1945 ensure that nothing similar would ever happen again? In what ways did this overriding political problem influence their national identities and accompanying psyches, and to what degree do these identities and psyches influence the way East and West Germans look upon and communicate with each other after unification? Or, formulated somewhat differently: What did the Germans actually learn from their role in creating the Nazi phenomenon and how did these learning processes shape the type of Germans who emerged after 1945 and reemerged in a somewhat different way after 1989 (Kupferberg, 1996a)?

After the fall of the Wall, the divided nation (Fulbrook, 1992) became one state again, but this does not mean that the two types of

Germans agree on what it means to be a German. Reunification on the contrary seems to have emphasized the extent of the cultural differences between them. Instead of bringing closure to the crimes of the Hitler era, reunification has had the effect of exposing once more this darkest chapter in German history (Kramer, 1996).

Never before in postwar German history has there been so much openness about the horrors of the Nazi past. This willingness to discuss these difficult issues freely is a healthy sign of the state of German democracy and is reassuring for its neighbors and allies. Less reassuring is the ease with which the radical right finds eager sympathizers, particularly in East Germany, where being nationalist and right wing has become the norm for a large segment of the youth. This again brings us back to the overall historical question that this book has tried to answer, namely, what moral and political lessons the East Germans learnt from the Nazi past, and how the national identity constructs that resulted from these historical learning processes shaped the East German mentality.

Although there is a great reluctance, particularly among East German sociologists, to acknowledge that there is such a thing as an East German mentality, a number of comparative studies indicate that the socialization patterns of the GDR still influence the thinking and behavior of East Germans and their attitude to West Germans, who are both admired and hated.

At the same time as they envy the wealth and productivity of their Western compatriots, the East Germans are convinced that the better ordered and more conformist lifestyle of the GDR was culturally superior to that of the "elbow society" of West Germany. The result is a strong cultural and political alienation from the dominant institutions of the Federal Republic.

One of the manifestations of this alienation is the widespread xenophobia and right-wing extremism among East German youth which seems to have its origins in both the Nazi ideal of a homogenous *Volksgemeinschaft* and in the Marxist dream of a harmonious classless society. However, any suggestions of such similarities are indignantly rejected and to protect themselves, the East Germans withdraw, seeking to recreate the innocence of a time when the world was so simple that a child could understand it.

Which brings us back to the core question: What is to be learnt from the Nazi past?

The problem seems to lie in a weak moral and civic ethos in German culture. This would explain why Germany capitulated to Hitler despite the fact that it was, in the period between the wars, a thoroughly modern society from a scientific, technological and industrial point of view. An explanation that focuses only upon the inability of Germans to cope with the stresses of a modern society tends to underestimate the moral dimension. What should be emphasized is that other nations have suffered comparable national humiliations or economic crises without losing their civic ethos. The French defeat by Bismarck's Germany, and the accompanying harsh war reparations did not destroy the spirit of France, nor did the Depression in the United States destroy the moral fiber of America.

This historical imbalance between the moral and the socioeconomic order was, as Adenauer correctly stated, mainly a result of a lack of the cultural individuality of the German nation. The Germans as a people were, like the East Germans of today, too dependent upon group pressure and group recognition to be able to develop the type of personal moral responsibility that is at the core of the civic ethos of modern societies.

In order to strengthen individuality individuals must participate in many groups, not be exclusive members of only one group. The East German preference for a group-oriented lifestyle delayed the process of individualization and today nourishes the inner wall.

The most important lesson to be learnt from the Hitler regime, according to Adenauer, was that the Germans had to become autonomous and morally responsible citizens and abandon their longing for feudal status (Kracauer, 1971; Kreimeier, 1996). To do this they had to learn how to live in a free, democratic and risk-oriented society (Beck, 1992). They had to combine the lessons of history with contemporary experience (Kolb and Fry, 1975). Adenauer's thinking was close to that of John Stuart Mill: It is only by participating successfully in a democratic society over a period of time that one can learn to appreciate the values and rules of a liberal democracy.

The political élite who held power in the Soviet-occupied sector of Germany had a different view of the situation. They regarded the rise of the Hitler regime in a liberal democracy as the inevitable result of a capitalist society (the "theory of fascism") (Craig, 1991). The defeat of Nazi Germany and their rise to power confirmed their deeply held belief in the "objective laws" of history. They saw themselves as the rightful rulers of post-war Germany, as the "victors of history" (Land and Possekel, 1994), because they alone had been able to predict events. They had predicted that voting for Hindenburg would lead to Hitler and that voting for Hitler would lead to war, and that the war would be lost, leaving the way open for the "dictator-ship of the proletariat" as predicted by Karl Marx in his theory of historical materialism.

Having introduced the "workers' and peasants' state," as the East German rulers called it for tactical reasons, they proclaimed East Germany to be the "better Germany." This had the political and moral effect of liberating them from any feeling of collective guilt or shame for what had happened during the Hitler years. The most mobile group, the new "socialist intelligentsia," willingly accepted the Marx-ist analysis of what had gone wrong in German history and eventu-ally became a pillar of the GDR.

Although East Germany called itself a "workers' and peasants' state," its most loyal citizens were to be found mainly among the educated middle classes, the professionals or the "intelligentsia." From a political point of view, this can be explained by the tight control of the communist authorities over access to higher educa-tion, where loyalty to the prevailing ideology was the key. There were rich rewards for these intellectuals provided they did not "dance outside the rows."

The reactions of members of the East German intelligentsia to the collapse of the GDR, which started with the refugee movement in the late summer of 1989 and ended with the fall of the Wall reveals their strong attachment to the life they were used to. What emerges clearly in interviews with them is how divorced they were from the mood of ordinary citizens. They were critical of the longing of the masses for a consumer society like that in the West. They would have preferred to continue the socialist experiment and felt dismayed, frustrated, sad and bitter, when it turned out that the ordinary citi-zens had different dreams of happiness.

These feelings of betrayal by their own people continue to color the way they view German unification. They have been too con-cerned with saving their own careers and legitimizing their roles to concede that they might have deceived themselves about the system they supported. Instead of examining their own role they project their bitterness upon their former leaders or upon the West German capitalists and political élites, arguing that these were forces that destroyed socialism. In this way they can avoid the inconvenient truth that Marxist socialism was mainly a project of the intelligentsia and conspicuously failed to capture the imagination and dreams of ordinary workers.

As the most loyal group in the GDR, members of the intelligentsia feared that their loyalty would be used against them. This rarely happened. Their greatest shock was to discover that their investment in higher education and careers suddenly looked inadequate, either because they had to compete with their more productive colleagues in academia, or, in the case of teachers, because they lost their undisputed social authority, or because the mass media had elevated writers and artists to a position they could only dream about in a free society. For these and similar reasons, they experienced the dismantling of the institutions of the GDR as a personal trauma.

This explains why they rarely talk of reunification. They speak about *die Wende*, the "turning point." Interestingly, the concept of a "turning point" was introduced by the sociologist Anselm Strauss who, in his book *Mirrors and Masks: The Search for Identity,* argues that a turning point can be likened to a train coming to a stop at a station. Like the train, individuals who have invested their future in a particular identity construct would like to continue in the same direction but they are forced to stop and rethink what it is they have invested in and why. This rethinking has been hard for the East German intelligentsia, who would have preferred the train to go on forever.

The strong identification of the intellectual élite with the totalitarian regime is one of the reasons why the GDR became the most stable and disciplined country in the Eastern bloc and why the sudden collapse of the regime came as such an unwelcome surprise. In contrast with other Eastern European countries such as Poland, Hungary and Czechoslovakia, moral factors played almost no role in the meltdown of the communist regime. It was the growing dissatisfaction among ordinary workers with the increasing gap in productivity and living standards between the two German states that undermined popular support for the regime and drove the masses out into the streets.

What ordinary East Germans did not accept was the Marxist contention that a centrally planned economy based upon state ownership would be economically more efficient and superior to a market economy. As the discrepancy between the promises of a better life for ordinary people and the reality of economic stagnation became increasingly clear, ordinary East Germans began increasingly to replace the dream of a classless utopia with the dream of a consumer democracy.

The internal differences between East German attitudes to unification have been grossly underplayed, particularly by sociologists, in their analysis and discussion of the events that followed it. Once we study the role of the intellectuals more closely we find that they were the prime socializing agents or intellectual mediators of the socialist, antifascist identity construct of the GDR (Fulbrook, 1997; Gculen, 1998) and as such contributed to shaping the psyche of the East Germans.

Although they do not want to be reminded of their role (Reich, 1992), they also do not want to abandon their commitment to the anti-fascist, socialist ideology (Hoerning and Kupferberg, 1999). On the one hand they want an entrée into the western-dominated professional labor markets, on the other, they are still emotionally attached to an ideology that gave their former lives deep meaning and purpose. This combination of pragmatically motivated denial and emotionally motivated affirmation fits the overall pattern of pretence or simulation so characteristic of the East German mentality.

This particular trait seems to be the longest lasting effect of the Marxist, antifascist identity construct. It has no doubt strengthened the inner wall that divides reunited Germany and is one explanation for why this metaphorical wall has shown little sign of coming down more than a decade after the fall of its more concrete counterpart.

This attitude can be interpreted as a rational way of adapting in a dictatorship – en element which was far stronger in the GDR than in other Central and Eastern European countries. As Havel points out, in most communist countries it was the ordinary citizens who colluded in the public lie for the most pragmatic of reasons—so that they would be left in peace. In those countries it was the intellectuals who, simply by speaking the truth and refusing to collude, brought the system down (Kupferberg, 1999).

The East German intellectuals had good reason to pretend—it helped them to forget the Nazi past and live in good conscience. German unification destroyed their peace of mind and forced them to face the fact that the crimes of the Nazi regime belonged to German history and were not something for which the West Germans exclusively were to blame. From now on they too will have to contemplate their past. The refusal to acknowledge this shared history is at the heart of the inner wall. A major rethink on the part of East Germans cannot be postponed forever. The full truth must eventually force its way into their minds and only when it does will it be possible to transcend the dividing inner wall.

This study has made me aware of the strong thread of continuity in German history. Whether one likes it or not, national traditions do not disappear easily, but it would be a grave mistake to assume that they should be preserved for their own sake or that no moral lessons can be learned from history. This has been my main argument against the different strands of cultural studies—the structuralist view with its determinist and nostalgic concept of culture, and the postmodernist view that is more dynamic but also unduly relativistic. No culture deserves to be preserved for its own sake—culture in itself does not have a moral value, only civic ethos has that. A culture with a weak or diminishing civic ethos does itself and humanity a service by ceasing to exist. For this reason I do not share the extreme relativistic view of postmodernism either. Different cultures are not equal in a moral sense—countries with a weak civic ethos have something to learn from countries with a stronger one.

Such moral lessons were not learnt in East Germany, mainly for historical reasons. But there are also sociological factors that have to be taken into account. The East German case represents not only what Havel called participation in the public lie but also massive self-deception among the educated élite. That this self-deception could continue for so long and indeed is present to this very day is disturbing and it ought to receive far more attention than has so far been the case.

References

Adler, Frank, and Rolf Reissig. "Sozialwissenschaftliche Forschung als `Modernisierungs-Ferment´ des Realsozialismus-eine gescheiterte Illusion?" *BISS PUBLIC* 4, 1991: 5–37.

Adorno, T.W., Else Frenkel-Brunswick, Daniel J. Levinson and R. Nevitt Sandford. *The Authoriatarian Personality*. New York: John Wiley & Sons, 1964.

Alheit, Peter. "Die Spaltung von 'Biographie' ind 'Gesellschaft.' Kollektive Verlaufskurven der deutschen Wiedervereinigung." In *Biographien in Deutschland*, edited by Wolfram Fischer-Rosenthal and Peter Alheit, 87-117. Opladen: Westdeutscher Verlag, 1995.

Anderson, Benedikt. *Imagined Communities. Reflections on the Origins and Spread of Nationalism*. London: Verso, 1991.

Anweiler, Oskar. *Schulpolitik und Schulsystem in der DDR*. Opladen: Leske + Budrich, 1988.

Arendt, Hannah. *The Origins of Totalitarianism*. San Diego, New York, London: Harcourt Brace Jovanovich, 1979.

Aron, Raymond. *The Opium of the Intellectuals*. London: Secker & Warburg, 1957.

____. *Democracy and Totalitarianism*. London: Weidenfeld & Nicolson, 1965.

____. *Main Currents in Sociological Thought 2*. Harmondsworth: Penguin Books, 1976.

Badke-Schaub, Peter, and Cornelius Buerschaper. "Der Schicksal der MANUTEX: Gruppenproblemløsen in Ost und West." In *Denken in Deutschland*, edited by Stefan Strogschnieder, 97-121. Bern: Hans Huber, 1996.

Bahrmann, Hannes, and Christoph Links. *Chronik der Wende*. Berlin: Ch.Links, 1994.

Baird, Robert M., and Stuart E. Rosenbaum. *Bigotry, Prejudice and Hatred. Definitions, Causes,and Solutions*. Buffalo, New York: Prometheus Books, 1992.

Bakunin, M. *Staatlichkeit und Anarkie*. Frankfurt am Main: Ullstein, 1979.

Baldwin, Peter. *Reworking the Past: Hitler, the Holocaust and the Historians´ Debate*. Boston: Beacon Press, 1990.

Bar-On, D. *Die Last des Schweigens: Gesrpäche mit Kindern von Nazi-tätern*. Hamburg: Rowohlt, 1996.

Barth, Fredrik. "Ethnic Groups and Boundaries." In *Ethnicity*, edited by John Hutchinson and Anthony D. Smith, 75-82. Oxford: Oxford University Press, 1996.

Bauer-Kaase, Petra, and Max Kaase. "Five Years of Unification: The Germans on the Path to Inner Unity?" *German Politics* 5 (1), 1996: 1-25.

Bauman, Gerd. *The Multicultural Riddle*. London and New York: Routledge, 1999.

Bauman, Zygmunt. *Modernity and the Holocaust*. Ithaca, N.Y.: Cornell University Press, 1993.

Beck, Ulrich. *Risk Society*. London: Sage, 1992.

____. *What is Globalization?* Cambridge: Polity Press, 2000.

Becker, Peter. "Ostdeutsche und Westdeutsche auf dem Prüfstand psychologischer Tests." *Aus Politik und Zeitgeschichte* 3 (24), 1992: 27-36.

Becker, Ulrich. *Zwischen Angst und Aufbruch. Das Lebensgefühl der Deutschen in Ost und West nach der Wiedervereinigung*. Düsseldorg: Econ, 1992.

Beier, Rosemarie. "Bericht zur mentalen Lage der Nation." *Aus Politik und Zeitgeschichte* 27, 1995: 1-18.

Belwe, Katharina. "Zur psychosozialen Befindlichkeit der Menchen in den neuen Bundesländern ein Jahnr nach der Vereinigung." *BISS PUBLIC* 8, 1992: 5-24.

Bender, Peter. *Unsere Erbschaft. Was war die DDR - was bleibt von ihr?* Hamburg and Zürich: Luchterhand, 1992.

Bendix, Reinhard. *Max Weber: An Intellectual Portrait.* Garden City: Anchor Books, 1962.

Benner, Dietrich, Hans Merkens, and Folker Schmidt. *Bildung und Schule im Transformationsprozess von SBZ, DDR und neuen Ländern-Untersuchungen zu Kontijutät und Wandel.* Berlin: Freie Universität Berlin, Institut für Allgemeine Pädagogik, 1996.

Berger, Peter, and Thomas Luckmann. *The Social Construction of Reality.* Garden City, New York: Doubleday & Anchor, 1966.

Berger, Peter, Birgitte Berger, and Hans-Joachim Kellner. *The Homeless Mind.* New York: Vintage, 1973.

Berger, Thomas U. "The Past in the Present: Historical Memory and German National Security Policy." *German Politics* 6 (1), 1997: 39-59.

Bergmann, Werner. *Schwierige Erbe: Der Umgang mit Nationalsozialismus und Antisemitismus in Österreich, der DDR und der Bundesrepublik Deutschland.* Frankfurt am Main and New York: Campus, 1995.

___. "Antisemitism and Xenophobia in Germany since Unification." In *Anti-semitism and Xenophobia in Germany after Unification,* edited by Hermann Kurthen, Werner Bergmann and Rainer Erb, 21-38. New York and Oxford: Oxford University Press, 1997.

___. and Rainer Erb. *Anti-Semitism in Germany: The Post-Nazi Epoch Since 1945.* New Brunswick and London: Transaction Publishers, 1997.

Berking, Helmuth. "Das Leben geht weiter: Politik und Alltag in einem ostdeutschen Dorf." *Soziale Welt* 46 (3), 1995: 342-353.

Bernstein, Richard J. *Hannah Arendt and the Jewish Question.* Cambridge: Polity Press, 1996.

Bessel, Richard, and Ralph Jessen, eds. *Die Grenzen der Diktatur: Staat und Gesellschaft in der DDR.* Göttingen: Vandenhoeck & Ruprecht, 1996.

Beyer, Hans-Joachim. "Die Generation der Vereinigung." *Aus Politik und Zeitgeschichte* 19, 1996: 30-39.

Beyerchen, Alan. "Anti-intellectualism and the Cultural Decapitation of Germany under the Nazis." In *The Muses Flee Hitler,* edited by Jarrell C. Jackman and Carla M.Borden, 29-44. Washington, D.C.: Smithsonian Institution Press, 1983.

Bion, Wilfred R. *Lernen durch Erfahrung.* Frankfurt am Main: Suhrkamp, 1992.

Bislev, Sven, and Katrin Erna Hjort. "Ökonomiopfattelse i en overgangssituation." In *Interkulturel Kommunikation,* edited by Katrin Hjort, Hanne Løngreen, and Anne-Marie Söderberg, 301-30. København: Samfundslitteratur, 1993.

Bittermann, Klaus. *Der rasende Mob: Die Ossis zwischen Selbstmitleid und Barbarei.* Berlin: Tiamat, 1993.

Björgo, Tore. "Terrorist Violence against Immigrants and Refugees in Scandinavia: Patterns and Motives." In *Racist Violence in Europe,* edited by Tore Björgo and Rob Witte, 29-45. London: MacMillan/New York: St. Martin's Press 1993.

Blank, Thomas. "Wer sind die Ostdeutschen? Nationalismus, Patriotismus, Identität - Ergebnisse einer empirischen Längdschnittstudie." *Aus Politik und Zeitgeschichte* 13, 1997: 38-46.

Bloch, Marc. *Feudal Society Vol. 1 and 2.* London and Henley: Routledge & Kegan Paul, 1978.

Bornemann, John. "Identity, Exile, and Division: Disjunctures of Culture, Nationality, and Citizenship in German-Jewish Selfhood in East and West Berlin." In *Jews, Germans, Memory: Reconstruction of Jewish Life in Germany*, edited by Y. Michael Bodemann, 131-159. Ann Arbor: The University of Michigan Press, 1996.

Brass, Paul. *Ethnicity and Nationalism: Theory and Comparison.* Aldershot: Gregg Rivals, 1991.

Brenner, Michael. *Nach dem Holocaust: Juden in Deutschland 1945-1950.* Munich: C. H. Beck, 1995.

Breuel, Birgit. "Den 3 Oktober markiert noch nicht das Ankommen in der neuen gemeinsamen Bundesrepublik." In *Erlebte Einheit*, edited by Eberhard Diepgen, 76-82. Berlin: Ullstein, 1995.

Broder, Henryk. *Der ewige Antisemit: Über Sinn und Funktion eines beständigen Gefühls.* Frankfurt am Main: Suhrkamp, 1986.

___. "Die Republik der Simulanten." In *Der rasende Mob: Die Ossis zwischen Selbstmitleid und Barbarei*, edited by Klause Bitterman, 94-103. Berlin: Tiamat, 1993.

___. *Erbarmen mit den Deutschen.* Hamburg: Hoffmann & Campe, 1994.

Brähler, Elmar, and Horst-Eberhard Richter. "Deutsche Befindlichkeiten im Ost-West-Vergleich."*Aus Politik und Zeitgeschichte.* B 40-41 (29 September) 1995: 13-20.

Brämer, Rainer, and Ulrich Heublein. "Studenten in der Wende?" *Aus Politik und Zeitgeschichte* 44, 1990: 3-16.

Browning, Christopher R. *Ordinary Men: Reserve Police Battalion 101 and the Final Solution in Poland.* New York: HarperCollins, 1992.

Brubaker, Rogers. *Citizenship and Nationhood in France and Germany.* New York: Cambridge University Press, 1992.

Brustein, William. *The Logic of Evil: The Social Origins of the Nazi Party, 1925–1933.* New Haven and London: Yale University Press, 1996.

Bubis, Ignatz. *Juden in Deutschland.* Berlin: Aufbau, 1996.

___, and Wolfgang Schäuble. *Deutschland wohin?* Frieburg: Herder, 1996.

Burgauer, Erika. *Zwischen Erinnerung und Verdrängung - Juden in Deutschland nach 1945.* Hamburg: Rowohlt, 1993.

Bürklin, Wilhelm. "Kontinuität und Wandel der deutschen Führungsschicht: Ergebnisse der Postsdamer Elitestudie 1995." Proceedings of the Conference at Potsdam University, Universität Potsdam, 1996.

Buruma, Ian. *Erbschaft der Schuld. Vergangenheitsbewältigung in Deutschland und Japan.* Hamburg: Rowohlt, 1996.

Böhm, Andrea. "Hass, nur Hass."*Die Zeit* 38, 10 September 1998.

Böhm, Jürgen, Joachim Brune, Herbert Flörchinger, Antje Helbing and Annegret Pinther, eds. *DeutschStunden: Aufsätze.* Berlin: Argon, 1993.

Cerulo, Karen A. "Identity Construction: New Issues, New Direction." *Ann. Rev. Sociol.* 23, 1997: 385-409.

Christ, Peter, and Ralf Neubauer. *Kolonie im eigenen Land: Die Treuhand, Bonn und die Wirtschaftskatastrophe der fünf neunen Länder.* Berlin: Rowohlt, 1991.

Claus, Jan U. "Addendum to 'Im Osten viel Neues: Plenty of News from the Eastern Länder.'" *Daedalus*, Summer 1997: 159-64.

Clausen, Detlev. "The House of the Hangman." In *Germans and Jews Since Holocaust*, edited by Anson Rabinbach and Jack Zipes, 50-64. New York and London: Holmes & Meyer, 1986.

Cohn, Michael. *The Jews in Germany. The Building of a Minority.* Westport, Conn. and London: Præger, 1994.

Colletti, Lucio. *From Rousseau to Lenin: Studies in Ideology and Society.* New York and London: Monthly Review Press, 1974.

Colquhoun, Robert. *Raymond Aron I and II.* London: Sage, 1986.

Connor, Walker. *Ethnonationalism: The Quest for Understanding.* Princeton, N.J.: Princeton University Press, 1994.

Coser, Lewis. *Continuities in the Study of Social Conflict.* New York: The Free Press/ London: Collier-Macmillan, 1968.

___. *The Functions of Social Conflict.* New York: The Free Press/London: Collier-Macmillan, 1969.

___. *Men of Idea: A Sociologist´s View.* New York: The Free Press/London: Collier-Macmillan, 1970.

___. *Greedy Insitution: Patterns of Undivided Commitment.* New York: The Free Press/ London: Collier-Macmillan, 1974.

Craig, Gordon A. *The Germans.* New York: Penguin Books, 1991.

Dahn, Daniela. *Wir bleiben hier oder Wem gehört der Osten.* Hamburg: Rowohlt, 1994.

___. *Westwärts und nicht vergessen: Vom Unbehagen der Einheit.* Hamburg: Rowohlt, 1997.

___. *Vertreibung ins Paradise.* Hamburg: Rowohlt. 1999.

Dawidowicz, Lucy, S. *The War Against the Jews.* Toronto: Bantam Books, 1986.

Deutsch, Karl. *Nationalism and Social Communication: An Inquiry into the Foundations of Nationality.* Cambridge, Mass.: MIT Press, 1966.

Diewald, Martin, and Karl Ulrich Mayer, eds. *Zwichenbilanz der Wiedervereinigung.* Opladen: Leske + Budrich, 1996.

Diewald, Martin, and Annemette Sørensen. "Erwerbsverläufe und soziale Mobilität von Frauern und Männern in Ostdetuscland: Makrostrukturelle Umbrüche und Kontinuitäten im Lebenslauf" In *Zwischenbilanz der Wiedervereinigung,* edited by Martin Diewald and Karl Ulrich Mayer, 63-88. Opladen: Leske + Budrich, 1996.

Döbert, Hans, and Roland Rudilf. *Lehrerberuf-Schule - Unterricht. Einstellungen, Meinungen und Urteile ostdeutscher Lehrerinnen und Lehrer.* Frankfurt am Main: Deutsches Institut für Internationale Pädagogische Forschung, 1995.

Ebaugh, Helen R. F. *Becoming an E: The Process of Role Exit.* Chicago and London: The University of Chicago Press, 1988.

Eberle, Henrik, and Denise Wesenberg. *Einverstanden. H. A.* Berlin: Schwarzkopf & Schwarzkopf, 1999.

The Economist. "Germany: Half-hidden Agenda." Survey, 21 May 1994: 3-34.

Eisenstadt, Shmuel Noah, and Bernard Giesen. "The Construction of Collective Identity." *Arch. Europ. Socil.,* 1995: 72-102.

Elias, Norbert. *Über den Prozess der Zivilisation I and II.* Frankfurt am Main: Suhrkamp, 1978.

___. *The Germans: Power Struggles and the Development of Habitus in the Nineteenth and Twentieth Centuries.* Cambridge: Polity Press, 1996

Elon, Amos. *In einem heimgesuchten Land.* München: Kindler, 1965.

Elzinga, Aat. "The Knowledge Aspect of Professionalization: The Case of Science-based Nursing Education in Sweden." In *The Formation of Professions: Knowledge, State and Strategy,* edited by Rolf Thorstendahl and Michael Burrage, 151-73. London: Sage, 1990.

Engler, Wolfgang. *Die Zivilisatorische Lücke. Versuch über den Staatssozialismus.* Frankfurt am Main: Suhrkamp, 1992.

___. *Die Ostdeutschen. Kunde von einem Verlorenen Land.* Berlin: Aufbau, 1999.

Ensel, Leo. *Warum wir uns nicht leiden mögen. Was Ossies und Wessies von einander halten.* Münster: Agenda, 1993.

Eppelmann, Rainer. *Fremd im eigenen Haus.* Köln: Kiepenheuer & Witsch, 1993.

___. "Zur inneren Einheit Deutschlanfs im fünften Jahr nach der Vereinigung." *Aus Politik und Zeitgeschichte.* B. 40 – 41 (29 September 1995):8-12.

Erikson, Erik. *Identitet - ungdom og kriser.* København: Hans Reitzel, 1982.

Eschwege, Helmuth. *Fremd unter meinesgleichen. Erinnerungen eines Dresdner Juden.* Berlin: Links Verlag, 1991.

Faktor, Jan. "Intellektuelle Opposition und alternativer Kultur in der DDR." *Aus Politik und Zeitgeschichte* 10, 1994: 30-7.

Falkner, Thomas and Dietmar Huber. *Aufschwung PDS. Rote Socken-zurück zur Macht.* München: Knaur, 1994.

Farin, Klau,. and Eberhard Seiden-Pielen. *Rassismus im neuen Deutschland.* Berlin: Rotbuch, 1992.

Fassbender, Ded, Steffen Roski, Christian Trapp, Uwe Ziemann. *Sozialer Wandel in den neuen Bundesländern.* Opladen: Leske + Budrich, 1993.

Findes, Hagen, Detlef Pollack, and Manuel Schilling. *Die Entzauberung des Politischen.* Leipzig: Evangelische Verlagsanstalt, 1994.

Fischer, Anderas. *Das Bildungssystem der DDR.* Darmstadt: Wissenschaftliche Buchgesellschaft, 1992.

Fischer, Fritz. *From Kaiserreich to Third Reich: Elements of Continuity in German History.* London: Allen & Unwin, 1986

Fischer-Rosenthal, Wolfram. "Schweigen - Rehctfertigen - Umschreiben. Biographische Arbeit im umgang mit deutschen Vergangenheiten." In *Biographien in Deutschland. Soziologische Rekonstruktionen Gelebter Gesellschaftsgeschichte,* edited by Wolfgang Fischer-Rosenthal and Peter Alheit, 43-86. Opladen: Westdeutscher Verlag, 1995.

Flood, Charles B. *Hitler. The Path to Power.* Boston: Houghton Mifflin, 1989.

Foucault, Michel. *L'archeologies du Savoir.* Paris: Gallimard, 1969.

___. *Overvågning og straf.* København: Rhodos, 1977.

___. *Dispositive der Macht.* Berlin: Merve Verlag 1979.

Freund, Julien. *The Sociology of Max Weber.* New York: Vintage Books, 1968.

Frey, Erich "Thomas Mann." In *Deutsche Literatur seit 1933. 1. Kalifornien,* edited by John M. Spalek and Joseph Strelka, 473-526. Bern and München: Francke Verlag, 1976.

Friedländer, Saul. *Nazi Germany and the Jews. Volume I. The Years of Persecution, 1933-1939.* New York: Harper Collins, 1997.

Friedrich, Walter. "Mentalitätswandlungen der Jugend in der DDR."*Aus Politik und Zeitgeschichte* 16-17, 1990: 25-37.

Fritze, Lothar (a). "Sehnsucht nach der DDR in den neuen Bundersländern?" *Frankfurter Allgemeine Zeitung,* 9 March 1995: 10.

_____(b). "Irritation in deutsch-deutschen Vereinigungsprozess." *Aus Politik und Zeitgeschichte* 27, 1995: 33-9.

Fuchs, Dieter, Edeltraud Roller, and Bernard Wessels. "Die Akzeptanz der Demokratie ses vereinigten Deutschland." *Aus Politik und Zeitgeschichte* 51, 1997: 3 - 12.

Fulbrook, Mary. *The Divided Nation: A History of Germany 1918-1990.* New York and Oxford: Oxford University Press, 1992.

___. *Anatomy of a Dictatorship: Inside the GDR 1949-1989.* Oxford and New York: Oxford University Press, 1997.

Gaschke, Susanne. "Brandenburg: Der alltägliche Schrecken." *Die Zeit* 38 (10 September 1998).

Gaus, Günther. *Wo Deutschland lieg: Eine Ortsbestimmung.* München: Deutscher Taschenbuch-Verlag, 1986.

___. *Zur Person.* Berlin: Edition Ost, 1999.

Gay, Peter. "Weima Culture: The Outsider as Insider." In *The Intellectual Migration,* edited by Donald Fleming and Bernard Bailyn, 11-93. Cambridge, Mass.: Harvard University Press, 1969.

____. *Weimar Culture.* New York: Harper & Row, 1970.

Gebhardt, Winfried, and Georg Kamphausen. "Mentalitetsunterschiede im wiedervereinigten Deutschland." *Aus Poltitik und Zeitgeschichte.* B. 16 (22), April 1994: 29-39.

Geiger, Theodor. *Die Soziale Schichtung des deutschen Volkes.* Stuttgart: Ferdinand Enke, 1932/1987.

Geissler, Rainer, ed. *Sozialer Umbruch in Ostdeutschland.* Opladen: Leske + Budrich, 1993.

____. *Die Sozialstruktur Deutschlands.* Opladen: Westdeutscher Verlag, 1996.

Genin, Salomea. "Wie ich in der DDR aus einer Kommunistin zu einer Jüdin wurde." In *Das Exil der kleinen Leute. Alltagserfahrungen deutscher Juden in der Emigration,* edited by Wolfgang Benz. Frankfurt am Main, 383-482: Fischer, 1994.

Gensicke, Thomas. "Mentalitätsentwicklungen im Osten Deutschlands seit den 70er Jahren." *Speyer Forschungsberichte* 110, 1992: 1-98.

____ "Die Stimmung ist besser als die Lage." In *Getrennt verein: Lebensverhältnisse in Deutschland seit der Wiedervereinigung,* edited by Wolfgang Glatzer and Heinz-Herbert Noll, 285-304. Frankfurt and New York: Campus, 1995.

Gerhmann, Axel, and Peter Hübner. "Sozialer Wandel statt Transformation? Über den Zusammenhang von beruflicher Zufriedenheit und schulinterne Wirkungsmechanismen bei Lehrerinnen und Lehrern im vereinigten Berlin." In *Zeitschrift für Pädagogik. 37 Beiheft. Kindheit, Jugend und Bildungsarbeit im Wandel,* edited by Heinz-Elmar Tenorth, 375-96. Weinheim and Basel: Beltz Verlag, 1997.

Geulen, Dieter. *Politische Sozialisation in der DDR: Autobiographische Gruppengespräche mit Angehöringen der Intelligentz.* Opladen: Leske + Budrich, 1998.

Gibas, Monika. "'Die DDR- das sozialistische Vaterland der Werktätigen!'Anmerkungen zur Identitetspolitik der SED und ihrem sozialisatorischen Erbe." *Aus Politik und Zeitgeschichte,* 39-40, 1999: 21-30.

Giddens, Anthony. *New Rules of Sociological Method.* London: Hutchinson, 1976.

____. *Central Problems in Social Theory.* Berkeley and Los Angeles: University of California Press, 1979.

____. *A Contemporary Critique of Historical Materialism.* London and Basingstoke: Macmillan, 1981

____. *The Constitutions of Society.* Berkeley and Los Angelese: The University of California Press, 1984.

____. *The Consequences of Modernity.* Cambridge: Polity Press, 1990.

____. *Modernity and Self-Identity.* Cambridge: Polity Press, 1991.

Giesen, Bernd, and Claus Leggewie, eds. *Experiment Vereinigung.* Berlin: Rotbuch, 1991.

____, and Kay Junge. "Nationale Identität und Staatsbürgerschaft in Deutschland und Frankreich." *Berl. J. Soziol* 4, 1998: 523-37.

Giordano, Ralph. *Die zweite Schuld oder Von der Last Deutscher zu Sein.* München: Knauer, 1990.

Gissendanner, Scott. "Die dritte Republik or the Same old Federal Republic? What the German Social Science Literature Has to Say about German Unification and Its Systemic Effects." Max Planck Gesellschaft. Arbeitgruppe Transformaitonsprozesse in den neuen Bundesländern. Arbeitspapiere 96/4, 1996.

Glaessner, Gert-Joachim. *Die Schwierige Weg zur Demokrati. Vom Ende der DDR zur Deutschen Einheit.* Opladen: Westdeutscher Verlag, 1992.

____, ed. *Der lange Weg zur Einheit.* Berlin: Dietz Verlag, 1993.

Glaser, Hermann, ed. *Die Mauer fiel, die Maur steht: Ein deutsches Lesebuch 1989-1999.* München: Deutscher Taschenbuch Verlag, 1999.

Glatzer, Wolfgang, and Heinz-Herbert Noll, eds. *Getrennt vereint: Lebensverhältnisse in Deutschland seit der Wiedervereinigung.* Frankfurt and New York: Campus, 1995.

Glucksmann, André. *Les maîtres penseurs.* Paris: Grasset, 1977.
___. *Köchin und Menchenfresser.* Berlin: Klaus Wagenbach, 1979.
Goffman, Erving. *The Presentation of Self in Everyday Life.* New York: Doubleday & Co, 1959.
Goldenbogen, Nora. "Juden in der DDR: Erwartungen - Realitäten - Wandlungen." In *Der Anfang nach dem Ende. Jüdisches Leben in Deutschland 1945 bis Heute,* edited by Günther B. Ginzel, 123-49. Düsseldorf: Droste Verlag, 1996.
Goldhagen, Daniel Jonah. *Hitler's Willing Executioner: Ordinary Germans and the Holocaust.* New York: Alfred A. Knopf, 1996.
Gordon, Sarah. *Hitler, Germany and the ".Jewish Question."* Princeton, N.J.: Princeton University Press, 1984.
Gouldner, Alvin W. *The Future of the Intellectuals and the Rise of the New Class.* London and Basingstoke: Macmillan, 1979.
Gouldner, Alvin. *Against Fragmentation. The Origins of Marxism and the Sociology of the Intellectuals.* New York and Oxford: Oxford University Press, 1985.
Granovetter, Mark. "The Strength of Weak Ties." *American Journal of Sociology* 78, 1973: 1360-80.
Greenfeld, Liah. *Nationalism: Five Roads to Modernity.* Cambridge, Mass.: Harvard University Press, 1992.
Grell, Brigitte, and Carola Wolf, eds. *Ein Ende ist immer ein Anfang.* München: Chr. Kaiser, 1992.
Gress, David. "Former West Germans and Their Past." *Partisan Review* 4, 1995: 534-44.
Groehler, Olaf. "Der Umgang mit dem Holocaust in der DDR." In *Der Umgang mit dem Holocaust. Europa-Israel-USA,* edited by Rolf Steininger, 223-45 Wien: Böhlau, 1994.
Grunenberg, Antonia. "Das Ende der Macht ist der Anfang der Literatur: Zum Streit um die Schriftstellerin in der DDR." *Aus Politik und Zeitgeschichte* 44, 1990: 17-26.
Gruner, Petra, ed. *Angepasst oder mündig?* Berlin: Volk und Wissen, 1990.
Gysi, Gregor. *Das war's. Noch lange nicht!* Düsseldorf: Econ, 1995.
Hacker, Jens. *Deutsche Irrtümer: Schönfärber und Helfershelfer der SED-Diktatur im Westen.* Frankfurt am Main and Berlin: Ullstein, 1994.
Hadril, Stefan. "Die Modernisierung des Denkens Zukunftspotentiale und 'Altlasten' in Ostdeutschland."*Aus Politik und Zeitgeschichte* 20, 1995: 3-15.
Hagan, John, Hans Merkens, and Klaus Boehnke. "Delinquency and Disdain: Social Capital and the Control of Right-Wing Extremism among East and West Berlin Youth." *American Journal of Sociology* 100 (4), 1995: 1028-52.
Hahn, Toni, and Gerhard Schön. *Arbeitslos - chancenlos? Verläufe von Arbeitslosigkeit in Ostdeutschland.* Opladen: Leske + Budrich, 1996.
Hall, Peter. *Cities in Civilization.* London: Phoenix, 1999.
Hall, Stuart "Cultural Identity and Diaspora." In *Identity-Community, Culture, Difference,* edited by Jonathan Rutherford, 19-39. London: Lawrence & Wishart, 1990.
___. "The Local and the Global." In *Cultural Globalization and the World System,* edited by Anthony D. King, 19-39. London and Basingstoke: Macmillan, 1991.
Händle, Christa. *Lehrerinnen im System und Lebenswelt.* Opladen: Leske + Budrich, 1998.
Hannerz, Ulf. *Transactional Places: Culture, People, Places.* London and New York: Routledge, 1996.
Harre, Elke. "Politischer Wandel und Gefühle im Umbruch." *BISS PUBLIC* 4, 1991: 116-22.
Hedetoft, Ulf. *Signs of nations: studies in the political semiotics of self and other in contemporary European nationalism.* Aldershot: Dartmouth, 1995.
Henderson, Karen. "The GDR and the East European Experience." *German Politics* 3 (2), 1994: 293-301.

Henrich, Rolf. *Der vormundschaftliche Staat. Vom Versagen des real existierenden Sozialismus.* Frankfurt am Main: Surhkamp, 1989.

Herf, Jeffrey. *Divided Memory: The Nazi Past in the Two Germanys.* Cambridge, Mass.: Harvard University Press, 1997.

___. "Germany's Holocaust Memorial." *Partisan Review* LXVI (3), 1999: 375–391.

Hermann, Armin. *Einstein.* Munich and Zurich: Piper, 1996.

Hertle, Hans-Hermann. *Der Fall der Mauer: Die Unbeabsichtige Selbstauflösung des SED-Staates.* Opladen: Westdeutscher Verlag, 1996.

Heurlin, Bertel, ed. *Germany in Europe in the Nineties.* Basingstoke and London: Macmillan/ New York: St. Martin's Press, 1996.

Heurlin, Bertel, ed. *Germany in Europe in the Nineties.* Basingstoke and London: Macmillan/ New York: St. Martin's Press, 1996.

Hilberg, Raul. *Perpetrators, Victims, Bystanders: The Jewish Catastrophe 1933-1945.* New York: HarperCollins, 1992.

Hilmer, R, and R. Müller-Hilmer. "Es wächst zusammen." *Die Zeit.* 40 (1) (October 1993).

Hirschman, Albert O. "Exit, Voice and the Fate of the German Democratic Republic." *World Politics* 45 (2), 1993: 173-202.

Hobsbawm, Erik. *Nations and Nationalism since 1780: Programme, Myth, Reality.* Cambridge: Cambridge University Press, 1991.

Hoerning, Erika M. "Aufstieg und Fall der Intelligenz der DDR: Transformation und Sozialisation." *Berliner Debatte Initial* 2, 1995: 21-32.

Hoerning, Erika, and Feiwel Kupferberg. "Die Anhaltende Loyalität er ostdeutschen Intelligenz." *Bios,* 1999: 28-49.

Hoffmann-Pawlowsky, Jutta, and Freya Voigt. *Lebenslinien.Geschichten von Frauen aus der ehemaligen DDR.* Frankfurt Oder: Frankfurter Oder Editionen, 1995.

Hollander, Paul. *Political Pilgrims. Travels of Western Intellectuals to the Soviet Union, China and Cuba 1928-78.* New York: Oxford University Press, 1981.

Hopf, Wulf. "Rechtsextremismus von Jugendlichen: Kein Deprivationsproblem?" *ZSE* 14 (3), 1994: 194-211.

Howard, Marc Alan. "Die Ostdeutschen als etnische Gruppe? Zum Verständniss der neuen Teilung der geeinten Deutschland." *Berliner Debatte Initial.* 4/5, 1995: 119-31.

Hoyer, Hans-Dieter. *Lehrer im Transformationsprozess.* Weinheim and München: Juventa, 1996.

Hradil, Stefan. "Die modernisierung des Denkens.Zukunftspotentiale und 'Altlasten' in Ostdeutschland." *Aus Politik und Zeitgeschichte* B 20 (12) (May 1995): 3-15.

Huaco, George A. *The Sociology of Film Art.* New York: Basic Books, 1965.

Hughes, Everett. *Men and Their Work.* New York: The Free Press of Glencoe, 1964.

___. *The Sociological Eye.* New Brunswick, N.J.: Transaction Publishers, 1984.

Hübner, Peter, and Axel Gehrmann. "Lehrerberuf und sozialer Wanderl. Ausgewählte Ergebnisse einer Berliner Lehrebefragung 1996." *Berl. J Soziol* 3, 1997: 307-30.

Huinink, Johannes, and Karl Ulrich Mayer. "Lebensverläufe im Wandel der DDR-Gesellschaft." In *Der Zusammenbruch der DDR* S, edited by Hans Joas and Martin Kohli, 151-71. Frankfurt am Main: Suhrkamp, 1993.

Huinink, Johannes, Karl-Ulrich Mayer, Martin Diewald, Heike Solga, Annemette Sørensen, and Heike Trappe. *Kollektiv und Eigensinn. Lebensverläufe in der DDR und danach.*Berlin: Akademie Verlag, 1995.

Huszar, George Bernard, ed. *Intellectuals.* New York: The Free Press, 1960.

Hutchinson, John, and Anthony Smith, eds. *Nationalism.* Oxford and New York: Oxford University Press, 1994.

Ignatieff, Michael. *Blood and Belonging: Journeys into the New Nationalism.* New York: The Noonday Press, 1995.

Jackman, Jarrel C., and Carla M. Borden, eds. *The Muses Flee Hitler: Cultural Transfer and Adaption 1930–1945*. Washington, D.C.: Smithonian Institution Press, 1983.

James, Harold. *A German Identity 1770-1990*. London: Weidenfeld and Nicolson, 1989.

Jarauch, Konrad H. *The Rush to German Unity*. New York/Oxford: Oxford University Press, 1994.

___. "Realer Sozialismus als Fürsorgediktatur.Zur begrifflichen Einordnung der DDR." *Aus Politik und Zeitgeschichte* B 20, 1998: 33-46.

Jesse, Eckhard. "Die Totalitarismusforschung und ihre Repräsentanten." *Aus Politik und Zeitgeschichte* 20, 1998: 3-18.

Joas, Hans, and Martin Kohli, eds. *Der Zusammenbruch der DDR.*. Frankfurt am Main: Suhrkamp, 1993.

Johnson, Paul. *Intellectuals*. London: Weidenfeld & Nicolson, 1988.

Joppke, Christian. "Why Leipzig? 'Exit' and 'Voice' in the East German Revolution." *German Politics* 2 (3), 1993: 393-414.

Kaelble, Hartmut, Jürgen Kocke, and Hartmut Zwahr. *Sozialgeschichte der DDR.*. Stuttgart: Klett-Cotta, 1994.

Kampe, Dieter. *Wer uns kennenlernt, gewinnt uns lieb. Nachfruf auf die Treuhand*. Berlin: Rotbuch, 1994.

Kanter, Rosabeth, M. "Commitment and Social Organization: A Study of Commitment Mechanism in Utopian Communities." *American Sociological Review* 33 (4), 1994: 499-517.

Katz, Jacob. *From Prejudice to Destruction. Antisemitism, 1700-1933*. Cambridge, Mass./ London: Harvard University Press, 1994.

Kay, Harvey J. *Why do the Ruling Classes Fear History*. New York: St. Martin's Griffin, 1997.

Kelly, G. A. *The Psychology of Personal Constructs*. New York: W. W. Norton & Co., 1955.

Kessler, Mario. *Die SED und die Juden - zwischen Repression und Toleranz*. Berlin: Akademie Verlag, 1995.

Kleinig, John. *Paternalism*. Totowa, N. J.: Rowman & Allanhead, 1984.

Klemm, Volker. *Korruption und Amtsmissbrauch in der DDR*. Stuttgart: Deutsche Verlagsanstalt, 1991.

Klessmann, Christoph. "The Burden of the Past in the Two Germanies." In *Studies in GDR Culture and Society 11/12. The End of the GDR and the Problems of Integration. Selected Papers from the Sixteenth and Seventeenth New Hampshire Symposia on the German Democratic Republic*, edited by Margy Gerber and Roger Woods, 195-209. Lanham and New York: University Press of America, 1993.

Klose, Dagmar. "Prägungen und Wandlungen ostdeutscher Identitäten." *Aus Politik und Zeitgeschichte* B. 41 (14) (October 1994): 3-11.

Knowlton, James, and Case Truett, eds. *Forever in the Shadow of Hitler?* N.J.: Humanities Press, 1993.

Knütter, Hans-Helmuth. "Antifascismus und politische Kultur in Deutschland nach der Wiedervereinigung." *Aus Politik und Zeitgeschichte*, B 9, 1991: 17-28.

Koch, Thomas. "The Renaissance of East German Group Awareness since Unification." In *Changing Identities in East Germany*, edited by M. Gerber and R. Woods, 189-210. Selected Papers from the Nineteenth and Twentieth New Hampshire Symposia Studies in GDR Culture and Society 14/15. Lanham/ New York/ London: University Press, 1996.

___. "Ostdeutsche Identitäten in der dualistischen Gesellschaft." *Berliner Debatte INITIAL* 8, 1997: 93-108.

___. "Ostdeutsche Identitäten in der dualistischen Gesellschaft." In *Sozialer Wandel in*

Ostdeutschland, edited by Michael Häder and Sabine Häder. Opladen: Westdeutscher Verlag, 1998: 38-63.

___, Jochen Mattern, Ursula Schöter, and Rudolf Woderich. *Ostdeutsche Lehrer Promotoren in Transformationsprozessen des Bildundswesens.* Berlin: Berliner Institut für Sozialwissenschaftliche Studien, 1994.

Kocka, Jürgen. *Vereinigungskrise.* Göttingen: Vandenhoeck & Ruprecht, 1995.

Köhler, Otto. *Die Grosse Enteignun: Wie die Treuhand eine Volkswirtschaft liquidierte.* München: Knaur, 1994.

Kohlhoff, Werner. "Die letzte Bastion der DDR." *Berliner Zeitung,* 2, 12 March 1999.

Kohn, Hans. *The Mind of Germany: The Education of a Nation.* New York: Charles Scribner, 1960.

Kolakowski, Leszek. *Die Hauptströmungen des Marxismus I.* München: Piper, 1977.

___. *Leben trotz Geschichte.* München: Deutscher Taschenbuch Verlag, 1980.

___, and Stuart Hampshire. *Socialismens idé. En omvärdering.* Stockholm: Rabén & Sjögren, 1977.

Kolb, D. A., and R. Fry. "Towards an Applied Theory of Experiential Learning. In *Theories of Group Processes,* edited by C .L. Cooper, 33-58. London: Wiley, 1975.

König, H., W. Kuhlmann, and K. Schwabe, eds. *Vertuschte Vergangenheit. Der Fall Schwerte und die NS-Vergangenheit der deutschen Hochschulen.* München: Beck, 1997.

Kracauer, Siegfried. *From Caligari to Hitler: A Psychological Study of the German Film.* Princeton, N.J.: Princeton University Press, 1971.

Kramer, Janet. *The Politics of Memory: Looking for Germany in the New Germany.* New York: Random House, 1996.

___ "Neo-Nazis. Chaos in the Head." *The New Yorker* 14 June 1993: 52-150.

Kreimeier, Klaus. *The UFA Story.* New York: Hill and Wang, 1996.

Krell, Gert, Hans Nicklas, and Anne Ostermann. "Immigration, Asylum, and Anti-Foreigner Violence in Germany." *Journal of Peace Research.* 33 (2), 1996: 153-70.

Kroboth, Rudolf. "Blicke auf den Nationalsozialismus im Schatten der Goldhagen-Kontroverse." *Lehren und Lernen* 8, 1997: 3-15.

Kuby, Erich. *The Russians and Berlin, 1945.* London: Heinemann, 1965.

___. *The Russians and Berlin.* London: Heinemann, 1968.

Kundera, Milan. *Skrattets og glömskans bok.* Stockholm: Bonnier, 1987.

Kupferberg, Feiwel. "At gentænke de østeuropæiske revolutioner." *Dansk Sociologi* 4 (2), 1993: 24-43.

___. "Biografisk självgestaltning." *Sociologisk Forskning,* Nr.4, s. 1995: 32-57.

___. "Managing an Unmasterable Past." *Society* 33 (2), 1996a: 69-79.

___. "Strategic Learning: East Germany as a 'Model Case' for Transformation Theory" *International Sociology* 11 (4), 1996b: 457-79.

___. "The Land of the Murderers." *Innovation* 10 (1), 1997: 85-105.

___. "Transformation as Biographical Experience: Personal Destinies of East Berlin Graduates Before and After Unification." *Acta Sociologica,* 1998: 243-67.

___. *The Break-up of Communism in East Germany and Eastern Europe.* Basingstoke: Macmillan/New York: St. Martin's Press, 1999.

___. "Nationale Identität als existentielle Entscheidung: Frauen in der DDR. In *Biographische Sozialisation,* edited by Erika M. Hoerning. Stuttgart: Lucius & Lucius, 2000: 325-41.

Kurthen, Hermann, Werner Bergmann, and Rainer Erb, eds. *Anti-semitism and Xenophobia in Germany after Unification.* New York and Oxford: Oxford University Press, 1997.

Land, Rainer, and Ralf Possekel. *Namenlose Stimmen waren uns vora: Politische Diskurse von Intellektuellen aus der DDR.* Bochum: Dieter Winkler, 1994.

Lane, Christel. *The Rites of Rulers*. Cambridge: Cambridge University Press, 1981.

Lappin, Elena. *Jewish Voices, German Words: Growing Up Jewish in Postwar Germany and Austria*. North Haven, Conn.: Catbird Press, 1994.

Lay, Conrad, and Christoph Potting, eds. *Gemeinsam sind wir unterschiedlich*. Bonn: Bundeszentrale für politische Bildung, 1995.

Lehnert, Herbert. "Bert Brecht und Thomas Mann im Streit über Deutschland." In *Deutsche Exilliteratur seit 1933. Band I. Kalifornien*, edited by John M. Spalek and Joseph Strelka, 62-88. Bern and München: Francke, 1976.

Lenhardt, Gero, and Manfred Stock. *Bildung, Bürger, Arbeitskraft*. Frankfurt am Main: Stuttgart, 1997.

Lerner, Daniel. *The Passing of Traditional Society*. New York: The Free Press, 1965.

Lessing, Doris. *Under My Skin: Volume One of My Autobiography, to 1949*. New York: HarperCollins, 1994.

___. *Walking in the Shade: Volume Two of My Autobiography, 1942-1962*. New York: HarperCollins, 1997.

Levine, Donald A. "Simmel as Educator: On Individuality and Modern Culture." *Theory, Culture and Society* 8, 1991: 99-117.

Lévi-Strauss. *Tristes Tropiques*. New York: Washington Square Books, 1977.

Lévy, Bernard-Henri. *Det menneskelige barbari*. København: Centrum, 1979.

Liebert, Ulrike. "Kein neuer deutscher nationalismus. Vereinigungsdebatte und Nationalbewusstsein auf dem 'Durchmarsch' zu Einheit." In *Die Politik zur deutschen Einheit. Probleme-Strategien-Kontroversen*, edited by Ulrike Liebert and Wolfgang Merkel, 51-94. Opladen: Leske + Budrich, 1991.

Lindner, Gabriele. *Die Eigenart der Implosion*. Berlin: Kolog, 1994.

Lipset, Seymor M. *Den politiska människan*. Stockholm: Aldus/ Bonniers, 1966.

___. *Political Man: The Social Bases of Politics*. Aldershot: Avebury, 1983.

Lowenthal, Martin. *The Jews of Germany: A Story of Sixteen Centuries*. New York and Toronto: Longmans, Green & Co, 1966.

Löwy, Michael. *Georg Lukaács—From Romanticism to Bolshevism*. London: New Left Books, 1979.

Lucas, Michael, and Adrienne Edgar. "Germany after the Wall." *World Policy Journal*. VII 1, 1989-90: 189-214.

Lüdtke, Alf. "'Helden der Arbeit'- Mühen beim Arbeiten. Zur missmutigen Loyalität von Industriearbeitern in der DDR." In *Sozialgeschichte der DDR*, edited by Hartmut Kaelble, Jürgen Kocka, and Hartmut Zwahr, 188-213. Stuttgart: Klett-Cotta, 1994.

Ludwig, Andreas. *Tempolinsen und P2*. Berlin: be.bra verlag, 1996.

Lyon, James K. *Bertold Brecht in America*. Princeton, N.J.: Princeton University Press, 1980.

Lyotard, Jean-Francois. *The Postmodern Condition: A Report on Knowledge*. Manchester: Manchester University Press, 1984.

Maaz, Hans-Joachim. "Psychosoziale Aspekte im deutschen Einigungsprozess." *Aus Politik und Zeitgeschichte* B 19 (3), Mai: 3–10, 1991.

___. *Der Gefühlsstau. Ein Psychogramm der DDR*. München: Knaur, 1992.

___. *Die Entrüstung*. München: Knaur, 1994.

___. "Wehe, Deutschland, wenn der Wohlstand knapper wird!" *Stern* No. 49, 1999: 116-118.

MacDonald, Keith. *The Sociology of Professions*. London: Sage, 1995.

Maier, Charles S. *The Unmasterable Past. History, Holocaust and German National Identity*. Cambridge, Mass.: Harvard University Press, 1988.

___. *Dissolution: The Crisis of Communism and the End of East Germany*. Princeton, N.J.: Princeton University Press, 1997.

de Maizière, Lothar. *Anwalt der Einheit.* Berlin: Argon, 1996.

Mannheim, Karl. *Ideology and Utopia.* London: Routledge & Kegan Paul, 1968.

Markovits, Inga. *Die Abwicklung.* Munich: C. H. Beck, 1993.

Marris, Peter. *Loss and Change.* London: Routledge & Kegan Paul, 1985.

Marshal, T. H. *Citizenship and Social Class and Other Essays.* Cambridge: Cambridge University Press, 1950.

Martenstein, Harald. "Die Zone zwischen den Zeilen." *Der Tagesspiegel* 9 (September 1999).

Marz, Lutz. "Dispositionskosten des Transformationsprozesses. Werden mentale Orientierungsnöe zum wirtschaftlichen Problem?" *Aus Politik und Zeitgeschichte* B 24, 1992 : 3-14.

Mathiopolous, Margarita. *Rendezvous mit der DDR..* Düsseldorf: Econ, 1994.

Matussek, Matthias. "Keine Opfer, keine Täter." *Der Spiegel* 10, 1999: 120-142.

____. "Sehnsucht nach dem Totalitären." *Der Spiegel* 11, 1999b: 46-58.

Mayer, Karl Ulrich. "Vereinigung Soziologisch: Die soziale Ordnung der DDR und ihre Folgen." *Berl. J. Soziol.* 3, 1994: 307-321.

____, and Heike Solga. "Mobilität und Legitimität. Zum Vergleich der chancenstrukturen in der alten DDR oder: Haben Mobilitätschancen zu Stabilität und Zusammenbruch der DDR beigetragen?" *Kölner Zeitschrift für Soziologie und Sozialpsyhologie.* 46 (2), 1994: 193-208.

____, Heike Solga, and Martin Diewald. "Kontinuitëten und Brüche in den Erwerbs-und Berufsverläufen nach der deutschen Vereinigung." Arbeitspapir, Max Planck Institut für Bildungsforschung, Berlin, 1996.

McAdams, A. James. "Germany after unification: Normal at last?" *World Politics.* 49 (2), 1997: 28-308.

McCarthy, Doyle. *Knowledge as Culture.* London and New York: Routledge, 1996.

McLellan, David. *Karl Marx. His Life and Thought.* Frogmore, St.Albans: Paladin, 1976.

Meier, Arthur, Sabine Hoffmann, Hildegard-Maria Nickel, Irmgard Steiner, Gerhard Wenzke. *Soziale Erfahrungen der Schuljugend in ihrer Bedeutung für deren Bewussseiensentwicklung und Erziehung.* Berlin: Akademie der Pädagogischen, Wissenschaften der DDR/ Abteilung Soziologie des Bildungswesens, 1983.

____. "Abschied von der sozialistischen Ständegesellschaft." *Aus Politik und Zeitgeschichte.* B 16-17 (13) (April 1990): 3-14.

Merkel, Wolfgang. "Restriktionen und Chancen demokratischer Konsolidierung in postkommunistischen Gesellschaften: Ostmitteleuropa im Vergleich." *Berl. J. Soziol.* 4 1994a: 463-85.

____, ed. *Systemwechsel 1.*Opladen: Leske + Budrich, 1994b.

Merkl, Peter. "German Nationalism, Identity, and Generations." Working Paper 3.4, University of California at Berkeley, Center for German and European Studies, 1992.

Mertens, Lothar. "Die SED und die NS-Vergangenheit." In Werner Bergmann, Rainer Erb and Albert Licthblau, eds, 194-211. *Schwierige Erbe. Der Umgang mit Nationalsozialismus und Antisemitismus in Österreich, der DDR und der Bundesrepublik Deutschland.* Frankfurt and New York: Campus, 1995.

Merton, Robert K. *Social Theory and Social Structure.* New York and London: The Free Press and Collier Macmillan, 1968.

____. *The Sociology of Science.* Chicago: The University of Chicago Press, 1973.

Meulemann, Heiner. "Aufholtendenzen und Systemeffekte. Eine Übersich über Wertunterschiede zwischen West- und Ostdeutschland." *Aus Politik und Zeitgeschichte.* B 40-41, (29 September 1995): 21-33.

____. "Die Implosion einer staatlich verordneter Moral.Moralität in West-und Ostdetuschland 1990-1994." *Kölner Zeitschrift für Soziologie und Sozialpsykologie:* 50 (3), 1998: 411-41.

Meuschel, Sigrid. *Legitimation und Parteiherrschaft in der DDR*. Frankfurt am Main: Suhrkamp, 1992.

Meyer, Hansgünter. "Neugestaltung der Hochschulen in Ostdeutschland." *Wissenschaftszentrum Berlin für Sozialforschung*, 1993: 93-402.

Mietzner, Ulrike. *Enteignung der Subjekte—Lehrer und Schule in der DDR: Eine Schule in Mecklenburg von 1945 bis zum Mauerbau*. Opladen: Leske + Budrich, 1998.

Milosz, Czeslaw. *The Captive Mind*. New York: Alfred A. Knopf, 1953.

Minkenberg, Michael. "German Unification and the Continuity of Discontinuities: Cultural Change and the Far Right in East and West." *German Politics* 3 (2), 1994: 169-192.

Misselwitz, Hans-Jürgen. "Annäherung durch Wandel Für eine neue Sicht auf die 'innere Einheit' und die Rolle der politischen Bildung." *Aus Politik und Zeitgeschichte* 7-8, 1999: 24-30.

Mitscherlich, Alexander, and Margarete Mitscherlich. *Die Unfähigkeit zu trauern*. München: Piper, 1977.

Mitscherlich, Margarete. "How do Germans Face Their Guilt?" *Partisan Review*, LXII (4), 1995: 527-534.

___, and Irene Runge. *Kulturschock: Umgang mit Deutschen*. Hamburg: Klein, 1993.

Moeller, Mikael, and Hans-Joachim Maaz. *Die Einheit beginnt zu zweit*. Hamburg: Rowohlt, 1993.

Mommsen, Wolfgang J. *Nation und Geschichte*. München: Piper, 1990.

Montada, Leo, and Anne Dieter. "Gevinn-und Verlusterfahrungen in den neuen Bundesländern: Nicht der Kaufkraft der Einkommen, sondern politische Bewerungen sind entscheidend." In Manfred Schmidt, and Leo Montada, eds. *Gerechtigkeitserleben im wiederbereinigten Deutschland*. Opladen: Leske + Budrich, 1999, 19-44.

Moore, Ruth. *Niels Bohr*. New York: Alfred A. Knopf. 1966.

Morin, Edgar. "Die Stars." In Dieter Prokop, ed. *Materialien zur Theorie des Films*. Frankfurt am Main: Fischer, 1971, 427-433.

___. "Filmen och fantasilivet." In Gösta Werner, ed. *Filmstilar*. Stockholm: Pan/ Norstedts, 1977, 64-176.

Mosse, W. E. *Jews in the German Econom*. Oxford: Clarendon Press, 1987.

Münkler, Herfried. "Antifascismus und antifascistischer Widerstand als politischer Gründungsmythos der DDR." *Aus Politik und Zeitgeschichte* 45, 1998: 16-29.

Muszinski, Bernhard. "Politische Bildung im vereigten Deutschland." *Aus Politik und Zeitgeschichte* 47, 1995: 3-12.

Mutz, Gerd. "Soziologische Analysen zum Transformationsprozess in Deutschland. Fünf Jahre nach der Wende." *Schweiz. Z. Soziol.* 221, 1996: 207-219.

Neckel, Sighard. "Etablierte und Aussenseiter und das vereinigte Deutschland. Eine rekonstruktive Prozessanalyse mit Elias und Simmel." *Berl. J. Soziol.* No. 2, 1997: 205-215.

Nelson, Richard R., ed. *National Innovation Systems: A Comparative Analysis*. New York: Oxford University Press, 1994.

Neumann, Thomas W. "'Die Lehrer sind natürlich insgesamt als Berufstand in der DDR sehr stark angegriffen worden.' Was Lehrerinnen und Lehrer heute mit der DDR-schule verbindet. In Heinz-Elmar Tenorth, ed. *Zeitschrift für Pädagogik. 37 Beiheft. Kindheit, Jugend und Bildungsarbeit im Wandel*, 397-410. Weinheim and Basel: Beltz Verlag, 1997.

Nickel, Hildegard Maria. "Frauen in der DDR." *Aus Politik und Zeitgeschichte* 16-17, 1990: 39-45.

Niedermeyer, Oskar, and Klaus von Beyme, eds. *Politsche Kultur in Ost-und Westdeeutschland*. Berlin: Akademie Verlag, 1994.

Niethammer, Lutz. *Die Volkseigene Erfahrung. Eine Archeologi des Lebens in der Industriprovinz der DDR*. Berlin: Rowohlt, 1991.

Niewyk, Donald L. *The Jews in Weimar Germany*. Baton Rouge and London: Louisiana State University Press, 1980.

Offe, Claus. *Der Tunnel am Ende des Lichts. Erkundungen der politischen Transformation im neuen Osten*. Frankfurt am Main and New York: Campus, 1994.

von Ollberg, Hans-Joachim, Botho Priebe, and Hartmut Wenzel. "Lehrerrolle und Lehreridentität in Wendezeiten: Herausforderungen und Aufgaben der Lehrerfort- und Lehrerweiterbildung in den ostdeutschen Bundesländern." *Gruppendynamik* 4, 1993: 339-358.

Orwell. George. In *The Collected Essays, Journalism and Letters of George Orwell*, edited by Sonia Orwell and Ian Angus. New York and London: Harcourt Brace Jovanovich, 1968.

Ostow, Robin. *Jews in Contemporary East Germany*. Basingstoke and London: Macmillan, 1989.

———. "Imperialist Agents, Anti-Fascist Monuments, Eastern Refugees, Property Claims: Jews and Incorporations of Eat German Social Trauma, 1945-54." In *Jews, Germans, Memory. Reconstruction of Jewish Life in Germany*, edited by Y. Michael Bodemann, 227-242. Ann Arbor: The Univiersity of Michigan Press, 1996a.

———. *Juden aus der DDR und die deutsche Wiedervereinigung*. Berlin: Wichern-Verlag, 1996b.

Parsons, Talcott. *Essays in Sociological Theory*. New York: The Free Press, 1964.

Paul, Christiane. "Kann sein dass ich einiges romantisiere." *Stern* 45, 1999: 76-80.

Pirker, Theo M., Rainer Lepsius, Rainer Weinert, and Hans-Hermann Hertle. *Der Plan als Befhel und Fiktion. Wirtschaftsführung in der DDR*. Opladen: Westdeutscher Verlag, 1994.

von Plato, Alexander. "'Eine zweite Entnazifixierung'?" Zur Verarbeitung politischer Umwälzungen in deutschland. 1945 und 1989." In *Wendezeiten-Zeitenwende. Zur "Entnazifizierung" und "Entstaliniesierung,"* edited by Rainer Eckert, Alexander von Plato, and Jörn Schütrmpf. Hamburg: Ergebnisse, 1991: 7-32.

———. "Von deutscher Schuld und Unschuld.Persönliche Umorientierungen in Zeiten politischer Umbrüche." In *Gemeinsam sind wir unterschiedlich*, edited by Conrad Lay and Christoph Potting, 13-17. Bonn: Bundeszentrale für politische Bildung, 1995.

Pohl, Klaus. "Planet Germany." *Der Spiegel* 33, 1994: 96-111.

Pollack, Detlef. "Das Ende eine Organisationsgesellschaft. Systemtheoretische Überlegungen zum gesellschaftlichen Umbruch in der DDR." *Zeitschrift für Soziologie* 19, 1990: 292-307.

———. "Zwischen alten Verhaltensdispositionen und neuen Anforderungsprofilen." In *Organisierte Interessen in Ostdeutschland*, edited by Volker Eichene, Ralf Kleinfeld, Detlef Pollack, Josef Schmid, Klaus Schubert, and Helmut Voelzkow, 489-508. Marburg: Metropolis-Verlag, 1992.

———. "Das Bedürfnis nach sozialer Anerkennung" *Aus Politik und Zeitgechichte* B13, 1997: 3-14.

———. "Das geteilte Bewusstsein.Einstellungen zur sozialen Ungleichheit und zur Demokratie in Ost- und Westdeutschland 1990-1998." Paper to the conference "Die unvollendete Einheit. Soziale Ungleichheit und Erwerbsbiographien in Ostdeutschland." Max Planck Institute for Human Development, Berlin, 17-18 November 1999.

———, and Gert Pickel. "Die Ostdeutsche Identität Erbe des DDR-Sozialismus oder Produkt der Wiedervereinigung." *Aus Politik und Zeitgeschichte* 41-42, 1998: 9-23.

Popper, Karl. *The Poverty of Historicism*. London: Routledge & Kegan Paul, 1972.

———. *The Open Society and its Enemies*. Volume 1 and 2. London: Routledge & Kegan Paul, 1966.

Porter, Michael. *The Competitive Advantage of Nations*. London and Basingstoke: Macmillan, 1990.

Powers, Thomas. "The Conspiracy that Failed." *New York Review of Books* XLIV (1) (January 9, 1997): 49-54.

Pritchard, Rosalind M.O. *Reconstructing Education. East German Schools and Universities after Unification*. New York and Oxford: Berghahn Books, 1999.

Pulzer, Peter. *The Rise of Political Antisemitism in Germany and Austria*. London: Peter Alban, 1988.

Putnam, Robert D. *Making Democracy Work: Civic Traditions in Modern Italy*. Princeton, N.J.: Princeton University Press, 1993.

Reich, Jens. *Abschied von den Lebenslügen: Die Intelligenz und die Macht*. Berlin: Rowohlt, 1992.

___. *Rückkehr nach Europa*. Munich: Deutscher Taschenbuch Verlag, 1993.

___. "East Germany: Mentality Five Years after Unification." In *Culture in the Federal Republic of Germany 1945–1995*, edited by Reiner Pommerin, 133-44. Oxford/Washington D.C.: Berg, 1996.

Reich-Ranicki. *Über Ruhestörer. Juden in der deutschen Literatur*. Stuttgart: Deutsche Verlags-Anstalt, 1989.

Reiher, Ruth, and Rüdiger Läzer. *Von "Buschzulage" und "Ossienachweis."* Berlin: Aufbau, 1996.

Reissig, Rolf, and Hans-Joachim Glaessner. *Das Ende eines Experiments*. Berlin: Dietz Verlag, 1991.

___, ed. *Rückweg in die Zukunft: Über den schwierigen Transformationsprozess in Ostdeutschland*. Frankfurt and New York: Campus, 1993a.

___. "Ostdeutscher Transformations - und deutscher Integrationsprozess neue Probleme und Erklärungsversuche." *BISS PUBLIC* 12, 1993b: 5–31.

Revel, Jean Francois. *Die totalitäre Versuchung*. Frankfurt am Main: Ullstein, 1977.

Richarz, Monika. "Juden in der Bundesrepublik Deutschland und in der deutschen Demokratischen Republik seit 1945." In *Jüdisches Leben in Deutschland seit 1945*, edited by Micha Brumlik, Doron Kiesel, Cilly Kugelmann, and Julius Schoeps, 13-30. Frankfurt am Main: Jüdischer Verlag bei Athenäum, 1986.

Rippl, Susanne. "Ostdeutsch, westdeutsch oder deutsch? Gruppenzugehörigkeit und ihr Einfluss auf das Selbstkonzept." *Gruppendynamik* Heft 2, 1997: 171-90.

___, and Klaus Boehnke. "Authoritarianism: Adolescents from East and West Germany and the United States Compared." In *After the Wall: Family Adaptions in East and West Germany*, edited by James Youniss, 57-70. San Fransisco: Jossey-Bass, 1995.

___, and Christian Seipel. "Autoritarismus und Fremdenfiendlichkeit bei ost-und westdeutschen Jugendlichen." *Zeitschrift für politische Psychologie* 6 (3), 1998: 273-88.

Ritter, Claudia. "Politische Identitäten in den neuen Bundesländern." In *Einheit als Privileg: Vergleichende Perspektive auf die Transformation Ostdeutschlands*, edited by Helmut Wiesenthal, 141-87. Frankfurt am Main and New York: Campus Verlag, 1996.

Robertson, Roland. *Globalization. Social Theory and Social Culture*. London: Sage, 1992.

Roesler, Jörg. "Probleme des Brigadealltags. Arbeitsverhältniss und Arbeitsklima in volkseigenen Betriben 1950-1989." *Aus Politik und Zeitgeschichte* B38, 1997: 3-17.

Rosenthal, Gabriele, ed. *Der Holocaust im Leben von drei Generationen*. Giessen: Psychosozial Verlag, 1997.

Rottenburg, Richard. "Der Sozialismus braucht den ganzen Menschen. Zum Verhältnis vertraglicher und nichtvertraglicher Beziehungen in einem VEB." *Zeitschrift für Soziologie* 20 (4), 1991: 305-32.

Rutherford, Jonathan, ed. *Identity: Community, Culture, Difference*. London: Lawrence & Wishart, 1990. Rutkoff, Peter M., and William B. Scott. *New School. A History of the*

New School of Social Research. New York: The Free Press/ London: CollierMacmillan, 1986.

Rytlewski, R. "Politische Kultur und Generationswechsel in der DDR: Tendenzen zu einer alternativen politischen Kultur." In *Politische Sozialisation Jugendlicher in Ost und West*, edited by B. Claussen, 209-24. Bonn: Bundeszentral für politische Bildung, 1989.

Sabath, Wolfgang, and Regina General. *Stefan Hey: Querköpfe.* Berlin: Elefantenpress, 1994.

Safranski, Rüdiger. *Martin Heidegger: Between Good and Evil.* Cambridge, Mass. and London: Harvard University Press, 1998.

Sartre, Jean-Paul. *Anti-Semite and Jew.* New York: Schocken Books, 1965.

Sarup, Madan. *An Introductory Guide to Poststructuralism and Postmodernism.* New York: Harvester Wheatsheaf, 1988.

Schabowski, Günter. *Der Absturz.* Berlin: Rowohlt, 1991.

Schäuble, Wolfgang. *Der Vertrag.* Stuttgart: Deutsche Verlagsanstalt, 1991.

Scheuch, Erwin. *Wie deutsch sind die Deutschen?* Bergisch-Gladbach: Gustav Lübke, 1991.

Schlosser, Horst Dieter. "Deutsche Teilung, deutsche Einheit und die Sprache der Deutschen." *Aus Politik und Zeitgeschichte* B 17-19 (April, 1991): 13-21.

Schluchter, W. "Umbau der Hochschulen in Ostdeutschland." *Berl. J. Soziol.* 1, 1994: 89-114.

Schluchter, Wolfgang. *Neubeginn durch Anpassung? Studien zum ostdeutschen Übergang.* Frankfurt am Main: Suhrkamp, 1996.

Schmidt, Rudi, and Burkart Lutz, eds. *Chancen und Risiken der industriellen Restrukturierung in Ostdeutschland.* Berlin: Akademie Verlag, 1995.

Schmitt, Manfred, and Leo Montada eds. *Gerechtigkeitserleben im wiedervereinighten Deutschland.* Opladen: Leske + Budrich, 1999.

Schmitz, Mikael. *Wendestress. Die psychosozialen Kosten der deutschen Einheit.* Berlin: Rohwolt, 1995.

Schneider, Peter. *Eduards Heimkehr.* Berlin: Rowohlt, 1999.

Schoenbaum, David. "1945 - Starting All Over." In *German Identity Forty Years After Zero*, edited by Wolfgang Pollack and Derek Rutter. Sankt Augustin: Liberal Verlag, 1986: 17-40.

Schoeps, Julius H, ed. *Ein Volk von Mördern?* Hamburg: Hoffmann & Campe, 1996.

Schramm, Florian, and Michael Schlese. "From Solidarity to Cooperation: The German Case." *Futures* (March 1992): 173-78.

Schröter, Ursula. "Ostdeutsche Frauen im Transformationsprozess." *Aus Politik und Zeitgeschichte* 20, 1995: 31-42.

Schubarth, Wilfried, Ronald Pschierer, Thomas Schmidt. "Verordneter Antifascismus und die Folgen."*Aus Politik und Zeitgeschichte* 9: 9-16.

Schubert, Wilfried. "Xenophobia among East German Youth." In *Anti-Semitism and Xenophobia in Germany after Unification,* edited by Hermann Kurthen, Werner Bermann, and Rainer Erb, 143-58. New York and Oxford: Oxford University Press, 1997:

Schulz, Marianne, and Jan Wielgohs. "DDR-identität zwischen Demokrati und DM." In *DDR Ein Staat vergeht,* edited by Thomas Blanke and Rainer Erd, 123-36. Frankfurt am Main: Fischer, 1990.

Schumann, Karl F. "Probleme der Assimilation von Bürgern und Bürgerinnen der ehemaligen deutschen Teilstaaten." *Deutschland Archiv* 25, 1991: 1193-1201.

Schutz, Alfred. *Collected Papers I-III.* The Hague: Martinus Nijhoff, 1973-75.

Schwarz, Barry. "Social Change and Collective Mamory: The Democratization of George Washington." *American Sociological Review* 56, 1991: 221-36.

Schweigler, Gebhard. *Nationalbewusstsein in der BRD und der DDR.*Düsseldorf: Bertelsmann-Universitätsverlag, 1975.

Schwitzler, Klaus-Peter. "Ältere und alte Menchen in den neuen Bundesländern in zehnten Jahr nach der Wende." *Aus Politik und Zeitgeschichte* 43-44, 1999: 32-39.

Seebacher-Brandt. "Nation im vereinigten Deutschland." *Aus Politik und Zeitgeschichte* 42, (21 October 1994): 3-9.

Seiring, Kerstin. "Ostdeutsche Jugendliche fünf Jahre nach der Wiedervereinigung." *Aus Politik und Zeitgeschichte* 20, 1995: 43-55.

Selucky, Radoslav. *Marxism, Socialism, Freedom.* London and Basingstoke: Macmillan, 1979.

Sichrovsky, Peter. *Born Guilty. Children of Nazi Families.* New York: Basic Books, 1988.

Simmel, Georg. *Über soziale Differenzierung.* Leipzig: Duncker & Humblot, 1890.

___. *Soziologie.* Leipzig: Duncker & Humblot, 1908.

___. *Das individuelle Gesetz: Philosophische Exkurse,* edited by M. Landmann. Frankfurt am Main: Surhkamp, 1968.

___. *The Philosophy of Money.* London: Routledge & Kegan Paul, 1978.

Simon, Annette. *Versuch, mir und anderen die ostdeutsche Moral zu erklären.* Giessen: Psychosozial Verlag, 1995.

Smith, Antony. *The Ethnic Origins of Nations.* Oxford: Basil Blackwell, 1986.

Snyder, Louis L. *German Nationalism: The Tragedy of a People.* Harrisburg, Pa.: Stackburg, 1952.

___. *Roots of German Nationalism.* New York: Barnes & Noble, 1996.

Solga, Heike. "Intergenerationale Mobilität: Von der Mobilisierung der Arbeiterkinder zur Selbstreproduktion der Intelligenz? Beitrag zum Kolloquiu." Paper to the conference "Annährung an die soziale Wirklichkeit der DDR." Bonn, 29 March 1993.

___. "Systemloyalität als Bedingung sozialer Mobilität im Staatssozialismus, am Beispiel der DDR." *Berliner Journal für Soziologie* 4, 1994: 523-42.

___. *Auf dem Weg in eine Klassenlose Gesellschaft.* Berlin: Akademie Verlag, 1995.

___. "The Fate of the East German Upper Service Class after 1989: Types of System Transformation and Changes in Elite Recruitment." In *Eliten, politische Kultur und Privatisierung in Ostdeutschland, Tschechien und Mitteleuropa,* edited by Ilja Srubar, 97-118. Konstanz: Universitätsverlag Konstanz, 1998.

Sommerfeld, Franz, ed. *Pioniere im neuen Deutschland. Westöstliche Porträts.* Hamburg: Rowohlt, 1993.

Sontheimer, Michael. "Land ohne Kinder." *Die Zeit* 41, 1994: 37.

Der Spiegel. "Stolz aufs eigene Leben." 27 3.07, 1995a: 40-52.

___. "Vor den Kop geschlagen." 29 17.7, 1995b: 50-3.

___. "Bei den Wessies ist jeder für sich." 10, 1999: 28.

Srubar, Ilja. "War der reale Sozialismus modern?" *Kölner Zeitschrift für Soziologie und Sozialpsychology* 43 (3), 1991: 415-32.

Staritz, Dietrich. *Die Gründung der DDR.* München: Deutscher Taschenbuch Verlag, 1995.

Staud, Toralf. "Mecklenburg: Die NPD auf dem Vormarsch." *Die Zeit* 38, 10 September 1998.

___. "Die importierte Moral." *Die Zeit* 15, 8 April 1999.

Steininger, Rolf. *Der Umgang mit dem Holocaust.* Wien: Böhlau Verlag, 1999.

Stern, Fritz. *The Politics of Cultural Despai: A Study in the Rise of the Germanic Ideology.* New York: Anchor Books, 1965.

___. *The Whitewashing of the Yellow Badge: Antisemitism and Philosemitism in Postwar Europe.* Oxford: Pergamon Press, 1992.

Stern, Susan, ed. *Speaking Out: Jewish Voices from United Germany.* Chicago: edition q, 1995.

Stock, Manfred. "Ostdeutsche Jugend in der Wertekrise." *Zeitschrift für Pädagogik* 42 (4), 1996: 623-36.

___. "Bildung zwischen Macht, Technik und Lebensstil. Das Beispiel der 'sozialistischen Intelligenz' in der DDR." In *Bildungsgeschichte einer Diktatur: Bildung un Erziehung in SBZ und DDR imhistorisch-gesellschaftlichen Kontext,* edited by Sonja Häder and Heinz-Elmar Tenorth, 295-333. Weinheim: Deutscher Studien Verlag, 1997.

Stojanov, Christo. "Das 'Immunsystem' des 'real existierenden Sozialismus.' *Aus Politik und Zeitgeschichte.* B 19 3. (Mai 1991): 36-46.

Stolpe, Manfred. *Schwieriger Aufbruch.* Berlin: Siedler, 1992.

Stratemann, Ingrid. "Psychologische Bedingunden des wirtschaftlichen Aufschwungs in den neuen Bundesländern."*Aus Politik und Zeitgeschichte* 24, 1992: 15-26.

Strauss, Anselm. *Mirrors and Masks: The Search for Identity.* New York: The Free Press, 1959.

Strauss, Herber A., and Norbert Kampe, eds. *Antisemitismus: Von der Judenfeindschaft zum Holocaust.* Frankfurt and New York: Campus, 1985.

Strohschneider, Stefan. *Denken in Deutschland.* Bern: Hans Huber, 1996 ed.

Szepanski, Gerda. *Die Stille Emanzipation: Frauen in der DDR.* Frankfurt am Main: Fischer, 1995.

Szilard, Leo. "Reminiscences." In *The Intellectual Migration: Europe and America, 1930–1960,* edited by Donald Fleming and Bernard Bailyn, 94-151. Cambridge, Mass.: Harvard University Press, 1969.

Tajfel, H. *Gruppenkonflikt und Vorurteil.* Bern: Huber, 1982.

___, ed. *Differentiation Between Groups: Studies in the Social Psychology of Intergroup Relations.* London: Academic Press, 1978.

___, and J.C. Turner. "An integrative theory of integroup conflict." in W.G. Austin and S. Worchel eds., 33–47. *The Social Psychology of Intergroup Relations.* Monterey: Brooks/Cole, 1979.

Talbot, R. J., and T. Rickards. "Developing Creativity." In *Management Development: Advances in Practice and Theory*, edited by Charles Cox and John Beck, 93-121. Chicester: John Wiley & Sons, 1984.

Thierse, Wolfgang. "Fünf Jahre deutsche Vereinigung: Wirtschaft - Gesellschaft - Mentalität." *Aus Politik und Zeitgeschichte* 40-41 (29 September 1995: 3-7.

Thomas, Michael, Thomas Koch, Gabriele Valerius, and Rudolf Woderich. "Abschlussberich zum Projekt 'Neue Selbständige' im Transformationsprozess: Herkunftsweg, soziale Charakteristika und Potentiale." Berlin: BISS, 1995.

Tillmann, Klaus Jürgen. "Staatlicher Zusammenbruch und schulischer Wandel." In *Transformationden der deutschen Bildungslandschaft*, edited by Peter Dudek and H.-Elmar Tenorth, 29-36. Weinheim and Basel: Beltz, 1994.

Traverso, Enzo. *The Jews and Germany.* Lincoln and London: University of Nebraska Press, 1995.

Trommsdorf, Gisela. "Identitätsprozesse im kulturellen Kontext und im sozialen Wandel." In *Transformationsprozesse in Deutschland*, edited by Heins Sahner, 117-147.Opladen: Leske + Budrich, 1995.

___, Gisela, and Hans-Joachim Kornadt. "Prosocial and Antisocial Motivation of Adolescents in East and West Germany." In *After the Wall: Family Adaptions in East and West Germany*, edited by James Youniss, 30-56. San Fransisco: Jossey-Bass, 1995.

Tudor, Andrew. *Image and Influence: Studies in the Sociology of Film.* London: George Allen & Unwin, 1974.

Veen, Hans-Joachim. "National Identity and Political Priorities in Eastern and Western Germany." *German Politics* 4 (1), 1995: 1-26.

___. "Inner Unity-Back to Community Myth? A Plea for a Basic Consensus." *German Politics* 6 (3), 1997: 1–15.

___, and Carsten Zelle. "National Identity and Political Priorities in Eastern and Western Germany." *German Politics* 4 (1), 1996: 1-26.

Vester, Michael. "Deutschlands feine Unterschiede." *Aus Politik und Zeitgeschichte* 20, 1995: 16-30.

Voskamp, Ulrich, and Volker Wittke. "Fordismus in einem Land: Das Produktionsmodel der DDR." *Sozialwissenschaftliche Information* 2, 1991.

Walther, Joachim. "Zwischen Amnestie und Amnesie: Schwierigkeiten im Umgang mit der DDR-Vergangenheit." In *Studies in GDR Culture and Society 11/1: The End of the GDR and the Problems of Integration. Selected Papers from the Sixteenth and Seventeenth New Hampshire Symposia on the German Democratic Republic*, edited by Margy Gerber and Roger Woods, 181-93. Lanham and New York: University Press of America, 1993.

Walz, Dieter, and Wolfram Brunner. "Das Sein bestimmt das Bewusstsein." *Aus Politik und Zeitgeschichte* 51 (12 December, 1997): 13-19.

Watson, Alan. *The Germans: Who Are They Now?* London: Mandarin, 1994.

Watts, Meredith. "Political Xenophobia in the Transition from Socialism: Threat, Racism and Ideology among East German Youth." *Political Psychology* 17 (1), 1996: 97-126.

Weaver, Bradden. "Rightist Violence as a Youth Phenomenon in United Germany." In *Dimensions of German Unification, Economic, Social, and Legal Analyses* edited by A. Bradley Shingleton, Marian J. Gibbon, and Kathryn S. Mack, 143-56. Boulder, Colo.: Westview Press, 1995.

Wedel, Mathias. *Einheitsfrust.* Hamburg: Rowohlt, 1995.

Weeks, Jeffrey. "The Value of Difference." In Jonathan Rutherford, ed. *Identity-Community, Culture, Difference.* Lawrence & Wishart, 1990.

Weinberg, Meyer. *Because They Were Jews. A History of Antisemitism.* New York: Greenwood Press, 1986.

Welsch, Helga A. "'Antifascistisch-demokratische Umwälzung' und politische Saüberung in de sowjetischen Besatzungszone Deutschlands." In *Politische Säuberung in Europa. Die Abrechnung mit Faschismus und Kollaboration nach dem Zweiten Weltkrieg,* edited by Klaus-Dietmar Henke and Hans Wollter, 84–107. München: München: Deutsche Verlagsanstalt, 1991.

von Wensierski, Hans-Jürgen. *Mit uns zieht die alte Zeit. Biographie und Lebenswelt junder DDR-Bürger im Umbruch.* Opladen: Leske + Budrich, 1994.

Westle, Bettina. *Kollektive Identität im vereinten Deutschland.* Opladen: Leske + Budrich, 1999.

Wetherell, Margaret, ed. *Identities, Groups and Social Issues.* London: Sage, 1996.

White, Michael, and John Gribbin. *Einstein: A Life in Science.* London: Simon & Schuster, 1997.

Wiesenthal, Helmut. "Post-Unification Dissatisfaction. Or: Why Are So Many East Germans Dissatisfied with West German Political Institutions?" Max Planck Gesellschaft Arbeitgruppe Transformaitonsprozesse in den neuen Bundesländern. Arbeitspapiere 96/6, 1996.

Wieworka, Michel. "Racism in Europe: Unity and Diversity." In *The Ethnicity Reader: Nationalism, Multiculturalism and Migration,* edited by Montserrat Guibernau and John Rex, 291-301.Cambridge: Polity Press, 1999.

Willems, Helmut. *Fremdenfeindliche Gewalt: Einstellungen, Täter, Konflikteskalation.* Opladen: Leske + Budrich, 1993.

von Wilpert. *Sachhwörterbuch der Literatur.* Stuttgart: Kröner, 1969.

Die Wirtschaft. Kombinate: Was aus ihnen geworden ist. Berlin and Munich: Verlag Die Wirtschaft, 1993.

Wistrich, Robert S. *Antisemitism: The Longest Hatred.* London: Thames Methuen, 1991.

Woderich, Rudolf. "Auf der Suche nach der 'verborgenen' Mentalität der Ost-Deutschen." *BISS PUBLIC* 3, 1991a: 121-32.

Woderich, Rudolf. "Zur Rekonstruktion der Lebenswelt." *BISS PUBLIC* 5, 1991b: 107-16.

___. "Mentalitäten im Land der kleinen Leute." In *Abbruch und Aufbruch*, edited by Michael Thomas, 76 – 90. Berlin: Akademie Verlag, 1992a.

___. "Mentalitäten zwischen Anpassung und Eigensinne." *Deutschlandarchiv* 25 (1), 1992b: 21-32.

Wolf, Christa. "Das haben wir nicht gelernt." In *Angepasst oder Mündig*, edited by Petra Grüner, 9-12. Berlin: Volk und Wissen, 1990a.

___. *Was Bleibt*. Frankfurt am Main: Luchterhand, 1990b.

Wolf, Hans-Georg. *Organisationsschicksale im deutschen Vereinigungsprozess: Die Entwicklungswege der Institute der akademie der Wissenschaften der DDR*. Frankfurt/ New York: Campus Verlag, 1996.

Wolle, Stefan. *Die heile Welt der Diktatur: Alltag und Herrschaft in der DDR 1971 - 1989*. Berlin: Links, 1998.

von Wroblewsky, Vincent, ed. *Zwischen Thora und Trabant: Juden in der DDR*. Berlin: Berlin: Aufbau, 1993.

Wüllenwerber, Walter, and Wilfried Bauer. "Besser-Ossie, Jammer-Wessie." *Stern* 42, 1999: 64-68.

Wyman, David S. *The Abandonement of the Jews*. New York: The New Press, 1998.

Yearly, Steven. *Sociology, Environmentalism, Globalization*. London: Sage, 1996.

Young-Bruehl, Elisabeth. *Hannah Arendt: For Love of the World*. New Haven, Conn.: Yale University Press, 1982.

Zapf, Wolfgang. "Modernisierung und Modernisierungstheorien." In *Die Modernisierung moderner Gesellschaften* edited by Wolfgang Zapf, 23-39. Frankfrut/ New York: Campus, 1991.

___. "Zur Theorie der Transformation." *BISS PUBLIC* 13, 1994: 5-9.

Zelikow, Philip, and Condoleezza Rice. *Germany Unified and Europe Transforme: A Study in Statecraft*. Cambridge, Mass., and London: Harvard University Press, 1995.

Zelle, Carsten. "Soziale und liberale Wertorientieurungen: Versuch einer situativer Erklärung der Unterschiede zwischen Ost- und Westdeutschen." *Aus Politik und Zeitgeschichte* 41-42, 1998: 24-36.

Index